A Student's Guide
to Legal Analysis

A Student's Guide to Legal Analysis

Thinking Like a Lawyer

Patrick M. McFadden

Professor of Law
Loyola University Chicago School of Law

ASPEN LAW & BUSINESS
A Division of Aspen Publishers, Inc.
Gaithersburg   New York

Printed in the United States of America

ISBN 0-7355-2395-9

1 2 3 4 5 6 7 8 9 0

Library of Congress Cataloging-in-Publication Data

McFadden, Patrick M.
    A student's guide to legal analysis: thinking like a lawyer / Patrick M. McFadden.
        p. cm.
    Includes index.
    ISBN 0-7355-2395-9 (alk. paper)
    1. Law—United States—Methodology.   2. Law—Study and teaching—United
States.   I. Title.

KF283 .M396 2001
340'.071'173—dc21   2001022365

About Aspen Law & Business
Legal Education Division

With a dedication to preserving and strengthening the long-standing tradition of publishing excellence in legal education, Aspen Law & Business continues to provide the highest quality teaching and learning resources for today's law school community. Careful development, meticulous editing, and an unmatched responsiveness to the evolving needs of today's discerning educators combine in the creation of our outstanding casebooks, coursebooks, textbooks, and study aids.

ASPEN LAW & BUSINESS
A Division of Aspen Publishers, Inc.
A Wolters Kluwer Company
www.aspenpublishers.com

For Elaine

Contents

CHAPTER 5: FROM QUESTIONS TO ANSWERS
(On Legal Argument)

Acknowledgments

I thank those who read and commented on this book during its many early stages: Diane Geraghty, Jeff Atkinson, Paul Lebel, Rod Smolla, Susan Grover, Neil Devin, Elaine Frangedakis, Jeff Kwall, Stanley Mamangakis, and my students at Loyola University Chicago School of Law. Thanks to Dean Nina Appel of Loyola Law School for her support in securing research leaves and funding to support this work. Thanks also to Elizabeth Frangedakis and Stanley and Alexandra Mamangakis for providing a quiet place to work during many summers of writing.

I acknowledge the permission kindly granted to reproduce an excerpt from Robert Bolt, *A Man for All Seasons* (1st Vintage International Edition 1990). Copyright 1960, 1990. Reprinted by permission of Vintage Books.

Introduction

The law is likely to overwhelm beginning students with its scope and complexity. The standard law school curriculum offers dozens of courses—impressive enough in sheer number—and each is only an introduction to the subject it covers. The aura of complexity is confirmed by the thousands of books, reporters, and periodicals that line the shelves of every law library, examining issues as diverse as the political rights of Aboriginal peoples in Brazil to the proper interpretation of construction contracts in Florida.

This complexity of subject matter, however, contrasts sharply with the essential simplicity of legal analysis. The law does indeed cover hundreds of subjects, but lawyers and judges work with these subjects in very limited ways. They ask and answer only a handful of questions about any legal matter:

- Is there a law? (questions of *obligation* and *right*)
- Has it been violated? (questions of *liability*)
- What will be done about it? (questions of *remedy*)

These questions can appear in many guises, but they are always the same.

This book demonstrates how these three questions recur in different areas of legal study and practice, including the first-year curriculum of law school. Among other goals, the book gives law students a way of organizing and thinking about their coursework generally and about the individual cases, laws, and regulations they confront every day. It shows how "everything fits." The book also introduces the dynamics of legal argument. Just as there are only a few legal questions, there are only a few reasons to answer those questions one way or the other. These reasons—the fundamental, often conflicting aspirations we have for legal regulation—make a great deal of legal argument predictable as well. By the end of the book, students will not only recognize the basic questions posed in a legal dispute, but the predictable reasons lawyers give for reaching one resolution or another.

Law deans and professors often say that one of the primary purposes of law school is to teach each student how to "think like a lawyer," but we are not always clear about what this means. The lack of clarity is unfortunate, because the meaning is simple. To think like a lawyer is to *ask the kinds of questions lawyers and judges ask* about the situations they confront, the questions described in this book.

As may be obvious by now, this book is quite different from other standard texts for law students. It is not a treatise in the normal sense, for it does not provide a summary of substantive legal rules, divided along traditional lines such as contract, property, and criminal law. Nor is it a study aid in the normal sense, for it does not explain how to brief a case, how to synthesize a group of cases, or how to prepare for and take a final examination. There is no substitute for detailed, substantive knowledge of the law or for clear-headed advice on how to study and take examinations, but they alone are not enough. What is missing, and what this book provides, is the "big picture"—the fundamental issues of law and the fundamental dynamics of legal argument. With these in hand, both the substance and mechanics of law study will be easier to grasp.

Some final words about scope and design. First, because the book is written for beginning students, no prior legal knowledge is presumed. A glossary of major, recurring terms has been provided at the back, in addition to an extensive index. For those who want to read more about the subjects raised in this book, a list of Suggested Readings has also been included. Second, because the book is written primarily for Americans, historically important branches of law, such as Roman law, and the domestic laws of other nations, such as British or Chinese law, have not been consulted systematically. This is an important limitation; a book set in the context of current American law makes assumptions about law and its practice that may seem natural, but are assumptions nonetheless. A book for Germans or Aleuts would be different. Finally, the book deals with only one, albeit crucial, aspect of the lawyer's work—legal analysis. Lawyers are more, however, than analytical thinking machines. They are counselors, confidants, and keepers of the peace; they are moral agents with professional responsibilities both to their clients and society more generally. We will see these other aspects of the lawyer's work in the course of this book, but the focus will be on legal analysis.

Despite inevitable limitations of context and method, the book's value should become apparent the first time a professor complains, after 30 minutes of confusing and frustrating classroom discussion, "But you're missing the forest for the trees!" This book is a map of the forest.

A Student's Guide to Legal Analysis

The Only Three Questions in Law

THIS CHAPTER

- **Sets the groundwork for understanding legal analysis by explaining:**
  - the essential nature of legal rights and obligations, and
  - how those rights and obligations are created

- **Describes the three types of legal questions that judges and lawyers repeatedly try to answer in every situation they confront:**
  - is there a law?
  - has it been violated?
  - what will be done about it?

- **Explains how these three questions affect not only lawyers, but also:**
  - *clients* (and what this means for their chances of success); and
  - *law students* (and how understanding these questions will help them read their assignments and prepare for classes more effectively)

THE LAW AND THE WORLD

All good questions, including legal questions, arise in a particular context. Before embarking on our examination of legal analysis, it will be useful to set the stage with some discussion about the law itself — how it works and what it seeks to accomplish. We begin with some fundamentals about what the law regulates and how those regulations arise.

The Law's Concern

The law concerns itself with observable human action. Note first that the law is concerned with *human* action: the law regulates people and nothing else. A city ordinance providing that dogs shall be leashed at all times is not addressed to the dogs but to their human owners. We speak of a "law of property," but that law does not regulate houses, office buildings, or public parks; it regulates people in their dealings with those things. Legal analysis, no matter how difficult or complicated it becomes, must eventually return to earth and answer the question, "What exactly are we asking people to do?"

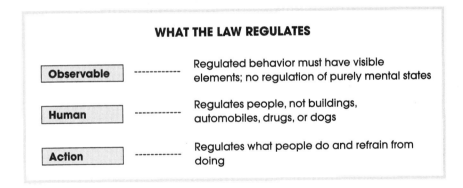

WHAT THE LAW REGULATES

Observable	-----------	Regulated behavior must have visible elements; no regulation of purely mental states
Human	-----------	Regulates people, not buildings, automobiles, drugs, or dogs
Action	-----------	Regulates what people do and refrain from doing

"People," however, are regulated in two ways: (1) directly, as individuals; and (2) indirectly, through the groups and associations they form. The law does not regulate just any group or association, but only certain types, few in number and carefully defined: international organizations, nation-states and their political subdivisions (states, counties, cities), certain business entities (corporations, partnerships, proprietorships, unincorporated associations), and a few others (e.g., estates and trusts). These formal groups and associations are commonly known as *juristic persons;* you and I are known as *natural persons.* Together, we are *subjects of the law.*

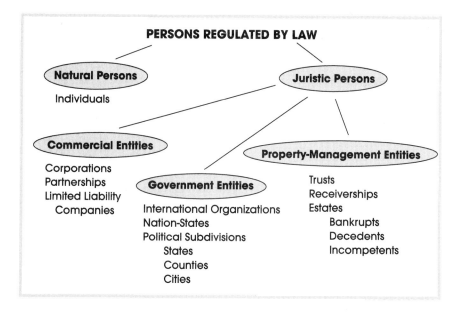

At first blush, the legal regulation of juristic persons seems to contravene the principle that the law regulates only human action: a nation-state is not a human and neither is a corporation. For each kind of juristic person, however, the law has developed a set of rules that connects the entity's actions and responsibilities with that of individuals. For each kind of juristic person, there are always rules about how and when to attribute individual action to the group (each partner in a general business partnership, for example, can bind the partnership), and how to distribute group responsibility among individuals (when a general partnership can't pay its bills, for example, each of the partners is individually liable). In this way we connect individuals to the group and the group to individuals. Ultimately, it is individuals who are regulated.

When the law regulates human beings, individually or in groups, it regulates only what is physically observable to others: shaking the candy machine; failing to pay taxes; selling groceries. There is no regulation of purely mental or internal states of affairs. This limitation on the law is not driven by a concern for freedom of thought, but is a matter of practical necessity. We cannot regulate what we cannot see (or hear or smell or touch or taste). We could not regulate pure thought even if we tried. This makes the law highly materialistic, tethering it firmly to the world of physically observable facts, of what was said and done. This does not mean that the law never refers to mental or internal states of affairs; the difference between first- and second-degree murder, for example, turns on the precise mental state of the accused. But there would be no murder at all without at least one physical act, observable (even if not observed) by others. Physical, observable human acts are the necessary prerequisites for legal regulation.

Obligation and Right

The law can only do three things with observable human action — require it, prohibit it, or permit it. Most of the time, the law either requires or prohibits action rather than permits it. It either forces conduct of certain kinds or limits the conduct otherwise possible. This constraining cast of the law is not the result of malevolence, but reflects the context in which the law works, a context dominated by the *principle of legality*. This fundamental principle provides that *all actions are legal unless made illegal*. As a consequence, the law spends little time gratuitously granting permission for things that are permissible in the first place. The principle of legality has important practical consequences as well. When a lawyer is asked whether a client can take a particular action, the lawyer's first and most common reaction is to ask, "why not?" No law is needed to make an act legal, just the absence of any prohibition.

Still, the law does explicitly grant permission in several contexts. Explicit permission is often given to clear up ambiguities, when the legality of an act has been drawn into question, or to carve out an exception from a more general prohibition. Beyond ambiguities and exceptions, one of the most common occasions for permission-granting concerns juristic persons. Traditionally, the principle of legality has applied only to individuals; juristic persons, unlike individuals, generally cannot act unless specifically authorized by law to do so. A corporation, for example, may not engage in a particular line of business un-

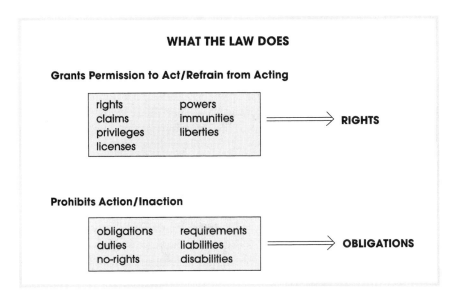

WHAT THE LAW DOES

Grants Permission to Act/Refrain from Acting

rights	powers
claims	immunities	⟹ **RIGHTS**
privileges	liberties
licenses	

Prohibits Action/Inaction

obligations	requirements
duties	liabilities	⟹ **OBLIGATIONS**
no-rights	disabilities

less its charter permits it. The federal government of the United States cannot do anything under domestic law unless the Constitution says it can.

When attached to a person, requirements and prohibitions (the constraining side of law) generate *obligations* of various sorts. Depending on the circumstances, they might be called *obligations,* or instead *duties, disabilities, requirements,* or *liabilities.* When attached to a person, permissions (the confirming or enabling side of law) generate *rights* of various sorts. Depending on the circumstances, they might be called *rights,* or instead *claims, privileges, licenses, powers, immunities,* or *liberties.* Over the years, there have been some important and interesting attempts to define and regularize this terminology. In 1913, in one of the most influential efforts, Professor Wesley Hohfeld suggested a standard nomenclature of eight "lowest common denominators" for describing and classifying legal relations — right, noright, privilege, duty, power, disability, immunity, and liability — the details of which will not concern us here.[1] Despite the analytical power of such efforts, however, neither Hohfeld's system nor anyone else's is employed consistently by lawyers and judges. To this day, American legal argument is filled with loose talk of "rights" and "duties," all sufficiently imprecise to set the late Professor Hohfeld spinning in his grave. But this doesn't mean that today's lawyers and judges are wrong. On the whole, we are just as precise as we need to be: Hohfeldian and other distinctions are useful for resolving difficult problems, but they are not needed most of the time. In this book, we will adopt the practice of the legal community, making only those distinctions we have to, when we have to, and using the words most commonly used by lawyers and judges themselves. When the law requires or prohibits an action, we will call this an obligation; when the law permits an action, we will call this a right. When finer distinctions are needed we will make them.

Many rights and obligations apply to persons without any effort or voluntary action on their part: I enjoy the right to free speech, for example, even though I never applied for it, and I am obliged not to commit murder, even though I never expressly agreed to limit my behavior in that way. Many other rights and obligations, on the other hand, are *conditional:* I am obliged to act in certain ways if (but *only* if) I wish to achieve a certain objective. No one is obliged, as a general matter, to form a corporation, but *if* I wish to do so, I must file certain papers with a government office. *If* I want the privilege of driving, I must apply for a license and take the required tests. Indeed, most of a lawyer's work outside the courtroom involves conditional rights and obligations, helping people to achieve objectives that they are not required to achieve, but once sought, require the fulfillment of particular obligations. As one can imagine, these rights

---

[1]Wesley Hohfeld, "Some Fundamental Legal Conceptions as Applied in Judicial Reasoning," 23 Yale L.J. 16, 28-58 (1913).

and obligations, though "conditional," are of utmost importance to the people concerned, for it is in this way that children are adopted, homes purchased, and businesses founded.

Rights and obligations, whether conditional or not, are clearly related. If someone has a right to receive a thing, someone else (generally speaking) has a correlative obligation to provide it. If, for example, I have a right to the mobile home I have just bought from you, you have an obligation to deliver it. Likewise, if someone has a right to do something, others (generally speaking) have a correlative obligation not to interfere. Thus, if I have a right to criticize my government for a recent action, the government has an obligation not to hinder or prosecute me. In sum, every right entails the existence of a complementary obligation; every obligation, a complementary right.

The close, reciprocal relation of rights and obligations does not mean that we can sensibly or usefully rid ourselves of one kind of talk or the other. Even if it were conceptually possible to translate all rights-talk into obligations-talk or vice-versa, the translations would often be unwieldy. "Joe has the right to possess his house," does mean (more or less) that "everyone is obliged to refrain from interfering with Joe's possession of his house," but why substitute thirteen words for eight? And why risk the error of translation? But there is more to the matter than linguistic economy. In many instances, one side of the right/obligation correlation is held by one person, the other side by an amorphous class of persons — not a very suitable subject for a right or obligation. Joe's right to possess his house turns into everyone's obligation not to interfere, but is only meaningful for that subset of persons who are actually in a position to interfere: neighbors, passers-by, the state of Texas, as the case may be. Likewise, Susan's obligation as a doctor to perform her work in a competent manner turns into a right to receive competent care, held by those whom Susan treats in her professional capacity, a class of persons whose membership changes daily.

In any particular instance, how do we know whether to formulate the relevant question as a rights problem or an obligations problem? As suggested above, the answer may come by deciding which formulation is simpler or more direct. Tradition, too, may play a role, as some formulations of a question may have been better accepted over time than the alternatives. Most likely, however, the formulation will depend on who has the problem. Any legal relation is properly understood as a relation between two or more people — with corresponding rights and obligations — but usually only one of them walks through the lawyer's door with a question. Only one of them marches to the courthouse to seek relief. And when that happens, it is most natural and effective to formulate the legal question from the puzzled or angry person's perspective, not the perspective of a person or persons unknown who may or may not hold a corresponding right or obligation. For example, if a client comes to ask whether she can build a second story on her house, the legal question is easily and meaningfully formulated from her perspective in "rights" language: does she have the right to build a second story? We are not focused on whether a *particular* person has a corresponding obligation to refrain from stopping her; but whether *anyone* can. In this particular case, to put the client's question in the language of obligations — "Does everyone, who is in a position to stop her, have an obligation to refrain from stopping her?" — admirably suggests why it is usually best to follow the client's or litigant's lead in deciding between rights-talk and obligations-talk.

Status and Contract

Both rights and obligations arise in essentially the same two ways: by *status* and by *contract.* One hundred years ago, Sir Henry Maine famously remarked that, "the movement of the progressive societies has hitherto been a movement from Status to Contract."[2] By this he meant that legal rights and obligations have come to be determined more and more by the will of the individuals, in agreement with each other (contract), rather than by membership in preexisting categories that define one's station or rank (status). Despite this movement, however, it remains true even today that status generates far more rights and obligations than does contract.

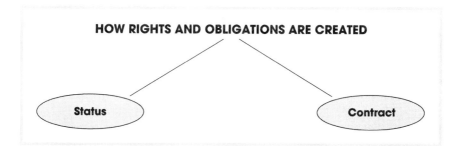

HOW RIGHTS AND OBLIGATIONS ARE CREATED

Status   Contract

The law has a thousand statuses, of extraordinary, fascinating variety — stockholder, mother, Vice-President of the United States, tenant, citizen of Alabama, plaintiff, etc. — and each is associated with a body of legal rights and obligations. Legal statuses vary dramatically in their *width,* that is, in how many people they cover. Width ranges from "person" at one end of the spectrum to (for example) a "party to a reorganization" as defined by section 368(b) of the federal tax code. There are over 250 million persons in the United States, but only several thousand parties to a reor-

---

[2]Henry Sumner Maine, *Ancient Law* 100 (Everyman's Library ed. 1927) (emphasis removed).

ganization in any one year. Legal statuses also vary in their *depth,* that is, in the number of rights and obligations they carry with them. One's status as a person imports a great many rights and obligations, while one's status as a party to a reorganization imports only a small group of tax-related consequences under the Internal Revenue Code. Width and depth are often related, as in the examples just given — some statuses are both wide and deep, others both narrow and shallow. But there is no necessary relation between width and depth. Trustee, for example, is a relatively narrow status (how many trustees do you know personally?), but the status comes with a relatively large number of explicitly delineated rights and responsibilities. "Male" and "female," in contrast, are both very wide statuses, but carry with them very few legal rights or obligations *per se.*

Each person occupies several different statuses simultaneously. On a particular morning, for example, one can wake to find oneself a stockholder, mother, Vice-President of the United States, tenant, citizen of Alabama, and plaintiff, subject to all of the rights and obligations carried by each status. But not all statuses are relevant at every moment of the day, and indeed most statuses are irrelevant almost all of the time — except when there is a legal problem. Lawyers and judges must know which statuses are relevant and when. If Susan wants to sue Joe because he sold her shoddy goods, for example, Joe's status as the executor of his grandmother's estate and as the father of two children are likely to be irrelevant; his status as a "merchant dealing in goods of that kind" might be pivotal. Lawyers and judges must therefore know what statuses there are, that is, which are legally recognized, and what rights and obligations are connected with each status. A great deal of law school training involves just this — learning about legal statuses and their relevance to common situations.

Rights and obligations are created not only by status, but also by agreement. When I agree to buy your 1978 Chrysler New Yorker for $500, you become obliged to transfer title and possession to me (conditioned on my payment of the agreed purchase price) and I, correlatively, become obliged to pay the purchase price (conditioned on your transfer of title and possession). In the broad scheme of things, however, the contractual creation of rights and obligations is much rarer than their status-driven creation. This disparity is reflected, among other places, in the law school curriculum. Of the all the courses typically offered in the first year, only one — contracts — is concerned primarily with the creation of rights and obligations by agreement. In none of the others — torts, property law, criminal law, and civil procedure — does agreement play a central role.

Even so, the contractual source of right and obligation is vitally important in selected areas of human endeavor, particularly in the buying and selling of goods and services. And that is no small matter in a society as thoroughly commercialized as our own. From a purely self-interested perspective, the contractual source of right and obligation is important to lawyers because business people generate a lot of work for them. But there are also more general, less mercenary reasons for contracts' significance. First, contracts and agreements create law where there was none before, and thus permit the stabilization and regulation of human interaction whenever two or more people wish it to occur. Second, contracts and agreements are the great safety valve of the law, permitting (at least sometimes) the modification of rights and obligations that would otherwise have existed by status. And finally, contracts and agreements can clarify what would otherwise have been doubtful or ambiguous. Contracts and agreements work at the margins of legal regulation, but are essential nonetheless.

The distinction between contract and status is not quite the same as that between voluntary and involuntary. First, rights and obligations founded in status are not always forced. Many statuses are optional, and one can enter or leave them at will — "theater patron," for example, or "stockholder." Still, there are many statuses about which one has no choice ("person," "Caucasian"), and statuses that, once entered, are hard to leave ("parent," "spouse"). Even those statuses that are relatively easy to enter and leave retain an element of coercion, since statuses typically come with a package of rights and obligations: if you wish to enjoy the rights of property ownership, for example, you must take on the obligation to pay property taxes.

Second, and conversely, many agreements are implied or imposed by the law, robbing them of any serious claim to voluntariness despite their nominal status as "agreements." For example, in residential leases, most states imply a *warranty of habitability,* that is, a promise from the landlord to the tenant that the premises are and will be maintained at a minimal level of safety and comfort. And courts will imply this promise even if the lease is silent or says something different. In such a case, the language of the obligation appears promissory, contractual, and voluntary, but is really compulsory and involuntary. (In such cases, one can argue that the obligation is really founded in status: the landlord in our example must maintain and repair the premises by virtue of being the landlord.) It is therefore useful to guard against two errors in one's study of law: the assumption that the holder of a status-based right or obligation had no choice in the matter and the assumption that a right or obligation cast in contractual language is thereby voluntary or consensual.

The Known and the Unknown

Rights and obligations, whether arising out of status or contract, are imposed both explicitly and implicitly. They are imposed explicitly whenever a legislature or court associates a particular right or obligation with a particular status, or whenever private parties agree to rights and obligations described in a particular document. From that base of explicit rights and obligations, others can be generated. If I have a right to keep you from setting foot on my property, I have a right to keep you from living there, too — the prohibition of the lesser intrusion implicitly including the greater one. Some extensions and additions are based on the correlative character of rights and obligations. As we have already seen, if Susan has a right, Joe (or someone else) has a corresponding obligation. Still other extensions and additions are based on analogies with similar statuses and contracts. Thus, for example, duties imposed on used-car dealers might, over time, "seep out" and be imposed on completely private parties who sell their cars to others.

Generally speaking, and within limits, we are willing to countenance extensions and additions to explicit rights and obligations. We do so in the name of interpretation and the methods we employ can roughly be described as legal logic. (Both topics will be addressed in later chapters.) Even at this point, however, it should be clear that extending and adding, moving beyond what we know to be the case, runs the risk of error and injustice. As lawyers and judges, therefore, we must try to get things right. This is why so much time in law school is spent on hypotheticals — new, imaginary cases whose resolution requires us to push beyond the rights and obligations that we know. *Hypotheticals* develop judgment, the ability to move *reliably* from the known to the unknown and to learn which extensions of known law are warranted and which are not.

THE ONLY THREE QUESTIONS IN LAW

We now know that the law regulates observable human action. It does so by creating obligations and rights, either out of status or by contract, either explicitly or implicitly. Against this background the fundamental nature of legal analysis snaps into focus.

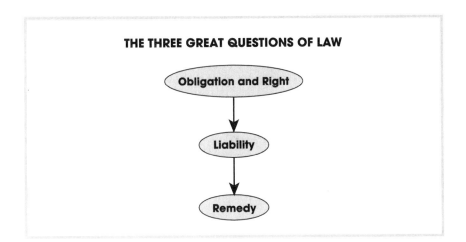

THE THREE GREAT QUESTIONS OF LAW

The Questions

There are only three legal questions. That is to say, there are only three kinds of questions that lawyers and judges try to answer:

1. Is there a law?
2. Has it been violated?
3. What will be done about it?

Not every legal situation raises questions of all three types, and indeed, even if all three types are raised initially, the answer to one question may eliminate the need to proceed further. If no law has been violated, there is no reason to worry about remedies; if there is no relevant law, neither questions of violation nor remedy are relevant. Still, every legal situation will raise at least one of these questions, or *it's not legal*. That doesn't mean a lawyer shouldn't answer it, or that the lawyer's answer won't be a good one. It just means that, in answering such a question, the lawyer moves beyond her distinctive calling *as a lawyer,* to a different field — perhaps of business or finance — where wisdom and truth will be judged on different grounds.

The three questions listed above have a particular cast. They are the questions of lawyers and judges involved in a lawsuit, in *litigation,* and litigation has the peculiar feature of looking both backward and forward. A problem has already arisen; certain actions and facts come to us from the past and cannot be changed. (We will say more later on the contingency of facts.) The resolution of the problem is still open; some result lies in the future and is yet unknown. This past-to-future, neck-twisting perspective is reflected in the way the questions are formulated: "*Has* the law been violated?" "What *will* be done about it?"

Legal questions look different, however, from the perspective of lawyers who do not litigate, but instead help their clients plan future activities — lawyers helping clients buy a house, adopt a child, construct a highway, or dissolve a partnership. Such work, sometimes called *transactional work* or *office practice* to distinguish it from litigation, is entirely forward-looking and filled with contingencies. For someone engaged in office practice, the three questions look more like this:

1. Are there any potentially relevant laws?
2. Would any of them be violated?
3. What might be done about those violations?

If a client wishes to take a particular action, the planning lawyer will often work through all three questions before giving advice.

Legal questions look different still in some planning situations, where legal violations can largely be avoided if the lawyers do their work right. In the drafting of a will or the transfer of property by deed, for example, the three question will look more like this:

1. What are the relevant laws?
2. How do we comply with them?
3. What happens if we don't?

Although the precise form of the three legal questions varies slightly from context to context, their essential character never changes. That is, in one form or another, lawyers and judges always raise questions about: (1) the law's existence; (2) its application; and (3) its consequences. This insight generates our final form of the three legal questions. When we ask about the law's existence, we know from our earlier discussion that we are asking about the existence of a relevant *obligation* or *right*. If such an obligation or right exists, we next want to know whether it was or will be violated by a course of conduct (past conduct in litigation, future conduct in planning). If such a violation has occurred or will occur, the person who violates the right or obligation will be liable, and thus it is proper to speak of the second inquiry as raising the issue of **liability**. Even after a person's liability has been established, it is not always easy to decide what to do about it, for there are several options. We can, for example, require the miscreant to pay money to the person harmed, pay money to the state, put everything back the way it was, or go to jail. We might even do nothing at all. This is the issue of *remedy*. Thus, no matter what one's legal job — judge, litigator, or transactional lawyer — every legal question will necessarily raise an issue concerning: (1) obligation and right; (2) liability; or (3) remedy. In the next three chapters we will examine each of these issues in turn.

The Three Questions, As Seen by Clients and Law Students

Before exploring each of the three legal questions in depth, it is important to see how they affect two groups of people — clients and law students. We turn first to clients, and more specifically to litigants (those involved in a lawsuit). It's hard to be a plaintiff, that is, the person who initiates a lawsuit. Plaintiffs consider themselves harmed or damaged and want action. They want heads to roll, large sums of money to be paid, things put back the way they were — probably all three. But they won't get these remedies unless they are proper. And there won't be any remedy at all unless there is liability. And there is no chance of liability unless a relevant obligation or right was violated in the first place. Plaintiffs, in short, must get a favorable answer to *all three* legal questions or they lose. Conversely, it is much easier to be a defendant (the person who is sued). Defendants win if they get a favorable answer to *just one* legal question, and any one will do: no law, no violation, or no remedy.

Clients in the planning stages have the easiest road of all. First, the planned actions — the adoption of a child, the building of a highway — might be permissible. They probably are. Like defendants in a lawsuit, planning clients "win" if they get a favorable answer to just one of the three legal questions. If there is no relevant law, or if the relevant laws would not be violated, or if the violated laws generate no effective remedy, the client can proceed as planned. Second, even if the planned actions are not permissible — the client having gotten "wrong" answers to all three questions — several options remain. The client can drop the current plans, modify them to expunge or minimize the legal difficulty, or charge ahead with the plans unchanged, but knowing the risks involved. (The last option is never one the client's lawyer can recommend, but it is often countenanced.)

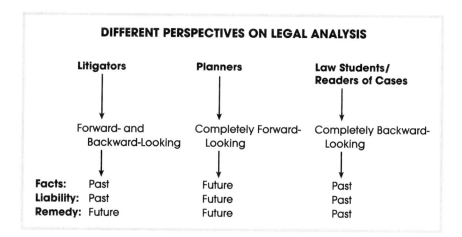

DIFFERENT PERSPECTIVES ON LEGAL ANALYSIS

	Litigators	Planners	Law Students/ Readers of Cases
	Forward- and Backward-Looking	Completely Forward-Looking	Completely Backward-Looking
Facts:	Past	Future	Past
Liability:	Past	Future	Past
Remedy:	Future	Future	Past

Law students face different challenges. We have already seen that practicing lawyers face different sets of questions regarding obligation and right, liability and remedy, depending on their role as litigators or transactional attorneys. Furthermore, because even die-hard litigators sometimes do planning and committed transactional lawyers sometimes litigate, most lawyers can see any type of question at any time. This is all sufficiently confusing, but the position of law students is even worse — not just because they don't know what to expect or when to expect it, but because law school training is confusing and sometimes flatly misleading on this point. There is a deep and important division between the reading of assignments, on the one hand, and classroom discussion, on the other. The failure to notice this division and to account for it during class preparation generates painful but needless anxiety. So here's the story; read carefully.

Law school assignments come from casebooks, and casebooks are filled with reports of cases decided in the past. Case reports are the "fossils" of litigation. Everyone involved in those cases, including the judges who wrote the opinions, were thinking like litigators, asking and answering questions from our original list: Is there a law? Has it been violated? What will be done about it? These were the questions that could be asked by those *in* the case. But law students are not the lawyers or judges involved. For them, and for anyone else reading the cases today, all the questions are in the past tense: Was there a law? Was it violated? What was done about it? These are the only questions that can be asked *about* a case. We will call this the "archaeological" perspective.

The archaeological perspective is the one necessarily taken by any reader of a case report. Completely backward-looking, it differs from the litigation perspective, which is both forward- and backward-looking, and from the planning perspective, which is entirely forward-looking. The archaeological perspective is the one necessarily taken by any reader of a case report, but *it is not the one taken by any lawyer in handling any legal matter.* The archaeological questions and answers are useless by themselves. It does no lawyer any good, by itself, to know that on May 17, 1954, Judge Clayton of the Missouri Court of Appeals refused to reverse the trial court decision holding Carlos Esquival liable to Friedrich Heimhofer on breach of contract for $62,500. These archeological facts must be translated into questions and answers needed by lawyers today.

What does this mean for studying cases and preparing for classes? First, one must begin with good archaeology. When reading a case, it is crucial to understand precisely what legal questions were raised and answered. This is the point of briefing the case, and the talent is essential. Without a firm archaeological understanding, nothing else will be possible. Second (and this is the key point), one must work at switching perspectives. For example, one could ask, "If exactly the same case (same facts, same parties) were litigated today, would the result be the same?" — the contemporary litigation perspective. Or ask, "If a client today wanted to do what the defendant did, would it still be prohibited?" — the contemporary planning perspective. These questions will tip you off to think about the possibility of changes in the law or perhaps changes in society that put a crucially different cast on the facts. From there, more difficult changes can be attempted, altering more than the dates (because, of course, no two cases are exactly alike). The point is to get in the habit of, and to gain skill in, moving from one perspective to another.

This should also explain the mystery of the law school classroom. In that forum, we are always concerned with archaeology (because, again, without a firm grasp of the archaeological facts, nothing else is possible). But the amount of time devoted to archaeology varies during the year. It is often the primary concern in the earliest weeks of the first year. During those weeks students will find the strongest correlation between what they read before class and what they talk about in class. As the weeks progress, however, classroom attention to archaeology diminishes not because it has lost its importance, but because there is (and always was) a great deal more to do. Classroom attention turns more frequently to the work of switching perspectives, to the work of making the fossils of litigation useful to litigators and transactional lawyers today. More and more, what is read before class and what is talked about in class diverge.

Again, the divergence is no mystery, and the new discussions can be prepared for with almost the same effectiveness as the earlier ones. Now the classroom question will often be, "What does this case (or administrative ruling or statute or regulation) tell us for someone litigating or planning today?" It is the sort of question that can be anticipated and therefore asked and answered at home. It just takes good archaeology and a growing talent for switching perspectives.

◆ IN SUMMARY

- The law regulates two kinds of persons, *natural* and *juristic*.

- The law regulates only physically observable behavior, although mental states can affect how that behavior is treated.

- The *principle of legality* holds that all actions are legal unless made illegal, but applies only to natural persons, not juristic ones.

- *Obligations* arise when the law requires or prohibits an action; depending on the context they can also be called duties, disabilities, requirements, or liabilities.

- *Rights* arise when the law permits an action; depending on the context, they can also be called claims, privileges, licenses, powers, immunities, or liberties.

- Obligations and rights are closely related, but we still need both ways of talking about legal relationships.

- Obligations and rights can be created:
  - by *status* or *contract* (with status the predominant method)
  - *voluntarily* or *involuntarily*
  - *explicitly* or *implicitly*

- Lawyers and judges consistently ask the same questions about any situation, questions about the law's:
  - existence (questions of *obligation* and *right*)
  - application (questions of *liability*)
  - consequences (questions of *remedy*)

- The precise form of the question depends on context, primarily on the distinction between *litigation* and *transactional work.*

- In law study, one must take the *archaeological* facts of decided cases and make them useful in litigation and planning today, by learning to switch perspectives.

Is There a Law?
(Questions of Obligation and Right)

THIS CHAPTER

- Takes up the first great question of legal analysis: Is there a law?

- Divides this inquiry into two questions:
  - has a relevant obligation or right been validly *created*? And if so,
  - has anything *happened* to it *since?*

- Describes the many questions that arise when:
  - *individuals* try to create legal obligations and rights by entering into contracts, making wills, creating trusts, and similar acts of private lawmaking
  - *governments* try to create legal obligations and rights by passing legislation, promulgating regulations, and similar acts of public lawmaking

- Describes the conditions under which legal obligations and rights, once created, can be:
  - *transferred*
  - *modified* or
  - *terminated*

- Explains how lawyers take account of these issues when representing their clients

The first type of legal question involves the *existence* of legal obligations and rights. Obligations and rights don't just happen; they must be created. Once created, many can be transferred, modified, or terminated. Because of these features, legal obligations and rights have something like a natural history or life-cycle: they are born, they live, they die. This chapter traces that natural history.

Lawyers and judges often debate the existence of particular obligations or rights. If someone claims, for example, that my client has violated a legal obligation, I might respond by denying that there was any obligation at all. Why? Because no such obligation was validly created in the first place or because it was later modified or terminated. Likewise, if another client believes that one of her rights has been violated by someone else, I will want to ensure that the right at issue was in fact validly created and that it has not been transferred, modified, or terminated since its creation. A judge will have to ask all these questions, too, if these cases ever get to court.

Everett's Case

To put these issues in context, let us assume throughout this book that we represent Everett Plainfield, who has been accused of striking a fellow employee at the tire plant where he works. As his lawyers, we might begin to analyze his legal situation by asking whether there are any obligations or rights that he might potentially have violated. There could, in fact, be at least three: some aspect of criminal law (subjecting him to prosecution by the local district attorney); some aspect of civil tort law (subjecting him to a lawsuit for battery by the person he allegedly struck); and some aspect of his employment contract (causing his termination by his employer). We'll explore each of these possibilities.

HAS AN OBLIGATION OR RIGHT BEEN CREATED AT ALL?

Legal obligations and rights are created in different ways, some of them more controversial than others. For over two thousand years, many lawyers have believed that at least some legal obligations and rights are imposed by nature. *Natural law* has taken many forms over time, and there is lively disagreement even today about its existence and content. At base, however, a belief in natural law requires a belief that law can exist in the absence of any officially recognized governmental action. Such law might come from God, from the very nature of human beings, or from some other source. Those who signed the Declaration of Independence, for example, claimed the existence of "inalienable rights" that no government could extinguish.

Natural law thinking continues to make its presence felt today, especially in the context of international human rights. There is a growing sentiment, for example, that individuals have a right not to be tortured, regardless of what any legislative body says about the matter. Another outcropping of natural law thinking can be seen in debates among members of the United States Supreme Court about whether there can be any recognizable, enforceable constitutional rights beyond those explicitly mentioned in the constitutional text. (A lawyer steeped in the natural law tradition would be more likely to think that there could be.) Subtler influences of natural law thinking can be found in the elaborate judicial interpretations of constitutional and statutory phrases such as *due process, equal protection,* and *fairness,* as courts fill these nebulous concepts with a substantive content that looks suspiciously like the universal values of natural law.

Despite its long history and remaining influence, natural law theory has been in more or less steady decline since the nineteenth century. It has been replaced by a competing theory that rejects the proposition that any part of law is given by nature, that any rule is pre-ordained. This competing theory, *positivism,* holds instead that law can only be created by the affirmative acts of duly authorized lawmakers. So complete has been positivism's victory that nowadays American lawyers and judges almost never refer to natural law in their arguments or decisions. Even less frequently do they claim it to be an independent source of legal obligation and right.

Custom is an equally controversial source of law. Many have believed that at least some legal obligations and rights are created out of patterns of behavior, long repeated, that generate legitimate expectations of continued compliance. Most of the law in preliterate societies was founded on custom, and indeed, early English courts were often guided by what was customary among the parties concerned. But the situation in the United States today is different. Custom, like natural law, is no longer regarded by most lawyers and judges as an independent source of legal obligation and right, although custom among *nations* is still considered a source of *international law.* In purely domestic matters, however, American judges and lawyers turn to custom only when directed to do so by a statute.

Everett's Case

Because they are so rarely invoked, we have assumed that neither custom nor natural law generates rights or obligations applicable to Everett's situation. Lawyers and judges almost always make the same assumption in contemporary practice.

Aside from controversial sources of law like custom and natural law, everyone agrees that legal obligations and rights can be created by governments, primarily through legislation, and by individuals, primarily through contractual arrangements. These sources of law fit more comfortably within the positivist paradigm and lawyers and judges in fact deal with them more frequently than any others. As a consequence, these are the forms of public and private lawmaking most discussed in this chapter.

We have already noted an important difference between the creation of legal obligations, on the one hand, and legal rights, on the other. A legal obligation can only be created by an affirmative act, but a legal right can exist without any affirmative act, the principle of legality "authorizing" natural persons to act as they wish without any official permission. This would suggest that legal discussion in this area tends to focus on legal obligations rather than legal rights, but the weight of discussion is not so lopsided as it might appear. First, the principle of legality does not apply to juristic persons, so the rights of corporations, partnerships, and other entities must be created by affirmative act. Second, even for natural persons, rights derived from the principle of legality are notoriously vague and it is therefore often useful to establish that a right has been created by affirmative act. In sum, despite the theoretical differences, the affirmative creation of both obligations *and* rights are of daily concern to lawyers and judges.

When working with questions about the creation of obligations and rights, lawyers and judges must distinguish between **public lawmaking** and **private lawmaking,** that is, between the work of governments on the one hand, and everyone else on the other. The problems typically generated by each source of law are similar in theory, but quite different in practice and terminology. Because private lawmaking is more frequently challenged than public lawmaking we take up the private mode of lawmaking first.

Note well, before we continue, that the distinction between public and private lawmaking is *not* the same as the distinction between status and contract. The distinction between status and contract turns on the *mechanism* by which obligations and rights are attached to persons. In the contract mechanism, rights and obligations are attached directly to particular persons, generally as those persons have agreed in some document; in the status mechanism, rights and obligations are attached to particular statuses, in and out of which people move. The distinction between public and private lawmaking, in contrast, turns on *who is involved* in the process; it is public lawmaking if a government or group of governments is at work, private if anyone else is.

It is true that public lawmakers almost always use the status mechanism (enacting legislation, for example, that applies to all pet owners) and that private parties almost always use the contractual mechanism, (a dog lover, for example, agreeing to purchase a collie), but there are important exceptions. Governments often enter into agreements with private individuals — for the building of highways or the production of aircraft carriers, for example — and they sometimes enact "private laws" that address named individuals rather than classes of persons. Conversely, private persons, like business corporations and condominium associations, sometimes issue rules and regulations whose tenor is clearly status-based and legislative. It is in areas like these, where governments and individuals step "out of character," that special problems arise and where one tends to find extra doses of judicial and scholarly hand-wringing.

Everett's Case

We recall that our client Everett faces at least three kinds of problems: prosecution under criminal law, a civil lawsuit by the alleged victim under tort law, and possible termination by his employer. The last of these threats, getting fired by his employer, would likely be based on his employment contract. We would therefore turn to that contract to see what it says about employee conduct on the job. Whatever it says, we might be able to avoid Everett's firing if we could show that there was something wrong with the creation of that contract or one of its provisions, and therefore that the supposedly binding right or obligation does not exist at all.

Problems in Private Creation

There is no doubt that private persons have lawmaking ability. When Susan agrees to purchase Joe's house, when Joe establishes a *trust* for his three children, when Susan writes a will, when Joe's new condominium association issues regulations, when Susan's corporation changes its bylaws, legal obligations and rights are created and modified. Some forms of private lawmaking are available only to natural persons (willmaking), some just to juristic persons (bylaw creation), and some are available to both (contracts, gifts, and trust formation). Some forms of private lawmaking require the assent of two or more parties (contracts) while others can be accomplished unilaterally (the formation of certain "grantor-trusts"). Despite the variety of contexts and forms, the private creation of obligations and rights raises predictable, recurring questions about authority, procedure, and results. Six of the most common issues are these:

1. *Capacity:* Did all the parties have the legal capacity to take the action they did?
2. *Agency:* Did someone (an agent) act in place of one of the parties? If so, was that representation legally effective?

3. *Mistake:* Did anyone misunderstand what they were doing, or make some other mistake about the nature of the transaction?
4. *Coercion:* Was anyone forced to act as he or she did?
5. *Formalities:* Were there any required formalities, such as a notarized signature, and if so, were those formalities observed?
6. *Public policy:* Do the resulting rights and obligations violate any overriding *public policy?*

Exercises of private lawmaking are likely to be valid if all six issues are settled satisfactorily. Conversely, the wrong answer to only one of them will usually destroy the private lawmaking effort.

Everett's Case

If there is a problem with any one of these aspects of Everett's employment contract with his employer, the contractual clauses harmful to Everett might be found void (because not validly created) and therefore unenforceable.

Problems of Capacity. Private lawmaking requires that all of the parties involved have the legal capacity to take the actions they have. Capacity questions are different for natural and juristic persons, so we must examine the two kinds of persons separately.

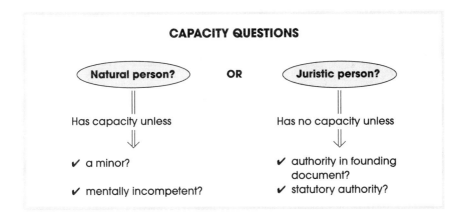

CAPACITY QUESTIONS

Natural person?	OR	Juristic person?
Has capacity unless		Has no capacity unless
✔ a minor?		✔ authority in founding document?
✔ mentally incompetent?		✔ statutory authority?

Natural persons. For natural persons, the principle of legality gives everyone the presumptive power to create obligations and rights whenever they wish. As a general rule, the power is limited only by youth and mental incompetence.

MINORITY. One's status as a minor modifies or precludes one's ability to enter into contracts, buy and sell property, and to make wills and trusts. Most disabilities are removed at the age of majority — 18 for most civil law purposes, but with many exceptions. In Illinois and in most other states, for example, one can vote at the age of 18 but cannot buy a bottle of whiskey until the age of 21. Most age limitations are set by the calendar, but some are determined on more amorphous grounds. The power to contract and the power to make certain gifts turn on whether the person has attained "the age of reason," a test much more likely to attract litigation and the concern of planners.

The age of majority tells us the age after which there is no problem, but doesn't tell us the nature of the problem before that age is reached. Persons under 18 can marry, for example, but only with permission. They can enter into contracts, but retain a right to nullify the transaction upon reaching majority. In contrast, persons under 18 are absolutely prohibited from making wills. Because of this variety, lawyers working with young people must be aware not only of the relevant age limitations, but the precise disabilities or consequences associated with each age.

Generally speaking, the law does not disable minors from *holding* privately created obligations and rights, but only from *creating* or *transferring* them without supervision. When adults are both willing and authorized to act for them, minors can engage in and become the subjects of private lawmaking activity. And indeed, the law has developed several techniques by which adults are authorized to act for minors. Parents, by virtue of their status as parents, can act for their children in many matters. More specialized techniques include the creation of guardianships and trusts, transfers of property under statutory Transfers to Minors Acts, and, in litigation, the appointment of guardians *ad litem*. Sometimes, however, no technique is available in a particular situation, because the kind of action at issue is not permitted on a representative basis. There are many alternative techniques for buying and selling property, for example, but none for willmaking.

Everett's Case

Everett is 32 years old, and began working for the tire company when he was 26. As a consequence, there was no age impediment to his entering into an employment contract with the tire company. If he had been younger than 18 when he was hired, some of these capacity issues may have arisen (along with laws prohibiting child labor).

MENTAL INCOMPETENCE. Like minors, those who lack mental competence are denied the power to create obligations and rights for themselves. Questions of mental competence can arise in two basic settings: in formal adjudications of a person's status as *mentally incompetent* (or other, similarly labeled category) and in *ad hoc* decisions regarding the mental competence of a person at a particular time. Like ages of majority, standards for mental competence vary from context to context. Willmaking is traditionally understood to have one of the lowest standards for mental competence in the civil law: a few minutes of lucidity, during years of abject confusion, are enough to make a will, so long as the willmaker knows some basic facts about his world and family. The standard for capacity to marry is said to be even lower. Higher standards, on the other hand, are required for contracting, gift-giving and trust-making. In formal hearings about a person's competence, the capacity to care for one's own body is often treated differently from the capacity to care for one's property — property dealings usually requiring a higher standard of lucidity. This is an old area of law, with many counterintuitive surprises.

Mental competence standards are notoriously difficult to apply, even after the verbal formula has been set. Decisionmaking often involves the review of ambiguous or conflicting evidence about a person's behavior over a long period of time. This puts a particular strain on, and raises questions about, evidentiary issues (what items of evidence can be heard?) and burdens of proof (who has it? is a preponderance of the evidence enough?). Even if all the appropriate evidence has been collected and heard, final determinations of competence are often hard to predict.

As with minors, mentally incompetent persons can act through representatives. And as with minors, the law has developed several techniques by which incompetent adults can be represented by competent ones. Court-obtained guardianships and privately created trust relationships are two of the most common examples. And again, representation may not be possible with respect to particular actions. There are alternative techniques for buying and selling property, but the mentally incompetent, like the young, cannot make a will through representatives.

Everett's Case

We have no evidence that Everett is mentally incompetent, either in the sense that he has been declared incompetent by some court or tribunal, or in the sense that he was in fact incompetent at the time of his hiring. Because Everett had passed the age of majority and was mentally competent at the time he began working for the tire company, we cannot question unfavorable clauses in his employment contract on the ground that Everett lacked capacity.

Juristic persons. Juristic persons can lack capacity, too, and this can hobble or defeat their ability to create private obligations and rights. A contract between two corporations, for example, could be rendered a nullity if either corporation lacked the relevant authority to make it. Capacity questions for juristic persons look quite different from capacity questions for natural persons. Age makes no difference to the powers of corporations and partnerships, and there is no sense in which they can become feeble-minded. Still, private juristic persons are not benefitted by the principle of legality and must be granted authority to act. This authority usually comes from their founding documents — articles of incorporation, a partnership agreement, a trust instrument, and sometimes from statutes. Capacity questions about private juristic persons are often cast as whether their actions were **ultra vires,** that is, "outside their power." If the lawmaking activity of a trust, corporation, or partnership is *ultra vires,* no obligations or rights will have been created.

Private juristic persons vary in their formality, that is to say, in how closely they are identified with the natural persons who make them up. A proprietorship, for example, is very closely identified with the person who owns it, and indeed, there are only a few instances in which it is important to know whether the owner is acting as Joe personally or as Joe's Steak House. Proprietorships are informal in their creation and operation. At the other end of the spectrum, publicly held corporations and large nonprofit organizations are not closely identified with their owners or managers, and such owners and managers are very careful in distinguishing whether they are acting in individual or corporate capacities. The entities themselves are quite formal in their creation and operation.

These differences have an effect on how often we ask capacity questions and how we go about answering them. The more formal a juristic entity, the more likely it is to raise capacity questions. When we do ask a capacity question about informal entities, we tend to answer it by reference to the persons who make them up. If we ask, for example, whether Joe's Steak House can give a donation to the Methodist Church, the answer is usually found by asking, "could Joe?" Questions about more formal entities tend to be answered by reference to documents — founding instruments, bylaws, and regulatory legislation. This is partly explained, of course, by the fact that we *have* more documents on formal entities and we might as well take a look at them. But the documentary emphasis is also explained on other grounds. The more different an entity becomes from a natural person, the more we lose our bearings on how to think about it, and capacity inquiries (like all other questions concerning it) become more formal and documentary in their approach.

Everett's Case

Everett's employer is a large corporation, and as a juristic person must have authority to enter into the kind of employment contract it has with Everett. If not, then the tire company lacked capacity, and Everett's employment contract may be called into question. It is virtually certain, however, that the company's charter grants it, expressly or by implication, the authority to hire employees and to enter into contracts with them regarding that employment.

Problems of Agency. It may be Susan and Joe at the table signing papers, but the partners in the new joint venture they are forming are Susan's dental floss company and Joe's Steak House. All juristic persons act exclusively through representatives, as do minors and mental incompetents most of the time. For all others — i.e., mentally competent adults — the use of agents is optional. The law gives many different names to representatives — *owners* in proprietorships, *partners* in partnerships, *officers* and *directors* in corporations and nonprofit organizations, *trustees* in trusts, *executors* and *administrators* in estates, *guardians* and *custodians* for minors and mental incompetents, or just plain old *agents*. Whatever the label, the law recognizes the possibility, and sometimes requires, that one person act for another. For our purposes, we will refer to all of these situations as *agencies*, and to the players as *agents* and *principals*.

AGENCY QUESTIONS

(**Need an agent?**)

Then ask:

Look for:

(1) agency validly created?

effective appointment, election, etc.?

(2) agent have capacity?

(see CAPACITY QUESTIONS)

(3) agency still in effect when action taken?

terminated by death of principal or other cause?

(4) agent acting within his or her scope?

agent doing the kind of work hired to do? serving the purpose of the agency?

Several things must hold true for an agent to create rights and obligations binding a principal. First, the agent must have capacity. Anyone can be a principal, but not just anyone can be an agent. A minor can have a guardian, but can't serve as one. In sum, both natural and juristic persons can be agents, but they must have: (1) *general* legal capacity, determined along the lines discussed in the immediately preceding section; and (2) legal capacity *to act as agents*. Only certain corporations, for example, are authorized to act as trustees.

Second, an agent can bind a principal only if the agency relationship was validly formed. Agency relationships are created in different ways, but they must be created. Directors of a corporation must be duly elected by the shareholders. Corporate officers must be elected by the directors or appointed by higher elected officers. Trustees must be named in the trust instrument, appointed by a court, or in some cases, named by other trustees. Partners must have joined the partnership. Literary agents must be hired by the authors concerned. Whatever the context of the agency, the agent must have been properly appointed in accord with the relevant rules.

Third, the agency relationship must still be in effect when the agent acts. This is an important qualification, because agency relationships can come to an end for many reasons. Some agencies are explicitly limited to a specific period of time; such agencies end when the period ends. In addition, most agencies end when either the agent or principal dies. Some end when the principal becomes incompetent. Literary agents who do not get top dollar for their clients' books are fired.

Fourth, the agent must act within the scope of the agency. Agents are appointed for broader and narrower purposes, but always for some purpose. Generally, agents no longer speak for their principals and cannot bind them when they act in areas or for purposes not contemplated in the original agency. An assistant treasurer in a corporation, though able to represent and bind the company in the hiring of accounting consultants, could not represent and bind the company in a merger agreement with a rival. My literary agent cannot bind me in the sale of my house.

As should be obvious by now, agency is both common and legally hazardous. It is thus a fertile source of litigation and a constant concern of planners. Every action or transaction involving a juristic person raises questions of agency, as do many actions or transactions involving natural persons. The problems are often compounded because *agents can represent and deal with other agents*. I might hire a literary agency, for example, which in turn employs the particular person who negotiates the sale of my book; that agent, in turn, will negotiate with an employee of a book publisher, who, in this particular case, might be working on behalf of one of the publisher's subsidiaries. Agency problems can arise at each step (and there will be plenty of people to sue if the book deal falls through).

Everett's Case

Everett dealt directly with the employer at his hiring, and thus there are no agency questions to raise on his side of the hiring transaction. But the employer, as a juristic person, necessarily works through agents. In theory, then, we could raise questions on the company's side of the transaction: Who exactly hired Everett? Who signed any papers that were signed? Practically speaking, however, it is unlikely (although possible) that the company made mistakes regarding agency in a simple hiring of personnel.

Problems of Mistake. Mistakes are part of life, and when an agent or principal makes a mistake in the course of private lawmaking — creating an easement, making a will, negotiating a contract — it can affect the transaction. Most areas of law that involve private lawmaking have developed doctrines for handling mistakes. The analysis and terminology varies from area to area, but the main issues are predictable. One issue involves the *consequences* of the mistake. Sometimes mistakes *void* the transaction at issue and sometimes they make it *voidable*. (When a transaction is void, it is treated as if it never occurred at all. When a transaction is voidable, it stands as a good transaction, but one or more of the parties involved can make it void at their option. Unless and until voided, however, the transaction is still good.) In still other cases, the mistake is either corrected or ignored entirely. Mistakes in contracts for example, can be ignored (the contract language standing as written), be corrected, or make the entire contract void. Mistakes in willmaking, in contrast, never make the will "voidable"; they either void the will (in whole or in part) or are corrected. Mistakes are thus treated differently from a finding that one or more of the parties to a transaction lacked capacity. When capacity is lacking, the transaction is almost always considered void — capacity representing an indispensable requirement for private lawmaking. Mistakes give rise to several more options.

Because of this variety of options, and because the precise options available vary from area to area (from contract law to property law to the law of wills, for example), it is hard to generalize about the substantive law of mistakes. Still, some principles tend to recur in all areas of law:

- Mistakes of agents (including lawyers) are sometimes dealt with more sympathetically than mistakes of principals. That is, a lawyer's mistake might more readily be corrected, or the transaction more readily voided or made voidable, in the interest of protecting the hapless client.

- In two-party transactions, mistakes made by both parties are generally treated more sympathetically than mistakes by only one. If only one of the parties makes the mistake, we are more likely to require the mistaken party to live with it.
- Mistakes about the law — what it says, what it requires — are treated less sympathetically than mistakes about facts in the world. That is, if a party has gotten the law wrong, he or she may be required to bear the consequences.
- Mistakes that arise from inattention or sloth are handled less sympathetically than mistakes that could not have been avoided with reasonable effort.
- Mistakes "helped along" by one of two parties to a transaction often give the innocent party a special claim to have the transaction voided or modified.
- Mistakes that affect only the parties to the transaction are more likely to be corrected than mistakes upon which other persons have innocently relied or, relatedly, mistakes made in documents that have entered a public records system.
- And finally, technical mistakes in the drafting of documents — spelling errors, mistakes in transcription (scrivener's error) — are often corrected, so long as one can show that there was truly a mistake of this sort.

Everett's Case

In the context of a hiring for a job, we would not expect either Everett or his employer to have made a mistake so fundamental as to call into question the validity of the employment contract or its termination provisions.

Problems of Coercion. Private lawmaking is voluntary and consensual. As a result, any hint of coercion in the formation of private obligations and rights raises the possibility that they will be found invalid or unenforceable. Sharp practice and sinister dealings can be found in all areas of life and each area of law tends to handle issues of coercion in slightly different ways, with different terminology. Depending on the area of law and the precise sort of coercion employed, the problem can be raised as a matter of *misrepresentation, fraud, undue influence, overreaching* or *unconscionability*. As with the law of mistakes, generalization is difficult, but several principles recur:

- The more immediate and threatening the coercion, the more likely that the private lawmaking will be affected. Putting a gun to the head of a home seller at the signing of real estate contract will void the contract; taunting him two weeks before will not.
- Coercive conduct that induces someone to enter into a transaction in the first place will generally make the whole transaction void or voidable; coercive conduct that affects only one of its terms will affect only the term involved. (Having made this distinction, it is often difficult to tell whether the entire transaction or just one of its terms was the product of coercion.)
- The existence of a willing or gullible participant can affect whether coercive conduct will have any affect at all on the transaction, or what its consequences will be. In property law, for example, a victim of theft can get his property back from the thief and anyone else the thief has sold it to, even if the later purchasers didn't know that the property was stolen. If instead of outright theft, the original victim was tricked into turning his property over to a con artist, the victim can still get his property back from the crook, but not from an innocent purchaser down the line.

Everett's Case

There are no facts here that suggest coercion in the formation of the employment contract. Absent other special circumstances, just needing a job is not enough.

Problems of Formalities. Private lawmaking often requires that certain formalities be observed. If one of those formalities is missing, we are likely to consider the transaction void. Typical formalities include a writing, signatures, witnesses, notarization, and the filing of papers in public offices. Different transactions require different formalities, and learning about these differences is an important subject in law school.

Formalities generally serve three purposes. They are meant to generate contemporary, relatively permanent evidence of a transaction (their evidentiary function); they remind the participants that serious business is afoot, that legal obligations and rights are about to be created (their ceremonial function); and, by requiring actions or steps that typically cannot be taken on the spur of the moment, they help to avoid overreaching and other forms of coercion (their protective function).

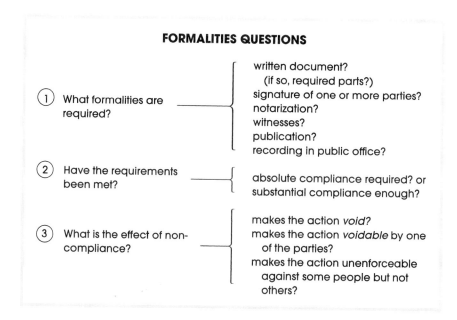

FORMALITIES QUESTIONS

① What formalities are required?
- written document?
  (if so, required parts?)
- signature of one or more parties?
- notarization?
- witnesses?
- publication?
- recording in public office?

② Have the requirements been met?
- absolute compliance required? or
- substantial compliance enough?

③ What is the effect of non-compliance?
- makes the action *void?*
- makes the action *voidable* by one of the parties?
- makes the action unenforceable against some people but not others?

The legal questions raised by formalities are of three types. First, precisely what formalities are required? Must there be a writing? There are different rules for contracts, deeds, trusts, wills, and corporate bylaws. If a writing is required, what must it contain? Again, there are different rules for contracts, deeds, trusts, and other private lawmaking efforts. Are signatures required? Most private lawmaking that requires a writing also requires signatures, but not necessarily everyone's. Written contracts, for example, are enforceable against the parties who *have* signed, even if not all of them have done so. Is authentication of some sort required? For some types of documents the law requires witnesses or attestation by a notary public. Must the document be filed with some public authority? Some do; some don't. Most first-year courses spend a significant amount of time reviewing the formalities required for different sorts of private lawmaking.

Second, have the required formalities been met? This raises not only the more obvious questions of fact (is there a writing or not? does it contain a description of the property or not?), but subtler issues of interpretation (is this an adequate description of the property? do the seller's initials count as a signature?). We sometimes interpret away minor failings in formalities by deciding that they aren't really failings at all.

Third, and finally, what is the effect of noncompliance? In some areas of private lawmaking, we explicitly recognize doctrines of **substantial compliance,** pursuant to which admitted deficiencies in the execution or content of required formalities will not affect a transaction's validity. In some states, for example, the law of wills has this feature. Even without such a doctrine, deficiencies in formalities can still be ignored, typically on one of two grounds: because the actions of the parties have proved the existence of the private lawmaking even in the absence of sufficient formalities; or because recognition of the transaction is necessary to prevent unfairness to one of the parties. Problems that cannot be ignored on these grounds make the whole transaction void or voidable, or affect the transaction as to some persons and not others. As an example of the latter effect, deeds not recorded in the public land office are still good as between the immediate parties (the buyer will win possession against the seller) but not against certain third parties who later acquire the subject property. (Just who those third parties are is a question fully explored in most first-year Property classes.)

Everett's Case

Employment agreements are contracts and thus subject to the general rules regarding the formalities required for any contract. Thus, we might be able to raise questions about whether a writing was required in Everett's case, and if so, whether he and the company signed anything. As it turns out, employment contracts raise some special and interesting issues on this score. Is an employee handbook, given to employees when they join the company, a part of the employment contract? If the company seeks to punish Everett for his action, we would want to know exactly what piece of paper, if any, the company is relying on.

Problems of Public Policy. There are some rights and obligations we don't let people create, even if they have capacity, make no mistakes, are free of coercion, and comply with all the relevant formalities. There are some obvious examples. You can't sell your children into slavery and you can't enter into a contract for the commission of a murder. But there are hundreds of subtler examples as well: you can't create certain interests in land; you can't buy an insurance policy on a stranger; you can't waive your right as a tenant to receive certain eviction notices from your landlord; and so forth. Each area of private lawmaking activity — from property and contract law in the first year to corporate law and wills and trusts in later years — contains a series of instances in which we simply deny to persons the results they wish to obtain.

It is very difficult to predict where and when these juristic brakes will be applied. We do know, however, who applies them: legislatures, in public laws that prohibit certain private agreements and actions; and courts, when they refuse to enforce prior agreements or documents because they violate public policy. It is always difficult to predict just where and when a legislature will act, and almost as difficult to predict when courts will declare a new class of actions or agreements against public policy. History tells us what old classes are prohibited, and hints at future ones, but these are only hints, the reading of entrails. Consequently, a great deal of legal study examines what has been prohibited in the past — where and how the legislature and the courts have in fact stepped in to upset the otherwise consensual, formally correct lawmaking of private persons.

Everett's Case

Employment contracts are more heavily regulated than other kinds of contracts, and thus raise special concerns of public policy whenever their provisions are sought to be enforced. Even so, if the provisions at issue in Everett's case simply require good conduct of employees while on the premises of the employer, it is unlikely that they violate any public policy or statute.

Problems of Public Creation

Day after day, the federal and state governments pass legislation and promulgate regulations. Even though filled with *political* controversy, this public lawmaking typically generates fewer *legal* challenges than the private lawmaking we just discussed. Even so, legal challenges do sometimes arise and are often highly publicized when they do. Nothing so interests the public as a claim that a particular law — such as an abortion law or a school busing plan — is unconstitutional.

Everett's Case

Everett is concerned with possible prosecution by the local district attorney and a lawsuit by the victim based on tort law. Both of these actions would be founded on publicly created law, created by the legislature and the courts, respectively. Public law, like private lawmaking in contracts, deeds, and wills, must also be validly created. We turn to those issues now.

Legal questions about public lawmaking come in three forms, concerning:

1. *Authority:* Was the public body at issue authorized to take the action it did?
2. *Procedure:* Did that body follow the proper procedure? and
3. *Substance:* Are the substantive results consistent with constitutional and similar requirements?

Problems of Authority. A public body must have the legal power to make the laws it does; if it does not, no obligations or rights will have been created by its actions. This legal power is commonly known as the *jurisdiction to prescribe,* and such jurisdiction is widely distributed among governmental institutions. At the international level, the United Nations, the European Union, and the World Trade Organization can create binding obligations on member nations. On the domestic level, prescriptive jurisdiction is scattered among the federal government, more than 54 state and territorial governments, and thousands of county, city, and other local governments. All but the smallest of these governments have created more specialized bodies to handle particular tasks or problems, generating hundreds of thousands of boards, commissions, and authorities, regulating everything from the distribution of fresh water to the color of this month's lottery tickets. Which of all these government bodies should be doing what? And how do we know when any particular government body has overstepped its bounds?

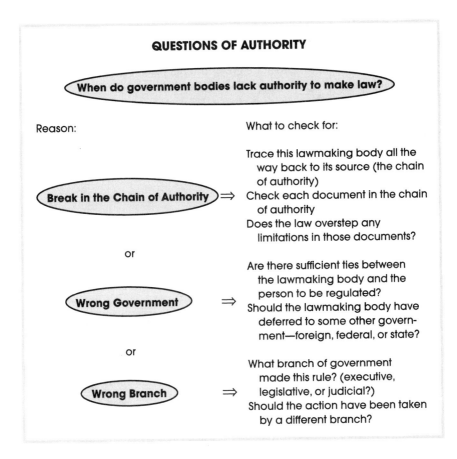

QUESTIONS OF AUTHORITY

When do government bodies lack authority to make law?

Reason:

Break in the Chain of Authority

or

Wrong Government

or

Wrong Branch

What to check for:

Trace this lawmaking body all the way back to its source (the chain of authority)
Check each document in the chain of authority
Does the law overstep any limitations in those documents?

Are there sufficient ties between the lawmaking body and the person to be regulated?
Should the lawmaking body have deferred to some other government—foreign, federal, or state?

What branch of government made this rule? (executive, legislative, or judicial?)
Should the action have been taken by a different branch?

Chain of authority limitations. Part of the answer to what a government can do depends on how it was created. Many governments are *constituted,* that is, formed directly by the natural or juristic persons who are to be its subjects. The United Nations, the federal government of the United States, and the governments of all American states have been formed in this way. The lawmaking authority of such a government is defined and limited by the constitution or charter (almost always a written document) under which it was formed. Powers not granted in that constitution are presumptively unavailable to the government concerned, a conclusion supported in both politics and law: the consent of the governed can only be manifested reliably in a written document to which formal assent has been given, and governments, as juristic persons, have no rights except those affirmatively granted to them. A constituted government, in sum, can create no legal rights or obligations unless its constitution says it can.

Other governments and public bodies, in contrast, are *created by legislation,* that is, they are formed by other governments. County and township governments are common examples of this type, having been formed by their respective state legislatures. The lawmaking authority of these governments is defined by the legislation under which they were created, and presumptively limited to the powers affirmatively granted. The analysis for these governments largely parallels that of constituted governments: we simply analyze founding legislation rather than a founding charter or constitution. But there is also an important difference: legislatively created governments are also limited by the constraints that apply to the government that formed them. A county government, for example, can only make laws consistent with both its founding legislation and the constitution of the state government that formed it.

Finally, some governments are formed in a hybrid way that combines both methods of creation. Such governments are constituted by the persons who wish to be governed by them, but pursuant to enabling legislation, legislation that both enables their creation and puts outer limits on their powers and scope. City governments are the prime example of this type. The city of Chicago, for example, was formed by a charter that sets out its lawmaking authority, but the charter was (and is) enabled, its terms limited (then and now) by state legislation. Such hybrid governments are limited in *all* the ways we have just seen: by their own charters, by the legislation under which they are formed and operate, and by the constraints that limit the sponsoring government. (The mode of creation for city government so closely resembles the one employed for business corporations that we are not surprised to hear them called "municipal corporations.")

However formed, national, state, and local governments often create subsidiary bodies — boards, commissions, panels, and so forth. As should be clear by now, the lawmaking authority of each such body is limited by its own founding documents, as well as by the constraints imposed on the government that formed it. In sum, each public lawmaking body can be located within a chain of governmental authority. In the United States the people have constituted the federal and state governments; and the federal government, along with other national governments, have together constituted international organizations such as the United Nations and the World Trade Organization. Radiating out from each of these constituted authorities are chains of legislatively created and hybrid governments. The "authority questions" one asks depends on where in the chains of authority the relevant lawmaking body appears. The lawmaking power of the Chicago Water Reclamation Board, for example, depends on its own charter, the legislation pursuant to which it was formed and operates, and the limitations generally imposed on the Illinois government.

As we have already noted, one looks for the answers to authority questions in documents of various sorts — a city charter, state enabling legislation, a state constitution, the federal constitution, and so forth — and the inquiry is primarily textual: does the relevant language from the relevant document grant the power to create the law at issue? But not all texts are treated alike. That is, the style of textual interpretation varies by document type. As one might expect, statutes are treated differently from constitutions, but we also commonly differentiate among constitutions. Because state governments are considered governments of general jurisdiction, the constitutions forming them are sometimes read expansively, so as to include all of the power needed to protect the health, safety, and welfare of the state's citizens. Because the federal government, in contrast, is traditionally viewed as a government of enumerated powers and limited jurisdiction, the power-granting clauses of the federal constitution are (in theory) more likely to be interpreted narrowly. Finally, because the United Nations and other international organizations are constituted by treaties, their founding documents are interpreted — neither broadly or narrowly, but differently — under internationally accepted rules of treaty interpretation. (See Chapter 3 for more on interpretation of texts.)

In summary, a public body's actions are limited by the chains of governmental authority by which it was created, each link in the chain backed by an authoritative document. If there is a break in the chain, that is, if one of those documents does not support the exercise of lawmaking power at issue, the challenged law will be invalid. Thus, for example, any rule promulgated by a federal agency can be voided on the ground that it violates the federal constitution, the document that formed the government that formed the agency.

Everett's Case

We would want to know precisely what sort of criminal laws the public prosecutor has in mind: federal law? state law? a city ordinance? Assuming that a state law is at issue, we would then ask ourselves whether the state legislature has the power to make such a law. That is, does the state constitution give the legislature such power? If not, the law would not have been validly created (it would be unconstitutional) and could not be used to prosecute Everett. Generally, however, state legislatures are constitutionally authorized to legislate in the area of criminal law.

Systemic limitations. Valid chains of authority are not enough. A government or other public body may lack lawmaking authority in a particular instance even when all the relevant documents in the chain appear to grant it. First, the exercise of authority may exceed certain overriding, universally recognized limits on prescriptive jurisdiction. One of the most important limits is this: a public body can only prescribe law for persons who have certain minimal ties with the legislating government, such as citizenship or physical presence within the territory. Thus, for example, one can question the power of the Illinois General Assembly to regulate the marriage requirements for Nepalese citizens living in Nepal. The exercise of such a power is unlikely to be sustained, even by the courts of Illinois.

Second, a government's nominal (document-sanctioned) authority to prescribe law may conflict with the lawmaking authority of other governments. The treatment of these conflicts depends, among other things, on the status of the two governments concerned. If the governments are of unequal status, the legal question is usually cast as one of *preemption,* and the lower-tiered government generally loses. State lawmaking is often questioned on this ground, because of its actual or potential conflict with federal authority. If the two conflicting governments are of equal status — both national or both state, for example — the legal question is usually cast as one of *comity,* or as calling for the application of *conflicts of law* rules, and who wins is harder to predict. Thus, the United States might refrain as a matter of comity from imposing anti-trust obligations on British companies in Great Britain, even though those companies also have a presence in the United States. Likewise, a Virginia court would usually refrain under conflicts of law principles from imposing its inheritance laws on a Virginia decedent and his only surviving heirs (also Virginians) regarding the ownership of an apartment building in San Francisco, deferring to California as the *situs* of the land at issue.

Everett's Case

Because Everett struck his co-worker in the state whose legislature has acted, Everett and his action have more than minimal ties needed to justify the legislature's prescriptive jurisdiction. No other state legislature would likely have sufficient ties to regulate this situation. It could be, however, that this state law conflicts with federal law or the federal constitution. In that case, the law itself (or its application here) would be deemed unconstitutional and could not be applied to Everett's action.

Branch limitations. Up until now, questions of lawmaking authority have been treated as if they were solely questions about governments as a whole: are Oklahoma wheat farmers, for example, properly regulated out of Geneva, Switzerland, Washington, D.C., or Oklahoma City? But many questions of lawmaking authority concern the proper allocation of power within governments, that is, between branches of governments. All governments perform functions of predictable types, which we traditionally classify as legislative, executive, and judicial. Work of all three types creates obligations and rights. Those engaged in the legislative function are the most obvious source, but those engaged in the executive function — administrators — often issue regulations in the course of carrying out their executive mandate, and those engaged in judicial functions — judges — continuously create, modify, and terminate obligations and rights in the name of developing and applying the *common law.*

All but the smallest governments segregate each function from the others. The larger the government, the clearer and more formal the segregation. The federal and state governments, as well as many county and city governments, have conceptually well-defined, physically separated departments to handle the three great branches of American government; officials of one-horse towns must keep the distinctions in their heads. Once segregated, we generally require that officials stick to the business in their own branch: legislators must legislate, executives execute, and judges judge. Inter-branch rivalry generates a great many legal questions and a great deal of litigation. Legislation is attacked because it interferes with executive or judicial functions. Executive action is questioned because it exceeds constitutional or legislative mandates. Judicial action is appealed because it looks executive or legislative in character. In sum, lawyers and judges might agree that the right *government* has created a right or obligation, but question whether it was the right *branch* that did so.

Everett's Case

As Everett's lawyers, we could question whether the legislature's passage of a criminal statute on assault and battery was better left to some other branch or organ of government. The answer in this case is no, since the regulation of behavior through criminal law is a classic function of the legislature. Indeed, if the executive or judicial branches tried to develop criminal law, such action would contravene the constitutionally required *separation of powers*.

Political limitations. There is one final but important twist in the creation of legal obligations and rights. Until now, we have discussed their creation by governments. But obligations and rights can also be created by the documents that formed those governments in the first place. The Bill of Rights of the U.S. Constitution serves as a preeminent example, creating a right to free speech, the freedom from unreasonable searches and seizures, and other rights and freedoms. State constitutions have similar provisions.

This *constitutional* creation of obligations and rights can also be subjected to questions of authority, but the questions are more political than legal in nature. Did the British subjects of the late eighteenth century have the authority to form a new, independent government on the North American continent? Did the representatives at the national constitutional convention of 1787 have the authority to adopt a document guaranteeing the freedom of speech, the freedom from unreasonable searches and seizures, and other rights? These questions are much different from those we have been asking so far, e.g., "Does the federal government have the power to regulate the production of wheat in Oklahoma?" The answer about wheat production depends on a text, the Constitution of the United States, and the meaning of the words we find there. There is no authoritative text, in contrast, for deciding the authority of the people of the United States to form a new government. That decision rests firmly in history, politics, and war. Although it might be objected that calling a particular inquiry "political" rather than "legal" is a word game, it reflects an important practical reality. Lawyers and judges are much more often called upon to answer questions about the federal regulation of wheat production than about the authority of several dozen men meeting in Philadelphia in 1787. It reflects the reality that, in law courts and law offices, constitutional rights and obligations are almost never questioned on the ground that prescriptive jurisdiction was lacking.

Everett's Case

In sum, the state legislature's passage of a criminal law, applicable to Everett in that same state, is not likely to raise any problems of public lawmaking authority. This still leaves open the question of the procedures followed by the legislature in passing that law.

Problems of Procedure. A public law is no law at all unless the proper procedures were followed in its creation or promulgation. Procedural questions involve the hunt for irregularities, although what is "regular" varies a great deal from government to government, from branch to branch, and from action to action. Well-trained lawyers typically know the basic procedures to be followed in each of the three main branches of the federal government and those of any other government or body with which they frequently deal. Most lawyers do not raise questions of this sort very often, but there are some that do. A major task of government lawyers, for example, is to ensure that governmental actions are procedurally proper. A segment of the private bar — usually working out of the national and state capitals — also examines procedural matters more frequently than others. Lawyers engaged in this business are required not just to master the procedures themselves, but to develop judgment in evaluating errors, for not every procedural gaffe invalidates a lawmaking action.

Executive branch procedures. Most of the litigation in this area concerns the actions of the executive branch. Federal and state governments distinguish between different kinds of executive action, and for each kind of action have developed a set of procedures to be followed in its execution. If, for example, the state fish and game commission wishes to issue new hunting regulations, it must follow legislatively designated procedures for rule-making. The department will likely need to publish proposed regulations, receive comments, and perhaps respond to those comments formally before adopting final regulations. One slip and the regulations might be deemed invalid. A different set of procedures applies to adjudicatory matters, case-by-case decisions in the executive branch that affect particular individuals. Such procedures often require notice to the affected party, provide for an opportunity to be heard, and specify how appeals from those decisions can be made. Such procedures would govern the action of the Internal Revenue Service when it seeks to assess your client for $360,000 in back taxes, penalties, and interest.

Executive branch procedures at the federal level are governed primarily by the Administrative Procedure Act, although specialized procedures supplement the general Act in many instances. State governments have a similar body of laws, often derived from the federal rules. Sometimes the legal

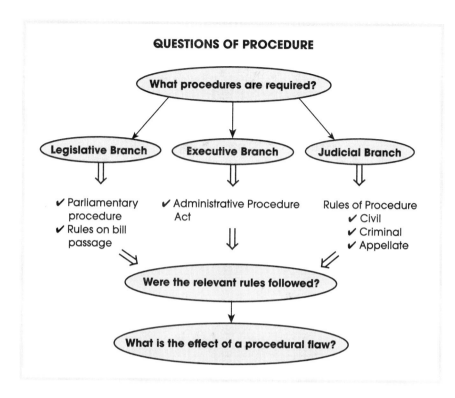

issues concern which of the different procedures should be followed, and sometimes the issue is whether the agreed-upon procedures have in fact been followed. Together these questions dominate the field of *administrative law,* an area of legal practice largely unknown outside of legal circles, but vital nonetheless. Our national scheme of regulation is characterized by a large, complex system of bureaucracies, employing hundreds of thousands of workers, and issuing a daily stream of regulations and decisions that affect us all — from when a new drug will be brought to market to whether my grandmother can get her social security payments reinstated. Administrative law is not only important socially, it's important professionally: both drug companies and my grandmother need good lawyers.

Legislative branch procedures. Procedural questions about legislative activity are raised less frequently. This may seem an odd statement, since legislators and their staffs often appear to be concerned with little else: whether a bill should be referred to a committee and, if so, which one; whether a particular amendment to a bill can be made by a handful of concerned legislators or whether the entire body must vote; whether a particular vote will be made by roll call; and so forth. But these are not usually the questions asked by lawyers and judges working outside the statehouse. A relatively small number of internal legislative gaffes can affect a law's validity — the lack of a quorum, for example, or an error in counting votes, so that a majority of votes is mistakenly recorded. Such problems are few enough and obvious enough that legislative bodies guard against them pretty effectively in the first place, and if they do occur, the legislation is rectified before it leaves the statehouse and becomes the subject of litigation.

Judicial branch procedures. Even more rarely is the lawmaking power of judges questioned on procedural grounds. Again, this may seem an odd statement, since judges and lawyers often appear to be concerned with nothing else. High-profile criminal trials, for example, bear witness to the extraordinary heights of procedural wrangling that can mark the American courtroom experience. And if there is a procedural problem, one side or the other can be expected to appeal whatever decision is rendered. All of these procedural matters are important (and will be discussed at length in the following chapter on liability) but they are not particularly germane to the present topic of lawmaking power. A judicial decision can certainly be understood to "make law" for the parties in the case, and procedural errors (if they result in a reversal of the decision) can be understood to "unmake" the law for the same parties. But judicial decisions have a much broader lawmaking power, and one that remains largely untouched by reversals on procedural grounds. The real power of judicial decisions lies in their precedential value, in their ability to be cited and used in later planning and litigation. In this context, a decision reversed on procedural grounds can still be cited for every other point it makes. The case still has life and makes law. Very rarely is the precedential value of a case questioned because of procedural problems that arose when the case was heard.

Constitutional procedures. Procedural questions can also be raised in the course of making and amending constitutions. Lawyers and judges seldom confront these questions either, because we don't make or amend constitutions very often. When we do, interesting questions arise. If the procedures used in such efforts comply with the requirements spelled out in the prior (or pre-amendment) document, then the new efforts are constitutional. If the prior document failed to specify how it could be replaced or amended, or if the specified procedures were not followed, then the new efforts are unconstitutional. Such conclusions, however, are more easily described than reached. Whether there was compliance with the specified procedures, or whether (in cases of noncompliance) the errors are significant enough to warrant a finding of unconstitutionality, are difficult questions to answer, especially because we have relatively little precedent for constitutional replacement and amendment. Even if we decide, as an initial matter, that the flawed procedures render the new efforts unconstitutional, we might accept their validity nonetheless. The founding of our own nation serves as a sufficient example of this point. Sometimes we ultimately decide to overlook even serious procedural flaws in new constitutional efforts and accept them as valid. The grounds upon which we do so lie far beyond the daily experience and special expertise of lawyers and judges. The judgments here are instead found in politics and power, and in the candidly recognized right of the victor — armed or not — to make the rules.

Everett's Case

Because Everett is threatened with prosecution under a state statute, a legislative act, we would obviously not need to ask questions about executive, judicial, or constitutional process. We could, however, examine the statute's *legislative history,* looking for irregularities in its passage. Such flaws are rare, but they sometimes occur. If we found them, they could render the statute a nullity, and Everett could not be prosecuted under it.

Problems of Substance. We have just seen how the creation of an obligation and right can be questioned on the grounds that the public body making it lacked authority or did not follow the right procedure. Lawyers and judges can also question the validity of a law because of its substantive content, that is, because of what the law actually seeks to accomplish. The substantive limits are found in "higher law," but the meaning of that term requires some explanation.

QUESTIONS OF SUBSTANCE

The Big Question

Do the legal rights and obligations created by this governmental body contravene any rule from a higher source?

General Pecking Order of American Law

Federal Law
  Constitution
  Congressional Statutes   (International Law)
  Agency Rules and Regulations

State Law
  Constitution
  Legislation   (Foreign Law)
  Agency and Regulations

Local Law
  Charter/Enabling Legislation
  Ordinances

There are several well-accepted sources of higher law. First, some constitutions are superior to other constitutions, an ordering usually made explicit in the documents themselves. The U.S. Constitution declares itself to be the "supreme Law of the Land . . . any Thing in the Constitution or Laws of any State to the Contrary notwithstanding." Consequently, a provision of a state constitution will not be recognized as valid if it contravenes a right or obligation contained in the federal constitution. Second, every constitution is "higher" than the work of the institutions it creates. Thus, federal legislation, administrative regulations, and judicial decisions will not be recognized as valid if they contravene the provisions of the federal constitution. Third, when governments create other governments, the work of the creating government is superior to the work of the created government. Thus, county and city ordinances will not be recognized as valid if they contravene the provisions of state legislation.

These principles can be applied in combination with each other. The obligations and rights created in state constitutions, for example, are superior not only to the work flowing from all the branches of state government, but limit the enactments of every county, township, and municipal government as well. The federal constitution being the supreme law of the land, the work of any federal entity trumps the work of any state entity. Because of this layering, normally uncontroversial examples of higher law can become controversial when applied in logically sound but politically sensitive combinations. Thus, when a low-ranking administrator from the Federal Commerce Commission takes an action contravening a provision of a state constitution, or when a federal judge orders a state legislature to redraw its electoral districts, litigation and appeals can be expected.

Other sources of higher law are controversial, even in principle. International law provides a good example. One view holds that international law is inherently, necessarily superior to domestic law; it is international law that gives each nation-state its status as such and defines its powers vis-à-vis other nation-states. On this view: (1) actions that violate international law cannot be excused on the basis that they were made pursuant to domestic law; and (2) domestic laws and practices, in order to be valid domestically, must conform with the substantive obligations and rights of international law. The officials of most national governments have accepted the first proposition, but not the second. They understand that domestically driven violations of international law will create liability to other nations, but they nonetheless defend the prerogative of each state to decide when and how to take account of international law when it makes domestic law.

Depending on how this prerogative is exercised, international law may or may not constitute a higher source of law capable of trumping domestic law. Different nations have given different answers to these questions, displaying a greater or lesser deference to international law. In some nations, principles of

international law are applied automatically and in preference to conflicting domestic law. U.S. practice on this point is complicated, and sorting it out is a
standard topic in international law courses at most U.S. law schools. In broad-
est summary, however, the American reception to international law is less cor-
dial than most. Only certain kinds of international law (self-executing treaties),
under limited circumstances (no later, conflicting federal legislation), reliably
trump federal or state legislation, and no kind of international law under any
circumstances is understood by the United States to trump the Constitution.

An even more controversial source of higher law is natural law. Earlier
in this chapter we saw that natural law was long considered an independent source of legal obligations and rights. Here, we are concerned about its
ability not just to generate binding law, but law so powerful it can override
the work of governmental bodies. Interest in natural law's power to override governmental action revived in the wake of World War II. A law cannot be valid and enforceable, Hitler's Germany taught us, simply because it
is passed by a governmental body with juristic authority, following the
right procedures, and acting in accordance with written constitutional law.
Stalin, Idi Amin, and Pol Pot, along with dozens of other murderous heads
of state, have repeated the lesson. Again and again we have seen the need
for grounds upon which to judge the legality of an act beyond asking questions of authority, procedure, and compliance with written constitutional
law. Despite the need for these additional grounds, however, American
lawyers and judges today almost never argue that natural law trumps governmental actions. Instead, they tend to rely on expansive, and sometimes
exorbitant, readings of legal phrases that are found in our federal constitution (especially *due process of law*), and use that constitutional passage, as
newly interpreted, to strike down legislative action.

Even when the sources of higher law are confined to the least controversial types and combinations, higher law questions account for a great
deal of contemporary litigation: Does a particular federal law violate the
federal constitution? Does a particular state regulation overstep a provision
of state law? These sorts of questions are bread-and-butter work for many
lawyers and judges, and law students see a lot of them during their law
school careers. The questions are common because they are hard to answer. Infringements on higher law are almost never direct or obvious. State
legislatures, for example, simply don't attempt to repeal the federal (and
state) constitutional right to equal protection of the law. The legislature
might, however, amend the state's laws on the inheritance rights of illegit-
imate children or change the state's Medicare reimbursement rules in
ways that raise equal protection concerns. There can be good faith differences on what constitutes an infringement of higher law, and on which
infringements are permissible anyway. When such differences occur, the
umpire of litigation is often required.

Everett's Case

Because Everett is threatened with prosecution under a state statute, we could examine its consistency with all other higher sources of law: the state constitution, federal agency regulations, international treaties, congressional statutes, and the federal constitution. If the substance of the state statute could not be squared with the substance of any one of these higher sources of law, the statute would be rendered a nullity, and could not be used against Everett.

HAS THE OBLIGATION OR RIGHT BEEN TRANSFERRED, MODIFIED, OR TERMINATED?

The creation of an obligation or right is only the beginning of the story. Once created, obligations and rights take on a life of their own, during which they can be transferred, modified, or terminated. These "post-creation" events are often extraordinarily important to clients, their lawyers, and eventually to judges. A client of mine may not have had a right originally, but can receive it later in a transfer. That same client may lose the right if it is subsequently transferred to someone else or is terminated. Likewise, obligations can move around from person to person or become extinguished. And in the midst of all these transfers, or even without a transfer at all, rights and obligations can be modified. Transfer, modification, and termination are all important, so we take them up separately.

Has the Obligation or Right Been Transferred?

Once created, legal obligations and rights can be transferred from one person to another. Joe can possess a particular right or obligation, not because it was created in him originally, but because it was created in someone else and validly transferred to him. Conversely, Susan can lose a right or obligation because it has been transferred to someone else. Giving advice about such transfers, and effecting (or stopping) them, lies at the core of the lawyer's work.

Questions of Transferability. One might assume that legal rights and obligations are generally transferable, but this is not the case. One cannot legally transfer one's right to vote nor the obligation not to commit murder. In fact, *most* legal obligations and rights cannot be transferred. Knowing which ones can and which ones can't is obviously important to lawyers and judges. If an obligation or right *can* be transferred, lawyers are usually involved in effecting that transfer. As a consequence, issues of transferability recur frequently in law school classrooms, as they do in practice.

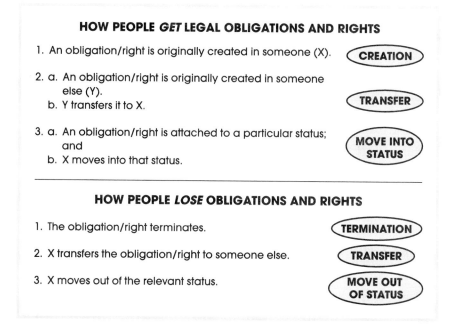

HOW PEOPLE *GET* LEGAL OBLIGATIONS AND RIGHTS

1. An obligation/right is originally created in someone (X). CREATION

2. a. An obligation/right is originally created in someone else (Y).
   b. Y transfers it to X. TRANSFER

3. a. An obligation/right is attached to a particular status; and
   b. X moves into that status. MOVE INTO STATUS

HOW PEOPLE *LOSE* OBLIGATIONS AND RIGHTS

1. The obligation/right terminates. TERMINATION

2. X transfers the obligation/right to someone else. TRANSFER

3. X moves out of the relevant status. MOVE OUT OF STATUS

Whether a right or obligation is transferable depends, in the first instance, on whether it arose as a matter of status or contract. Status-based rights and obligations are usually harder to transfer. Theoretically, status-based obligations and rights can be transferred in two ways: "in bulk," that is, by transferring the status that generates a bundle of obligations and rights, or individually, by transferring an obligation or right that a particular status generates. Transfers in bulk, however, are uncommon because most statuses are not transferable. Try as I might, I cannot transfer away my status as a person: I simply move out of that status when I die. Other statuses work the same way. I can move in or out of the statuses of minor, widower, and mental incompetent, for example, but cannot transfer that status to someone else. If a status cannot be transferred, then no individual right or obligation based on that status can be transferred either. Thus, because my status as a U.S. citizen cannot be transferred, I cannot transfer to someone else (separately, as it were) my right to vote, my freedom of speech, or my obligation to pay income taxes. (These might be given up, waived, or terminated, but not transferred.)

Only property statuses are regularly and easily transferable: stockholder, proprietor, homeowner, and so on. Rights and obligations associated with these statuses can presumptively be transferred in bulk, as can individual rights and obligations generated by those statuses. As the owner of a home, I can transfer my home ownership to another or I can carve out and transfer lesser interests, such as possessory rights to the basement apartment for one year. But lawyers must be on the lookout for exceptions. Despite the fact that the underlying status is transferable, public policy or contractual constraints may prohibit the transfer of obligations and rights growing out of that status. A prior agreement with my neighbor or zoning laws may prevent me from renting out my basement apartment, even though such a transfer is available in principle.

The transfer of contract-based obligations and rights is a bit simpler to analyze, because we can bypass the complications of status transfers and their availability. Obligations and rights that arise originally in a contract or agreement are presumptively transferable, subject only to contractual prohibitions and public policy limitations. Contractual prohibitions, if they exist, will generally be easy to spot, appearing in the same place where the obligations and rights were created in the first place. Less obvious are transfer limitations that are implied, and sometimes flatly imposed, on grounds of public policy. For example, the duties under a personal service contract cannot generally be delegated. If I agree to have you cut my hair, you can't substitute your cousin Vinny as the barber (at least not without my permission). It is hard to predict when legislative or judge-made prohibitions on transfer will occur, so most law school courses are careful to flag them.

Everett's Case

Everett's obligation not to commit assault and battery arises out of his status as a person, not as a matter of contract. Because his status as a person cannot be transferred to anyone else, his obligation not to commit assault and battery cannot be transferred either. In contrast, his employer's contractual right to demand suitable conduct of its employees while on the premises might be transferable to others in the context of the sale of the tire factory to a new owner.

Questions of Valid Transfer. If a particular right or obligation is transferable, its holder may wish to do so. Lawyers and judges then shift their attention to issues like those we saw in the creation of obligations and rights.

Voluntary transfers among private persons. For transfers among private persons, we can ask: Do the parties involved have sufficient capacity to make the transfer? Are any agents for the parties duly authorized to act? Has there been a mistake? Has either party been coerced in any way? Have all the formalities of transfer been observed? Are the substantive results of the transfer acceptable? The standards to be applied in answering these question are also similar to those we ask when obligations and rights are created in the first place. Thus, whatever level of mental competence is required to make a contract is also required to transfer rights under it. Mistakes or coercion in the transfer of a property right are likely to be handled in the same way as mistakes and coercion in its creation. Even the formalities of transfer are likely to be the same. The *equal dignity rule,* found by name or in substance in most areas of private lawmaking, creates the presumption that whatever formalities are required in the creation of an obligation or right are likewise required in its later transfer, modification, or termination. Thus, if a contract must be written and signed in the first place because of the *statute of frauds,* the assignment of rights in that contract must presumptively be in writing as well.

The basic questions we ask about all consensual transfers are essentially the same, but details vary a great deal between different kinds of transfers — each kind having its own indigenous set of requirements. For example, we "assign" contractual rights, but we "delegate" contractual duties, and assignment and delegation operate under slightly different principles. In property law, we recognize a massive array of transfer techniques — grant, gift *inter vivos,* gift *causa mortis,* sale, pledge, bailment, bequest, conveyance, devise, license, assignment, lease, and intestate distribution, among others. The terminology alone requires sorting out and mastery. More important, these differences in terminology represent substantive differences in doctrine. If the wrong technique is chosen, the transfer will be void, even though the transfer could have been accomplished in some other way. Even if the right technique is chosen, a failure to meet all the relevant requirements will void the transfer as well. Woe to the lawyer who tries to transfer a parcel of land by deed when it should have been transferred by will, or having correctly chosen a will, fails to meet all the special requirements for willmaking!

Involuntary transfers among private persons (succession). Until now, all of the transfers under discussion have been *consensual,* but some rights and obligations are transferred by operation of law, without the consent or voluntary action of the original holder. We often speak of this process as "succession," and the new recipients as "successors." The most common occasion for succession is death. When a person dies, some of the decedent's rights and obligations — primarily those growing out of property and contract — pass first to the decedent's *estate* (a legal entity that is created immediately and automatically upon the death of a natural person) and then to the decedent's heirs and will-takers. Analogous transfers occur when corporations and other business entities are terminated. When that happens, some of the rights and obligations of the entity devolve to others, such as shareholders and partners. Certain forms of financial and mental distress can also be a cause for succession. Trustees in bankruptcy, for example, succeed to many of the rights and obligations of people and entities that become bankrupt. Mental incompetence, followed by the appointment of a personal representative, can also transfer rights and obligations from the incompetent to incompetent's estate, to be managed by the representative. In sum, an important question in these matters is whether a particular event triggers a transfer by operation of law. Death, bankruptcy, and incompetence can trigger succession; an attack of nausea cannot.

A second question then arises: if succession has been triggered, has the particular right or obligation at issue been transferred in that succession? The answer to this question varies depending on the triggering event, whether it is death, insolvency, etc. Generally speaking, financial rights and obligations are subject to such transfer, but more personal rights and obligations are not. Thus, for example, a trustee in bankruptcy obtains certain rights in the bankrupt's property, but does not acquire his right to vote. A decedent's business obligations are likely to devolve to the decedent's estate, but not her obligation to pay child support, which generally dies with the decedent. Lawyers and judges must therefore understand not only the causes of succession, but its precise implications.

Everett's Case

If the tire company sold the factory to a new owner, we might raise questions about whether that new owner could enforce the previous owner's rights to take action against Everett. Were the contract rights from Everett's employment contract property transferred to the new owner? If Everett were to die before these issues were settled, we could raise questions about whether a contractual obligation to pay a fine passed to Everett's estate, involuntarily, by succession.

Transfers by public bodies. The distinction between private persons and public bodies, so important in the creation of legal rights and obligations, is relevant here as well. Governments and other public bodies rarely transfer legal rights and obligations. Instead, they busy themselves with status-based legislation: obliging or empowering whole classes of persons to do things or refrain from doing them. Once those rights and obligations are created, governments also terminate or modify them, again for whole classes of persons, a process discussed in the next section of this chapter. But a transfer of an obligation or right is in its nature bilateral — moving from one legal person to another — and governments seldom act in this way. They often oversee or regulate transfers between private parties, but are seldom involved as direct participants.

Still, transfers by public bodies sometimes occur. A government owning property may wish to sell it. A government that has contracted for the purchase of supplies may wish to assign the contract to someone else. Most dramatically of all, perhaps, a government can forcibly acquire property from private persons in eminent domain proceedings. When governments do seek to transfer obligations and rights, their attempts raise the same kinds of questions as governmental attempts to create them: Does the government have the authority to effect the transfer? Has it followed the proper procedures? Are the substantive results of the transfer acceptable? Thus, if a state highway authority seeks to condemn my client's property in an eminent domain proceeding for use in a new toll-road, I will carefully examine the authority of the state officials, ensure that they have followed all the procedures necessary for a condemnation action, and evaluate whether the compensation offered meets the relevant constitutional and statutory requirements.

Has the Obligation or Right Been Modified?

Lawyers are often called upon to help modify obligations and rights that have already been created. Judges are often called upon to decide if a particular attempt at modification was successful. In principle, *any obligation or right can be modified.* This feature distinguishes modifications from transfers, which are often impossible. Modifications, however, raise a special question of their own, the question of *who* can do the modifying.

Who Can Modify? In general, the persons who initially create an obligation or right have the power to modify it. If the legislature has made a law, it can amend it. If two people enter into a contract, they can later change its terms. Conversely, anyone who did *not* initially create an obligation or right cannot, as a rule, modify it. If, for example, the state government requires all able-bodied men and women to serve for two years in the national guard, the same government can change the length of service to one year, but I — able-bodied though I may be — cannot. If Joe and Susan contract for the sale of Susan's dental floss at Joe's Steak House, Joe and Susan can modify the obligations and rights created thereby, but I (once again) cannot.

Even so, there are cases in which those other than the original creators of obligations and rights can modify them. One group of such persons are lawful assigns and successors, the transferees we met in the previous section. On the public side, governments sometimes move their areas of competence — between governments, between branches in the same government, and between agencies in the same branch. If the move is otherwise lawful, the new governmental actor has the old actor's power to modify preexisting obligations and rights. In Chicago, for example, some aspects of public school regulation were moved from the state to local authorities, and some state-created obligations and rights can now be modified locally. On the private side, successions and assignments are more common: a landlord dies and is succeeded first by an administrator and then by heirs; a party to a long-term contract assigns its rights to a new customer, and so on. In each case, the new parties can modify obligations and rights they did not originally create, on the same terms as the original parties.

Another class of non-original parties capable of modifying preexisting rights and obligations are "higher authorities." For governments, these are superior governments — superior, that is, in the area at issue. If the area is interstate commerce, the federal government can modify state-created rights and obligations. For private parties, higher authorities are governments with the lawful jurisdiction to prescribe. A privately created right to buy goods from China, for example, can be modified by import quotas imposed by the federal government.

Was the Modification Effective? After the "who" question has been answered, the success of any modification turns primarily on the answers to questions we have seen twice before. If the modification is attempted by private persons, natural or juristic, we will ask questions about capacity and agency, whether anyone has made a mistake or was coerced, whether the proper formalities were complied with, and whether the substantive results of the modification contravene any public policies or laws. If the modification is attempted by a public body, we will ask questions about its jurisdiction to prescribe, whether the proper procedures were followed, and whether the substantive results are acceptable in light of any higher law. Questions about form and procedure are generally guided by the equal dignity rule; whatever was required to create an obligation or right in the first place is required to modify it later. Questions about substantive results are generally guided by the same standards as applied at creation: whatever results could not have been obtained originally cannot be obtained later by modification.

It should be noted that the law is especially cautious in permitting *unilateral* modifications of rights and obligations. This is obviously true when the obligation or right was originally created by two or more persons. Thus, one of the parties to a contract cannot ordinarily change its terms without the consent of the other(s). But unilateral modification can be difficult even when the right or obligation was created unilaterally. In other words, even though I might be able to create a right or obligation on my own, without the express consent of others, I may not be able to modify it without such consent, or may not be able to modify it at all. The unfriendly reception to unilateral modification manifests itself in many forms. In the private context, it shows up in the irrevocability of gifts, in the presumption that trusts cannot be modified by their creators unless a right to modify was originally retained, and in the inability of a landowner, once she has created an easement, to modify its terms. In the public context, it shows up in rules against *ex post facto* laws, the presumption against the retroactive application of legislation, and rules against takings without due process and adequate compensation. The "reliance" interest of others — the interest of others in things staying the way they are — often overrides the original creator's ability to change what he or she did alone in the first place. Lawyers, judges, and law students must always be on guard for such limitations.

Everett's Case

The state legislature can modify its laws on criminal assault and battery, and Everett and his employer can together modify Everett's obligations regarding his conduct on company premises, in both cases because those who initially created an obligation are the ones empowered to modify it. The state legislature could not, however, change the criminal law applicable to Everett's case after the fact and neither Everett nor his employer could change the employment contract unilaterally.

Has the Obligation or Right Been Terminated?

Obligations and rights don't last forever. Once created, they come to an end, or are brought to an end, in many ways. Some terminations are voluntary, others involuntary. Some are explicit, while others are implied. Issues of termination are vitally important in the law. My clients cannot exercise rights that they have previously lost. On the bright side, they cannot violate obligations that have ceased to exist. It should be obvious that lawyers and judges are almost daily concerned with the termination of obligations and rights — in planning them, effecting them, fighting them off, or simply deciding if and when they have occurred. There are at least seven ways that an obligation or right can come to an end. We will examine each one briefly.

Expiration by Its Own Terms. Governments and private parties often limit the duration of their lawmaking efforts, and as a consequence, many obligations and rights expire by their own terms. Transitional tax legislation, for example, typically lasts for only a few years, with obligations and rights changing each year; the owner of real property might grant a neighbor an easement for five years; a chain of retail stores and a producer of camping equipment might sign a three-year supply contract; and so forth. Equally significant, and much more often litigated, are cases of implied time limits. Judge-made law appearing in older cases can sometimes be attacked on the ground that it was based on social conditions that no longer exist and hence the old rules are no longer valid. Statutes, too, can fall into disuse over time and are sometimes denied enforcement for that reason. (Old case-law is usually easier to discard than old statutes.) In private lawmaking, if the parties have not specified the duration of their efforts, "reasonable" time limits are often implied.

Conditions Fulfilled. Many obligations and rights are conditional, and come to an end when a particular condition either is fulfilled or ceases to exist. The obligation to file an income tax return, for example, disappears when one's income falls below a certain level. Perhaps the biggest class of conditional obligations and rights are those found in contracts. Individual obligations and rights within a contract are commonly conditioned on the happening or continued existence of specified states of affairs, and generally (often implicitly) conditioned on the physical possibility of performance, the absence of fundamental changes of circumstances, acts of God, and material breaches by one of the parties.

Obligation or Right Satisfied. Obligations and rights can disappear because they are satisfied. Your right to receive a deed to my house and my obligation to provide it both disappear at closing when I hand over the deed; your obligation to pay back the money I lent you and my right to receive it both disappear when you fork over the dough. Not all obligations and rights, of course, are subject to satisfaction and expiration in this way. Neither my obligation to refrain from murder nor my right to vote will disappear when I walk peacefully to the polls and cast my ballot in the next general election.

Later Affirmative Acts. Generally speaking, those persons who are empowered to modify an obligation or right are also empowered to terminate it. Consequently, those who created the obligation or right in the first place, as well as their successors and assigns, are presumptively capable of ending it. Attempts at such termination raise all the same questions as attempted modifications: Has the presumptive power to terminate been limited for any reason? Were the proper procedures and formalities adhered to? Is the termination substantively acceptable?

An interesting set of issues always arises when the holder of an obligation or right seeks to terminate it *as the holder* (and not in the capacity as its creator). Sometimes this is permitted and sometimes not. For example, I am the holder of the right to have my attorney present during police interrogation, but the right's creator is the federal government. Likewise, I am the holder of the obligation to pay property taxes, but its creator is the state of Illinois. What if, in these cases, I wished to terminate my rights and obligations? Creators of rights and obligations can do so, but what about holders? Generally speaking, rights can be terminated by their holders, but obligations cannot. I can unilaterally *waive* my right to have an attorney present while being questioned by the police, but I cannot unilaterally terminate my obligation to pay property taxes. Even in the waiver of rights, however, the results are mixed. Privately created rights are generally easier to waive than publicly created ones. I can waive my right to receive the property devised to me in my Aunt Clara's will, but I can't waive my right to a fair trial or — in some states — my right as a tenant to habitable premises. The answers vary according to the right, and it is the lawyer's job to know which rights are terminable by the holder and which are not.

Terminations by creators, successors, and holders can either be express or implied. Both kinds of termination raise the issues just discussed, but implied terminations raise additional issues and are a major source of litigation. The form of the question is usually the same: Are the actions of one or more relevant parties tantamount to a waiver (or termination or rescission or revocation) of the obligation or right at issue? The answer to the question turns on a mix of considerations: the exact nature of the actions taken; the knowledge and intent of the persons taking those actions; the knowledge and reaction of any other relevant parties; the likelihood that the actions and reactions can be explained on other grounds; the existence of detrimental reliance or other sorts of perceived unfairness, and so forth. Not only are the considerations varied (and their exact relation to each other often unclear), their application in any particular case is highly dependent on the particular facts presented. Out of such a mix comes a great deal of litigation whose outcome is often hard to predict. Law school classes spend a lot of time on implied waivers, estoppels, and similar doctrines.

Holder Expires. Obligations and rights can be terminated when the holder expires. For natural persons, death terminates all legal obligations and rights. Some obligations and rights, as we saw in the last section, are passed on to others by operation of law, but none remain with the dead. In courses in torts, criminal law, and decedent's estates, therefore, one occasionally finds grisly inquiries into the exact time of death of particular persons (who died first in the fiery car crash?) since one's ability to hold rights and obligations depends on being alive. Similarly, for juristic persons, obligations and rights not transferred to others by operation of law are terminated when the entity is terminated. The winding up of the corporation and the dissolution of a public body, for example, are significant because they terminate all the obligations and rights held by those entities.

Holder Leaves the Relevant Status. Obligations and rights can terminate when the holder leaves the relevant status. As we have just noted, death terminates all the holder's obligations and rights. This is true regardless of whether those rights and obligations are founded in status or contract. Status-based obligations and rights can also be terminated (usually with less human drama) whenever the holder leaves the status upon which they are based. My right to vote in Illinois elections ends when I cease to be a citizen of the state. My obligation to take the car in for biannual emissions testing ends when I sell the car to someone else. Again, this mode of termination is only possible for status-based obligations and rights, and its likelihood of occurrence depends on how easy it is to move out of the relevant status: it is much easier to leave the status of stockholder than the status of parent.

Correlative Right or Obligation Terminated. Finally, an obligation or right can be terminated because its *correlative right* or *obligation* has been terminated. The explicit termination of one results in the implicit termination of the other. Thus, if my contractual obligation to buy your pinky ring terminates for any reason, your obligation to sell it to me expires as well (a blessing, I am sure, to us both).

Everett's Case

By legislative repeal (later affirmative act), Everett's obligation not to commit assault and battery could have terminated before he struck his co-worker at the tire factory. Likewise, his contractual duty of suitable behavior while on company premises could have terminated before that fateful day by mutual agreement of the parties. Neither possibility is likely, and no other common ground of termination is applicable. The situation looks bad for Everett, unless for some reason he did not *violate* the obligations that seem to exist. That is the subject of the next chapter.

IN SUMMARY

- Historically, lawyers and judges have recognized at least four sources of law:
  - *natural law*
  - *custom*
  - *governmental action*
  - *private action*

- Only the last two — *affirmative actions* by governments or individuals — are well accepted today.

- It is important to distinguish between *public* and *private* lawmaking, for they raise different issues and are handled with different terminology.

- The distinction between public and private lawmaking is different from the distinction between *status* and *contract*.

- Private parties can create legal obligations and rights only so long as:
  - all the actors involved have *capacity*
  - the parties are involved directly or through authorized *agents*
  - no one makes a *mistake*
  - no one is *coerced*
  - all the required *formalities* are met
  - the resulting rights and obligations violate no overriding *public policy*

- Public entities can create legal obligations and rights only as long as:
  - they have the *authority* to do so
  - they follow the proper *procedure*
  - nothing about the *substance* of their lawmaking efforts contravenes overriding constitutional or statutory requirements

- *Getting* obligations and rights: People can be subject to legal obligations or enjoy legal rights either because they were *created* in them originally or later *transferred* to them.

- *Losing* obligations and rights: People who are already subject to legal obligations or enjoy legal rights can lose them because they are *transferred* to someone else or are *terminated*.

- Only some obligations and rights can be transferred, but all of them, in principle, can be modified or terminated.

- Transfers can be *voluntary* or *involuntary*.

- Transfers and modifications generally follow the *equal dignity principle:* whatever was required to create the obligation or right in the first place is required for its transfer or modification

- Transfers come in all types, depending on the nature of the obligation or right at issue, and lawyers must be careful to use the *right technique* for the transfer desired.

- With important exceptions:
  - any right or obligation can be modified later
  - only the persons who created the obligation or right can modify it

- Obligations and rights can come to an end in many ways:
  - the obligation or right *expires* by its own terms
  - a condition is *fulfilled*
  - the obligation or right is *satisfied*
  - the parties take *affirmative acts* to terminate it
  - the *holder* of the obligation or right *expires*
  - the *correlative* right or obligation comes to an end

Has the Law Been Violated?
(Questions of Liability)

THIS CHAPTER

- Takes up the second great question of legal analysis: Has the law been violated?

- Divides this inquiry into three questions:
  - who decides whether an obligation or right has been violated? (*decisionmaking authority*)
  - how is the liability decision made? (*procedure*) and
  - was the obligation or right in fact violated? (*substance*)

- Describes the way that lawyers and judges interpret the law, and how that process changes depending on whether that law comes from legislative activity (statutes) or judicial activity (case-law)

- Describes the way that lawyers and judges find facts, with special emphasis on how legal fact-finding differs from fact-finding in everyday life

---

- Shows how decisions about legal liability can be affected by a host of additional legal doctrines that add to or block the liability otherwise present

In the last chapter we reviewed the questions lawyers and judges ask when they are concerned about the *existence* of an obligation or right. We saw that they can ask questions about whether an obligation or right was created at all and whether it has since been transferred, modified, or terminated. In that analysis we were not particularly concerned about the *substance* of the law at issue. We were not, for example, very interested in what a commercial contract required the parties to do, but with whether any contract had been formed at all — whether all the parties had capacity, complied with the proper formalities, and so on. In that sense, the inquiries from the last chapter were rather formal or technical in nature. Those formal and technical inquiries are vitally important — without a relevant law to work with there is not much room for further lawyering — but now we turn to questions that focus the lawyers' and judges' attention on the substance of legal obligations and rights. In this chapter, we assume that the obligations and rights exist, and instead try to *apply* them to clients and litigants.

Application is important for several reasons. We don't *really* know what our laws mean until we see them applied. Books and papers — and the rules we extract from them — are one thing; the law in action is another. Out in the world, a legal term may have a meaning we don't expect (often a *term of art*). Out in the world, judges might regularly interpret the exception to a particular rule so broadly that, despite appearances, the rule almost never applies. The law is full of such surprises. If lawyers are to do a good job for their clients — to gauge their chances of success in litigation or to advise them wisely on whether proposed courses of action are permissible — they must have mastered not only the linguistic forms of the law (the *black letter law*), but the history of its application as well. We often refer to this knowledge as "seasoning," and one can tell immediately, in both practice *and on a law school exam,* whether a person knows only the black letter law or has a sense of how that law is applied in the world. This is one of the primary reasons for studying cases and hypotheticals in law school. Case reports show how the language of the law has actually been applied and hypotheticals produce a group of related cases for further study of applications. In the final analysis, the application of law is important because that is what judges and lawyers are specially trained to do, and what clients and litigants rely on them to do well.

Applications, whether in the context of litigation or planning, inevitably raise questions of *liability*. Litigators argue about whether their clients, by action or inaction, have violated their own obligations or anyone else's rights. Planning lawyers often begin with their clients' objectives and ask which ways of attaining them are least likely to violate any law. In all these cases, both litigators and planners are constantly concerned with actual or potential violations of law. Because legal violations usually generate legal liability, it is natural to characterize this aspect of legal analysis as the search for liability.

Sometimes when we apply the law to a particular situation and find noncompliance, liability does not arise. This is because some obligations and rights are contingent. Only if you want to leave your house to your cousin Vinny must you make a will. If you do not follow the law of wills — violate the law of wills — say, by not signing the document, you will not incur legal liability. You will simply fail to achieve your objectives. In cases like these, a planning lawyer would not discuss the problem in terms of liability, but rather in terms of *compliance:* what must we do to comply with the law of wills? For this reason, the process of applying the law to the situations of clients would be more precisely characterized as the search for either liability or compliance. To save space and trees, however, we will shorten this more precise formulation to the search for liability.

To avoid some confusion, we should note that the word "liability," as used in this chapter, differs from other uses found in legal discussions. Sometimes the word is used to describe a duty to act in a particular way. I might say that I am "liable" under a contract with WalMart to provide 7,000 camping tents by the end of April. In this book, however, this is merely a legal obligation to provide the tents and liability refers to the situation when an obligation or right has been violated. Liability, in the sense of this book, arises only when April passes and I still have not delivered the tents.

There are three basic questions concerning liability:

1. who decides whether an obligation or right has been violated? (questions of authority);
2. how is the liability decision made? (questions of procedure); and
3. was the obligation or right in fact violated? (questions of substance).

We take them up in this order.

HAS THE LAW BEEN VIOLATED?

Decisions of Legal Liability

(1) WHO makes it? (authority)

(2) HOW is it made? (procedure)

(3) WHAT result is proper? (substance)

Everett's Case

Recall from Chapter 2 that we represent Everett Plainfield, who has been accused of striking a fellow employee at the tire plant where he works. We saw that he is threatened with criminal prosecution, a civil lawsuit by the victim, and the possibility of being fired, having potentially violated his obligations under criminal law, tort law, and his employment contract, respectively. Everett may not, however, have violated any of these laws or obligations. We will explore this possibility in the pages that follow.

WHO DECIDES WHETHER AN OBLIGATION OR RIGHT HAS BEEN VIOLATED?

Depending on the circumstances, an authoritative decision on liability can be made *privately;* that is, between the parties themselves. Alternatively, an authoritative decision on liability can be made *publicly,* that is, by one of the thousands of government officials who make such decisions — officials not only in the judicial branch (masters, magistrates, and judges of all sorts), but also in the executive branch ("front-line" bureaucrats, their superiors, appeal boards, commissions, and administrative law judges, among others). Private and public decisionmaking raise different issues and must be treated separately.

Private Decisionmaking

Lawyers and their clients ask and answer liability questions every day in many contexts:

- A client asks her lawyer whether she can legally rent out one of her back bedrooms to boarders. The lawyer quickly checks zoning and other relevant laws, gives an affirmative answer, and the client takes on a boarder.

- A middle-sized commercial client has a contract dispute with one of its suppliers: the last two shipments of aluminum hydroxide have arrived damaged and tainted, and the supplier has denied any responsibility. Both sides consult their lawyers and a settlement is negotiated: small price reductions on the next two shipments of aluminum hydroxide, along with a new system of early notification for shipment problems.
- A prosecuting attorney reviews a case file to decide what the defendant should be charged with, or whether any charges should be brought at all; she decides against bringing any charges and the defendant is released.

In all of these situations, as in thousands of other matters handled by lawyers, liability questions are asked and answered without any recourse to courts. In decisionmaking between the parties immediately concerned, *negotiation* and *settlement* are always proper. The parties themselves, in other words, are always authorized to make liability judgments. Lawyers can be involved, too, because they represent the parties.

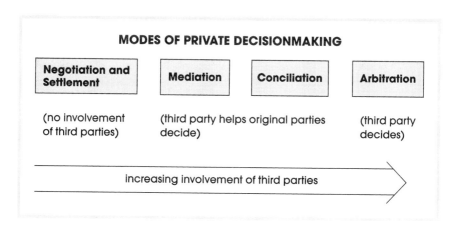

MODES OF PRIVATE DECISIONMAKING

Negotiation and Settlement	Mediation	Conciliation	Arbitration
(no involvement of third parties)	(third party helps original parties decide)		(third party decides)

increasing involvement of third parties →

In contrast, other forms of private decisionmaking — *mediation, conciliation,* and *arbitration* — generally require a special agreement of the parties. In mediation and conciliation, third parties are called in to help the disputants reach a settlement. In arbitration, the third parties decide on the proper resolution of the dispute (the *award*) and announce it to the parties. These alternative techniques introduce third parties who do not, strictly speaking, represent the principals, and their authority to act, not to mention their practical effectiveness, therefore depends on the express consent of the parties. Such consent can be given before or after the dispute arises. Whenever a liability question arises between parties, they can agree at that time to employ the efforts of others or they can agree to such services ahead of time. Nowadays, for example, many commercial contracts contain arbitration clauses, provisions calling for mandatory arbitration in the event of a future dispute about the contract or its performance.

Whenever third parties are called in, questions of decisionmaking authority can arise: Was there a valid agreement to involve such persons? Can that agreement now be invoked? What exactly does the agreement empower those persons to do? In addition, the use of third parties, especially arbitrators, is occasionally questioned on grounds of public policy, the use of arbitrators being prohibited because a statute has explicitly or implicitly required the judicial settlement of disputes of that type. In any event, *alternative dispute resolution* is becoming increasingly common and questions about it, like those above, are being raised as well. Law school curricula are beginning to reflect this change, sometimes in the form of special courses devoted to the topic, and more commonly in the growing number of references to mediation, conciliation, and arbitration in more traditional courses. These are useful developments, because lawyers are now frequently asked to invoke or fight off the use of these techniques in the course of their work.

Everett's Case

Criminal charges would involve the state government as a party, and thus no purely private means of determining Everett's liability would be available. The alleged victim's tort suit and the tire company's employment action could, on the other hand, be handled without recourse to any public body. We might negotiate a settlement with both the alleged victim and the company, with or without admitting any legal liability. If negotiations failed, we could suggest mediation, conciliation, or arbitration of the claims. If the other parties agreed, the issue of Everett's liability could be resolved without government involvement.

Public Decisonmaking

If the parties cannot reach a liability decision on their own, they might turn to courts and judges — judges of general jurisdiction and judges of special jurisdiction, trial court judges and appellate court judges, state judges and federal judges, masters, magistrates, umpires, chancellors, and referees. It is important to note, however, that many government officials make liability decisions outside the context of handling other people's disputes. Many executive branch officials make such decisions: zoning officers, public prosecutors, officials of the federal Securities and Exchange Commission, and the guy down at the Motor Vehicle Department who decides whether your three types of identification are sufficient. In each case, these officials make decisions about whether a law has been violated (or has been complied with). And whatever level of government they represent, whatever branch they represent, public decisionmakers provoke questions of *authority*, questions about whether they are in fact authorized to make determinations of liability.

Authority questions are often raised about public officials because public decisionmaking is nonconsensual. Unlike its private counterparts, authority in public decisionmaking does *not* depend on the mutual consent of the disputing parties, but on the public official having *jurisdiction to adjudicate*. It is usually in someone's interest to resist that jurisdiction: the defendant accused of purse-snatching; the supplier whose customers have been receiving tainted aluminum hydroxide; the homeowner with cash-paying boarders the city says she can't keep. Anyone who wants to resist a decision of legal liability has an interest in attacking the authority of the person who might impose it. Even if the attack on authority is unsuccessful, it will usually serve to delay the ultimate imposition of liability.

Finding the right public decisionmaker is crucial. A decision made without jurisdiction to adjudicate is no decision at all; it cannot be enforced anywhere by anyone. If I get a judgment against you in a California state court, for example, and it is later determined that the court did not have jurisdiction to hear the case, the court's decision will not be enforceable. Finding the right decisionmaker is no less crucial when there are several authorized decisionmakers to choose from. Some decisionmakers are more sympathetic to plaintiffs (or defendants or corporations or air-crash victims) than others; some decisionmakers work a thousand miles away, others are six blocks down the street; some can get the job done within a year, others will take ten. There are, in short, many practical reasons to find the "right" forum, and lawyers spend a lot of time in the search.

All government officials attract the same kinds of objections to their decisionmaking authority — wrong government (state versus federal, for example), wrong branch (executive versus judicial, usually) or wrong person within the branch. Despite these similarities, questions about executive branch officials and judges arise in different contexts and with different emphases. We thus take them up separately.

Objections to Executive Branch Decisionmaking. We often question the *substance* of executive branch decisions regarding legal rights and obligations: "Excuse me, officer, but I really think you've made a mistake." "If you'll just look at the envelope, sir, you'll see that my return was mailed before April 15th." But questions about decisionmaking *authority* are seldom raised: "Officer, what makes you think you can just pull people off the highway like that?" We seldom question executive branch authority — not just to avoid offense and curry favor — but because executive branch officials know their jobs. They tend to perform the same sorts of functions and make the same kinds of decisions every day. They come to learn the range of permissible activity within their areas of responsibility and tend to stay within that range. Only those at the very top of a department, agency, or government regularly face decisions that could push the bounds of previously accepted authority. When questions of authority do arise, they are usually of two types: has this matter been placed properly in the executive branch and is the official who actually made the decision the proper one?

Is there constitutional or statutory authority for the executive branch to act? Authority for executive branch action can be either constitutional or statutory, but it must be one or the other. That is, executive branch officials cannot take action unless the relevant constitution or laws authorize it. Many statutes provide explicitly for their enforcement by particular offices or departments in the executive branch and outline what sorts of decisions officials can make in the course of that enforcement. Such detail in a constitution is rarer, but sometimes is found. When the authority to act is given explicitly, any further legal questions tend to fall into two main patterns. First, is the executive decision at issue actually described in the relevant constitutional clause or statute? Second, was the granting of authority *itself* valid? For example, did the legislature have the power to give the executive branch the authority it tried to give?

Sometimes constitutional or statutory authority for executive action is implied rather than expressed. It is often implied from the very fact of the executive branch's existence and its obvious reason for being. (If not to execute the laws, then what's it for?) A lot of the reasoning in this area is a matter of common sense, but is traditionally treated as a matter of textual interpretation. Many executive branch powers of the federal government, for example, have been found in the first line of Article II of the Constitution: "The executive Power shall be vested in a President." The implied authority to execute a law, in turn, usually includes an implied authority to make (at least initial) decisions about whether that law has been violated. One can attack an implied authority to make liability decisions on the grounds that: (1) the decision at issue is not really necessary to execute the law at issue; or (2) that the underlying law is itself invalid.

Is this the proper official within the executive branch? Even though a decision about a particular matter is properly located in the executive branch, there can still be questions about the official who actually made it. If the official taking the action is not the person explicitly empowered to do so under a constitutional or statutory provision, then questions of this sort can always be raised. It will then be incumbent upon the official (or her attorneys) to establish a series of authoritative links connecting the official with the relevant constitutional or legislative language. Inquiries of this type are usually described as raising problems of *delegation,* such as whether an executive authority over highways, implicitly given to the governor, was properly delegated to the chief of the Bureau of Roads in the state Department of Transportation. One can attack purported delegations on the grounds that (1) one or more "links" in the chain of delegation are missing or invalid; or (2) the decisionmaking power has been put in the wrong place (in the governor's office, for example, rather than in an independent commission).

Everett's Case

A prosecutor's decision to proceed with prosecuting our client for assault and battery is not likely to be challenged successfully on grounds that she lacks the authority to act in this way. The executive branch is clearly the branch in which law enforcement resides, and public prosecutors are the ones within that branch authorized to make decisions about whether to go forward with any particular case.

Objections to Judicial Branch Decisionmaking. As noted earlier, the decisionmaking authority of executive branch officials is seldom challenged. Questions about judicial authority, on the other hand, are raised frequently. Indeed, in almost every piece of litigation, the parties and the judge spend at least some of their time worrying about this authority, the jurisdiction to adjudicate. The reason is not that judges stray from their proper roles more often than Presidents and department heads, but that litigants often fight between themselves about the proper forum. Plaintiffs, who have the first choice of forum (by filing suit in one court rather than another), understandably pick a court that is most favorable to them. Defendants just as understandably resist — not just to get a more favorable court, but simply for the purpose of delay. When these disputes arise, questions of judicial authority must be raised and answered.

The fundamental question of judicial authority is simple: in which court (if any) should the case be heard? And the most important factor in reaching the answer is simple as well, for jurisdiction to adjudicate is primarily *territorial*. A court is part of a government, and the government represents a political entity — a nation, a state, or a city — with territorial boundaries. Accordingly, a court can only hear cases that have sufficient contacts with the relevant territory. If those contacts do not exist, then the court cannot be used. To settle issues of jurisdictional authority, therefore, we often examine the physical locations of the parties — their residences, domiciles, and places of business — and the physical location of the

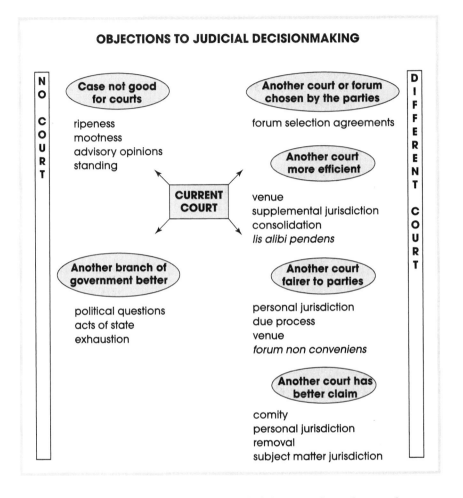

OBJECTIONS TO JUDICIAL DECISIONMAKING

NO COURT

Case not good for courts

ripeness
mootness
advisory opinions
standing

CURRENT COURT

Another branch of government better

political questions
acts of state
exhaustion

Another court or forum chosen by the parties

forum selection agreements

Another court more efficient

venue
supplemental jurisdiction
consolidation
lis alibi pendens

Another court fairer to parties

personal jurisdiction
due process
venue
forum non conveniens

Another court has better claim

comity
personal jurisdiction
removal
subject matter jurisdiction

DIFFERENT COURT

actions that have allegedly given rise to liability — where the accident occurred, where the contract was made or breached, where the murder took
place, and so on. The analysis focuses on territory, territory, and territory.
We are relatively less concerned about political connections and similar
facts — the citizenship of the parties, for example, or the government that
created the obligation alleged to have been violated. (An important exception to this territorial principle lies in the division of authority between
federal and state courts in the United States. Because there is always a territorial overlap between any federal court and at least one state court, the
division of responsibility between those courts is generally settled on non-
territorial grounds, such as the citizenship of the parties or the nature of
the dispute.)

Jurisdiction to adjudicate — the judicial authority to apply law — is
different from the jurisdiction to prescribe — the legislative authority to

make law, discussed in Chapter 2. It is quite possible, for example, to have a case heard in a state or nation that does not have the power to make the law applicable to that case. Two residents of California could sue each other in California courts over an automobile accident in New Zealand (because both have strong physical ties to California), even though the California General Assembly has no authority to extend its substantive tort law thousands of miles across the Pacific. The California court, in this instance, would likely hear the case and apply New Zealand tort law.

Despite their relatively simple foundations, questions about jurisdiction to adjudicate have generated a highly specialized vocabulary. This is the land of *mootness, ripeness, standing,* and *forum non conveniens;* the land of *general appearances, special appearances, long-arm statutes* and *removals;* and, of course, the land of *jurisdictions* — *general jurisdiction, special jurisdiction, personal jurisdiction, subject matter jurisdiction* and *ancillary jurisdiction,* among others. The legal questions we ask, using this vocabulary, can be grouped into six categories:

- Is the dispute amenable to judicial settlement?
- Have the parties made an effective choice of court or nonjudicial forum?
- Is the chosen court administratively efficient?
- Would a proceeding in the chosen forum be fair to all the parties?
- Does another court have a better claim to the case? and
- Is there a better branch of government for the hearing of this matter?

Thus, if a client of mine were sued in Hawaii state court, I might try to avoid the litigation entirely by arguing one or more of the following: the case is moot; the parties had earlier agreed that all disputes would be settled in Alaska courts; this case duplicates a lawsuit already proceeding in Alaska; my client has no contacts with the state of Hawaii; the *federal* court sitting in Hawaii is the proper forum for this kind of case; and this case raises sensitive issues better handled by the executive or legislative branches. If any of these arguments succeeds, the case will be dismissed and my client will have escaped or at least delayed a possible finding of liability. Issues of jurisdiction to adjudicate are so important and recur so often that we will briefly cover each one. Law school courses in civil procedure and advanced litigation cover these topics in much greater depth.

Is the dispute amenable to judicial settlement? We want to ensure that our courts hear only those cases for which judicial settlement is particularly appropriate. This generally means that we want to see (1) opposing parties (2) with real interests in the outcome (3) of a live controversy. Without these elements the wisdom of judicial settlement, especially in our adversarial system, decreases significantly. Thus, requests for *advisory opin-*

ions are almost certain to be rejected. When litigants don't have a real interest or stake in a lawsuit, they are likely to be dismissed for lack of *standing*. A lawsuit can also be dismissed if the issues are not ready for adjudication, either because a decision would be premature (the problem of *ripeness*) or because the decision would come too late to make any difference (the problem of *mootness*).

Have the parties made an effective choice of court or nonjudicial forum? Private parties can always agree to bring their disputes to a particular court or to eschew court action entirely and instead rely on alternative methods of dispute resolution such as binding arbitration. Many commercial contracts, especially international ones, contain *forum selection clauses* that attempt to direct the course of any future litigation between the parties. Judges have the last word on their own jurisdiction and are not bound by these private agreements, but they regularly enforce such clauses. Still, there are exceptions. In some state courts forum selection clauses are not enforced at all (or not enforced in certain types of cases), and most judges, regardless of court, will examine such clauses for overreaching or unconscionability, as well as for violations of public policy.

Is the chosen court administratively efficient? Our courts, like any institution, are concerned with doing their work as efficiently as possible. We have many courts, both state and federal, sitting in many places. We have an interest in spreading the work around, in sending cases to those courts best able to handle them, and in designing jurisdictional systems to accomplish these ends. These concerns explain the common practice of creating different courts for different purposes — a tax court, a small claims court, a court of international trade, a police court — and allocating cases accordingly. These concerns also help to explain *venue* rules (for choosing the proper courthouse within a multi-court system) and *supplemental jurisdiction* (giving courts the ability to decide otherwise impermissible claims because they are related to permissible claims in the same litigation). Administrative concerns also help to explain rules regarding *consolidation* (pulling similar cases together into one case) and the *lis alibi pendens* doctrine (pursuant to which courts can refuse to hear cases that are already proceeding in different forums). Each of these concerns might cause a court to refuse a case brought before it, and instead to dismiss or transfer it.

Would a proceeding in the chosen forum be fair to all the parties? Our courts are concerned that no one be forced to attend a proceeding too far from home or defend himself in a place that could not reasonably have been anticipated. Courts see these issues as matters of due process or fundamental fairness, which find expression in our rules of *personal jurisdiction* (permitting courts to decide only those cases with parties having minimal physical connections with the court's territory), venue rules (helping to decide which court within a physical territory is appropriate) and the *forum non conveniens* doctrine (pursuant to which courts decline to hear cases because the court is excessively inconvenient for one of the parties).

Does another court have a better claim to the case? Because courts work within a system of governments, both national and international, they need to ensure that no other court system has a better claim to the matters presented — better in a substantive sense other than administrative efficiency and fairness to the parties. Concerns about the division of responsibility between American and foreign courts are reflected in *comity* analysis, pursuant to which an American court might defer to the courts of another nation. Concerns about the division of responsibility between federal and state courts are reflected primarily in our rules of *subject matter jurisdiction*, defining the kinds of cases that can or must be heard in federal courts. Concerns about the division of responsibility among state courts are reflected in rules about personal jurisdiction (again, permitting courts to decide only those cases with parties or events having connections with the court's territory), *long-arm statutes* (pursuant to which each state defines what sorts of cases can be heard in its courts) and in *due process* analysis (which limits extravagant claims to jurisdiction).

Is there a better branch of government for the hearing of this matter? Finally, courts are concerned about whether the disputes brought to them ought to be handled instead by the legislative or the executive branches. Concerns of this type are reflected primarily in the *political question doctrine* (under which our courts will decline to hear cases because they are more properly settled by the President or Congress), the *act of state doctrine* (under which American courts will decline to hear cases that question the legality of certain actions by foreign governments, partly on the theory that the President is better suited to handle such claims) and the requirement of *exhaustion,* the requirement in some cases that potential litigants exhaust their administrative remedies in the executive branch before filing a lawsuit in the judicial branch.

Everett's Case

The criminal case, the civil tort suit by Everett's alleged striking victim, and (let us say) our own lawsuit against Everett's employer to overturn his firing, could potentially be brought in any number of courts, both federal and state. In each case the prosecutor/plaintiff will attempt to choose the forum most favorable to its cause, and the defendant will seek to have the case dismissed on one or more of the grounds just discussed.

In sum, lawyers and judges have a lot to argue about in jurisdictional matters, and argue they do. For several reasons, jurisdictional rules and jurisdictional arguments are some of the most difficult and complicated in the practice of law. First, because judges and litigants pay constant attention to these matters, there is constant pressure for change — to fiddle with the rules just a little bit more, to draw just one more distinction, to create just one more exception. This constant pressure for change tends to make the rules complex. Second, almost every doctrine or rule is founded on several concerns simultaneously. For example, federal rules about subject matter jurisdiction — rules describing the cases to be heard in federal courts — reflect not only the desire to divide responsibility between federal and state courts, but the administrative desire to divide work among federal courts and the desire to treat litigants fairly. Adjusting a rule or pressing an argument for one purpose always has effects, sometimes adverse effects, on the other purposes. Third, and finally, jurisdictional rules and reasoning come from many sources: international law, federal and state constitutions, federal and state statutes, rules of court and judicial precedents, among others. Although this hardly distinguishes the law of jurisdiction from other areas of law, jurisdictional law is especially contorted by the simultaneous involvement of many different lawmakers. That is, views on which cases courts should hear seem to depend a great deal on whether the rule-maker is a minister of foreign affairs, a drafter of a constitution, a legislator, a supreme court justice, or a judge in the trenches who simply wants to clear the docket. Treaties, constitutions, statutes, court rules, and judicial decisions thus tend to push jurisdictional boundaries in different directions.

HOW IS THE LIABILITY DECISION MADE?

We have just reviewed the questions lawyers and judges ask when deciding *who* can determine legal liability. We have seen that the parties concerned (with or without their lawyers) can always make such liability decisions and that other private parties — mediators, conciliators, and arbitrators — can become involved when the parties agree. Public decision-makers, in contrast, can make liability decisions only when they have jurisdiction to adjudicate, a power that depends on the answers to a number of subsidiary questions. For executive branch officials, we are primarily concerned with the existence of constitutional or statutory authorization; for judges, we are primarily concerned with the application of complex jurisdictional rules and doctrines.

We now assume that the "who" question has been answered, and proceed to ask the "how" questions, that is, questions about the *procedures* to be followed by the authorized decisionmaker. Questions about procedure are of three main types: What procedures are required? Have the required procedures been followed? What will be done about procedural violations? We will examine each of these questions briefly, followed by a discussion of how lawyers and judges react to procedural disputes.

What Procedure Is Required?

Legal decisionmakers typically follow a predetermined set of procedures in their work. The detail and complexity of these procedures varies from decisionmaker to decisionmaker. At one end of the spectrum, when parties decide a case through negotiation and settlement, procedural rules are at a low ebb. Which of the parties proposes what solutions, when they do so, how the final settlement is agreed upon, and how that settlement is finalized in documents, are all within the control of the parties themselves. Any procedures in negotiation and settlement tend to be created *ad hoc,* the parties and their lawyers making them up as they go along. At the other end of the spectrum lies decisionmaking in federal and state courts, which is characterized by highly detailed, highly stylized procedures that must be followed at every turn.

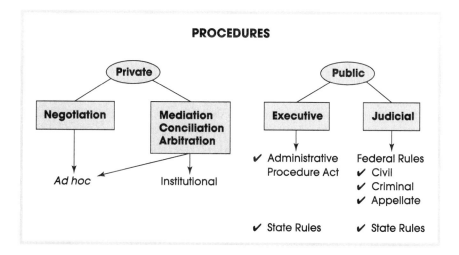

We sometimes refer to these differences as differences in *formality.* Negotiation and settlement are the least formal types of legal decisionmaking, courtroom litigation the most formal. The level of formality is largely determined by the extent to which the parties to the dispute control its resolution. When party control is at its peak, as in negotiation and settlement, procedural rules are largely nonexistent. The body of rules increases when third parties become involved. In conciliation and mediation, where a third party helps the disputants arrive at a settlement, the conciliator or mediator typically operates under a small set of rudimentary guidelines. In arbitration, where a third party is called upon to reach a decision for the parties, the arbitrator typically operates under a larger body of rules. In the courtroom, where decisionmaking power is granted exclusively and irrevocably to others (the judge, jury, and appellate courts), procedural rules grow to the largest size of all. In short, the greater the power of an independent decisionmaker, the more numerous and detailed the procedural rules that the decisionmaker must follow.

Procedures in Private Decisionmaking

Negotiation and settlement. As just noted, when private parties negotiate and settle liability questions, no particular procedure is required. As a consequence, procedural questions in this context are more practical than legal. Who does what, and when, are matters of personal choice. Whether I call for negotiations at all, whether I set time limits, whether I demand a response of a particular sort, are all decisions I can make on my own. Or I can sit down with the other party and work out a plan. How one proceeds raises questions of style and effectiveness, but not of legal propriety.

Mediation, conciliation, and arbitration. In mediation, conciliation, and arbitration, questions of procedure begin to acquire a legal cast. Each form of dispute resolution must be initiated by agreement, and that agreement can specify the procedures to be followed. The procedures can be decided *ad hoc,* as the decisionmaking moves along, or the parties can agree to follow some standardized procedures, such as those issued by the American Arbitration Association. In any event, the parties enjoy substantial freedom to set their own procedures, and oversight by judges or others is generally lacking. Procedural agreements can be brought under judicial scrutiny if a court case on the same matter is ultimately filed, but even then courts are reluctant to meddle. Weighed down by their own heavy caseloads, our courts generally seek to encourage out-of-court settlement, and if they become too eager to review and overturn the procedures chosen by the parties themselves, they will discourage the parties from making the settlement attempt in the first place. Once the procedures are agreed upon, however, each party has the right to insist that they be followed, and court review of procedural *violations* is more common.

Procedures in Public Decisionmaking. Procedures become dramatically more detailed in public decisionmaking.

Executive branch decisionmaking. Executive branch decisions, at both the federal and state levels, are governed by basic constitutional requirements of due process and, depending on the circumstances, by more specific guarantees like the effective assistance of counsel. At the statutory level, general requirements governing executive branch procedures are imposed by the federal Administrative Procedure Act and its state-law analogues. Federal and state agencies are also likely to be governed by legislation particularly tailored for them, and that legislation often contains procedural provisions for those agencies. In addition, all federal agencies and many state agencies have procedural rules that they, with legislative oversight, have themselves created and follow. These rules, taken together, are known as *administrative law*, and as we have noted previously, practice in this area is vitally important in the modern state.

Judicial branch decisionmaking. In the courthouse, federal judicial practice is governed by specific constitutional provisions on procedure, a series of congressional statutes, and a body of rules adopted by the federal courts themselves: the Federal Rules of Civil Procedure, the Federal Rules of Criminal Procedure, the Federal Rules of Evidence, and so on. In addition, federal appellate courts and trial courts have adopted local rules that govern additional matters within their particular circuits and districts. State judicial practice is also governed, at a very general level, by the federal constitution, but more specifically and directly by state constitutions and statutes. State courts, like federal courts, also have court-generated rules, which can apply both statewide or locally.

In public decisionmaking by executive and judicial officials, the parties themselves have relatively little power to set their own procedures, but there are exceptions. The Federal Rules of Civil Procedure, for example, sometimes allow and even encourage the parties to agree among themselves about certain procedures to be followed, especially in the pretrial discovery of evidence. These agreements, however, are subject to close scrutiny by the court that will ultimately hear the case.

Everett's Case

There are many fora in which Everett's liability to the state, his victim, and his employer might be determined, ranging from the most informal settlement negotiations to the most formal court proceeding. Each forum has its own rules, with the greatest level of procedural details found in state and federal court proceedings.

Have the Required Procedures Been Followed?

At a workaday level, most questions about whether the required procedures have been followed are easy to answer. Procedures tend to involve well-understood actions: the filing of a complaint, the entry of a document into evidence, the filing of an appeal within 60 days of final judgment, and so on. Either the paper was filed in time or it wasn't. Procedural errors tend to arise because someone made a mistake — obvious as a mistake — caused by a lapse in care or judgment.

Even so, questions about compliance with procedural requirements raise subtler issues as well. First, not all procedural rules are straightforward, and there can often be questions of whether the required action has been taken. From a trial court, for example, one cannot appeal an interlocutory order but can appeal a final judgment. Many trial court decisions fall into a gray area between those two alternatives and thus raise difficult questions of appealability. Second, even if a procedural rule is clear on its face, it can often raise subtle questions of compliance. The Federal Rules of Civil Procedure, for example, are quite clear that certain defenses are waived if they are not raised in the first responsive pleading, but what about defenses that are raised *implicitly* in that first pleading? Third, and finally, the required procedures *may not be the ones written in the rule book.* The overriding requirements of due process and fundamental fairness limit all of our written rules, and it can sometimes be argued that a particular procedure, at least as applied to a particular case, violates the due process rights of one of the parties. To give an example, every state has rules about how defendants are to be notified that a case has been filed against them. There are usually several alternatives, but a traditional method has been the periodic publication of a notice in a local newspaper. In recent years, however, the United States Supreme Court has called publication notice into question, on the ground that it is not sufficiently calculated to give notice to defendants, and thus represents an unconstitutional denial of the defendants' right to due process.

What Will Be Done about Procedural Violations?

A final source of procedural dispute concerns the consequences of procedural violations. Most of the time, the consequences are clear because the rules that require a particular action also specify what will happen if the action is not taken. In these cases, the question of consequences will not arise, unless they are attacked as so severe that they represent a denial of due process or fundamental fairness. In many cases, however, procedural rules either do not mandate a particular consequence for their violation or allow for a variety of remedies to be determined on a case-by-case basis. The most notorious example of this situation arises when evidence against a criminal defendant has been admitted to trial improperly. Was the admission of evidence sufficiently serious that the defendant's conviction should be overturned, and if so, with what implications for a new trial?

Everett's Case

In whatever forum we find ourselves, we will be careful to follow the correct procedures applicable to that forum. If the decision goes against our client Everett, we will review all the procedures that have gone on before, in search of irregularities important enough to void the decision.

Lawyers and judges approach procedural questions with an enthusiasm that borders on fetishism. There are many reasons for this state of affairs. First, procedure is our special province. The problems of litigants and clients come to us in dazzling variety, even though we work to catalog, characterize, and generalize among classes of such problems. The procedures by which those problems can be resolved, on the other hand, are relatively constant and unchanging. Special procedures for decisionmaking are one of the distinctive characteristics of law. These procedures are central to the lawyer's trade and we take them seriously. Second, those who master the procedural rules put themselves in a relative position of power over their less-well-tutored opponents. Lawyers serve their clients well by knowing procedure cold. Third, a procedural win is often just as good as one based on substance. If I can get the case against my client dismissed on procedural grounds, this is often just as effective as a final decision of no liability. A procedural victory may even be better, as such victories can often be obtained earlier in a case than a final judgment. Fourth and finally, procedure is often complicated and difficult to master, and we naturally tend to inflate the importance of subjects we've spent the longest time learning. (The same natural tendency is at work in many Property professors' treatment of the Rule Against Perpetuities; your author stands guilty as charged.)

The importance of procedure often blinds us to its dysfunctional aspects, its incongruities, its idiocies. As lawyers and judges we must therefore be especially sensitive to these problems. We must always ask ourselves, "Is all of this necessary?" And if it is not, we must work to make things better. Procedure is our special province; it represents us, and we have a particular interest in making sure that it represents us well. But more is at stake than professional vanity. If legal procedures fail us, the law will too.

WAS THE OBLIGATION OR RIGHT, IN FACT, VIOLATED?

We began this chapter by reviewing *who* can decide liability questions — the parties, their lawyers, mediators, conciliators, arbitrators, bureaucrats, and judges. We then asked *what procedures* those persons must follow. We are now ready to examine the actual process of decisionmaking — how someone decides whether an obligation or right has in fact been violated. The issues here lie at the heart of legal process. We will focus on *judicial* determinations of liability, even though this gives a distorted picture of where such determinations actually take place. As we have seen again and again, parties, lawyers, and executive branch officials all make liability decisions. Judges operating in the courtroom represent only one type of decisionmaker in one forum. There are, however, at least two justifications for focusing on judicial determinations of liability. First, judicial decisionmaking is clearly important in its own right; a great deal of law practice involves courtroom argument and the preparation for such argument. Second, legal decisionmakers other than judges tend to mimic judicial decisionmaking as they go about their work. A planning lawyer, for example, will review her client's situation (including the possibility of liability) by thinking like a judge: would her client be found liable in court if she followed the proposed course of action?

The process of determining legal liability is usually described as *applying the law to the facts*. This description presupposes a firm grasp of the difference between law and facts. Lawyers and judges typically operate with a philosophically naive but perfectly serviceable formulation of these concepts. The law is that corpus of rights and obligations generated by legislatures and courts. The facts are everything else that has happened in the world or is true of the world. Philosophers and philosophically inclined lawyers sometimes ridicule these formulations, and sometimes it is hard to tell whether something is a fact question or a law question, but most of the time the simple distinction works.

In the daily business of courtroom decisionmaking, the distinction between law and facts has a very practical consequence for the division of labor between judge and jury. The process of applying the law to the facts presupposes three steps: an ascertainment of the law; an ascertainment of the facts; and the application of the ascertained law to the ascertained facts. In American practice, the judge always ascertains the law; the jury, if there is one, ascertains the facts; and both the judge and jury share the work of application. The shared enterprise of application varies from case to case. Juries, when they are used, are usually asked to apply the law to the facts and thereby reach a *general verdict*. They are asked to find the defendant guilty or not guilty of a crime, or one party liable or not liable for the breach of a civil obligation. In some cases, however, a jury can instead be asked to reach a *special verdict,* that is, to answer only specific questions about the case. It could be asked whether the defendant possessed 100 or 1000 kilograms of marijuana at the time of her arrest (a real case). If a determination of liability is not one of the questions posed in a special verdict, the jury does not answer it. Even when the jury does apply the law to the facts — by general or special verdict — the final determination of liability is made by the judge. Legal liability is established only when the court (i.e., the judge) *gives judgment* and not before. Jury verdicts are relevant but not always dispositive. This point is clearest in the case of the *judgment notwithstanding the verdict,* or JNOV. Even after a jury has found the defendant liable, the losing party can ask the judge to hold otherwise. If the motion for JNOV is granted, the status of the defendant's liability is determined by the court's judgment, not the jury's decision.

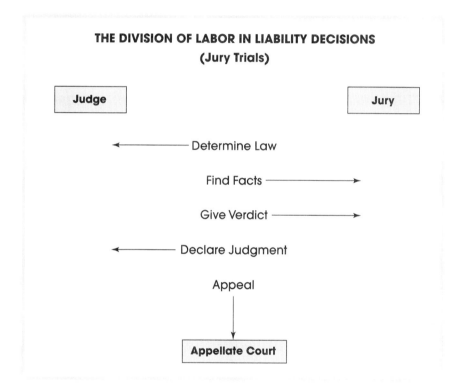

THE DIVISION OF LABOR IN LIABILITY DECISIONS
(Jury Trials)

In nonjury trials, which are common, judges do everything: they ascertain the law, ascertain the facts, and apply the law to the facts. Even then, judges usually keep the steps separate, addressing them individually in written or oral opinions. This is sometimes the result of a statute or rule of court requiring separate treatment, but even without such a rule, judges typically maintain the distinctions. This comes in part from the judge's obligation to explain her decision; detailed treatments of the facts, the law, and its application to the facts provide a sturdy framework for such explanations. The tenacity of the distinction between law and facts is also explained by its importance in appellate practice. When one or both parties to a lawsuit feels aggrieved by a trial court's final judgment, and appeal that decision to a higher court, the higher court (the ***appellate court***) will review both the trial court's findings of fact and determinations of law. Appellate courts, however, treat findings of fact much more deferentially than determinations of law. Facts, whether initially determined by a judge or jury, are overturned on appeal only if they are *against the manifest weight of the evidence,* constitute an *abuse of discretion* on the judge's part or represent a similarly egregious error. Determinations of law, on the other hand, can be overturned whenever appellate judges disagree with the judge below.

Even outside the world of trial practice, lawyers and other decision-makers typically think in terms of law and facts when they determine issues of legal liability. When parties to a dispute attempt to negotiate a settlement, there is likely to be some discussion about the state of the law and the state of the facts, even if no formal statement of either will be included in the final agreement. Planning lawyers, as well, almost reflexively break down questions of potential liability by thinking through the applicable facts and the applicable law. The dichotomous focus on law and facts recurs constantly in legal practice, whenever determinations of legal liability, current or potential, must be made.

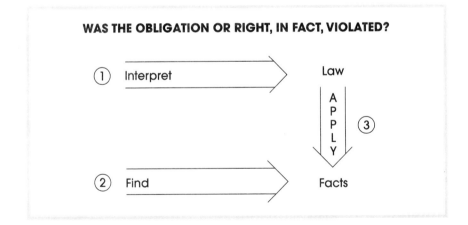

Law-finding and fact-finding are highly stylized endeavors. Both are ancient features of legal process and professional traditions have affected their operation in many ways. Some of those effects are predictable and easily understood; others are not. Each kind of inquiry — into law and facts — has its own special attributes and will be discussed separately.

Everett's Case

We have now reached a critical stage in our analysis of Everett's situation: deciding whether or not he is actually liable for violating his obligations under criminal law, tort law, and his employment contract. This inquiry breaks down into two main questions: (1) How exactly is Everett required to act under these rules? and (2) What exactly did he do?

What Does the Law Require?

To "find law" requires both a determination that a particular law exists (the formal inquiry) and a determination of its meaning (the interpretive inquiry). The formal inquiry has already been discussed in the previous chapter. This leaves the question of interpretation: What action (or restraint from action) does the obligation or right require? In legal discussions, interpretive questions are never asked in the abstract. When we ask, "What action or restraint from action does this obligation or right require?" we are not asking for a general review of all possible actions in the world, seeking to draw a line between those required and those not. We always have a particular action in mind. Does the language in my lease that prohibits subleasing prohibit me from taking on a boarder? Does the city ordinance that requires all pets to be licensed apply to the horse I have stabled in my garage at the back of my lot? The questions are always focused, asking whether a particular right or obligation permits or prohibits a particular action. We approach such questions in one of two ways, depending on whether the obligation or right comes from an *authoritative text* or from *judicial decisions*.

Everett's Case

In analyzing Everett's case, we will not ask general questions about criminal, tort, and contract law, but narrowly focus our inquiry to ask whether Everett's striking his co-worker violates his obligations under each of those laws. Our analysis will be different for his criminal law and contract obligations, on the one hand, and his tort law obligations, on the other. The first two are based on authoritative texts (criminal statutes and the employment contract) and the last on the common law (judicial decisions on tort liability).

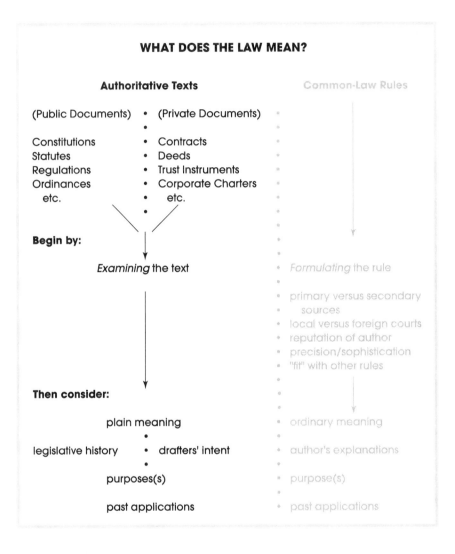

WHAT DOES THE LAW MEAN?

Authoritative Texts   Common-Law Rules

(Public Documents)   • (Private Documents)
                     •
Constitutions   • Contracts
Statutes   • Deeds
Regulations   • Trust Instruments
Ordinances   • Corporate Charters
   etc.   •   etc.
                     •

Begin by:

          Examining the text   • *Formulating* the rule

                                            • primary versus secondary
                                                sources
                                            • local versus foreign courts
                                            • reputation of author
                                            • precision/sophistication
                                            • "fit" with other rules

Then consider:

          plain meaning   • ordinary meaning
                •
legislative history   • drafters' intent   • author's explanations
                •
          purposes(s)   • purpose(s)

          past applications   • past applications

Statutes and Other Authoritative Texts. Many obligations and rights are created in documents that provide the precise wording of the obligation or right at issue. Constitutions, statutes, administrative regulations, city ordinances, contracts, wills, trusts, and deeds are all authoritative texts. Anyone who interprets them *must adhere to the exact language used in them.* If a contract says, "eighteen (18) short-tons of grade A winter wheat shall be delivered to purchaser by January 18, 1997," the interpreter must begin with *precisely* those words and no others. If a city ordinance provides that "all owners of domestic pets must annually obtain from city authorities a license for such ownership," the interpreter must begin with precisely those words and no others. The interpretation of authoritative texts is thus driven by a search for the meaning of *particular* words or phrases. (A little later, we will see that judicial decisions — case precedents — do not work this way, and that lawyers and judges are *not* tied to the precise language used in previous cases.)

Everett's Case

Suppose that Everett's employment contract with the tire company gives the company the power to terminate him "for cause," and further defines "cause" as (among other things) "commission by Employee of an act involving moral turpitude." In interpreting this obligation, we must begin with precisely these words and no others. We would likely start by exploring the meaning of "moral turpitude." Likewise, suppose the relevant criminal statute on "assault" provides that "no person shall knowingly cause or attempt to cause physical harm to another." Again, because we are dealing with an authoritative text, we must start with precisely those words and not a summary or paraphrase. We would likely start by exploring the meaning of the words "knowingly," "cause," and "physical harm."

The search for the proper meaning of a word or phrase is an inquiry into its *use*. We can think of word usage as falling along a spectrum: some usages are well accepted, others less so, and beyond them lie others that no native speaker would accept. We can usually make uncontroversial judgments about usages at either end of the spectrum. The collie I got from the humane society is a "domestic pet"; my station wagon is not. Thus, the pet licensing ordinance would apply to my collie but not to my car. Between these core and spurious usages lie more controversial cases. What about the horse I have stabled in my garage at the back of my lot? Is it a "domestic pet" subject to licensing? A great deal of interpretive debate in the law concerns such penumbral usages. When disagreements arise, we handle them in predictable ways, asking predictable questions. We start by summarizing the three great modes of textual interpretation, and then examine each one in more depth.

The interpretation of a word or phrase begins with the working presumption that core usages are intended, spurious usages are not, and penumbral usages require further analysis. We see the presumption, for example, in the *plain meaning rule* of statutory construction, the rule that statutory language should be interpreted to mean what ordinary people in their daily affairs would understand it to mean. Similar *canons of construction* are applied to private documents like contracts, wills, and trusts. In both public and private documents we presumptively apply language in its everyday sense.

But this is only a working presumption, and we sometimes reject the tyranny of plain meaning. We sometimes do so when the drafters of the word or phrase were in fact using it in a different way. We then might change course and ask what the drafters had in mind. We note immediately that this represents a dramatic change in our analysis. Plain meaning turns on how ordinary people talk. The second approach looks to the drafters and to *their* usage, with little regard for what the rest of us think. An examination of *drafter's intent* can thus be characterized as a switch from a public to a private approach to meaning.

We also depart from the tyranny of plain meaning to look at the *purposes* for which an obligation or right is created. Purposes are different from the drafter's intent, though they are often confused. The purposes for which a particular piece of language has been drafted, whether in a statute or a contract, may be ascertained with either the public or private approach to meaning. That is, we can ask either: what would a *reasonable person* (anyone, all of us, etc.) wish to accomplish by such language? (the public approach) or what did *these particular drafters* seek to accomplish? (the private approach). As such, purposive interpretation represents yet a third way of approaching interpretive questions.

What is the plain meaning of the words? We have already seen that word usage falls along a spectrum, ranging from core uses to penumbral uses to spurious uses. If a proposed interpretation of a word or phrase falls at either end of the spectrum (a core or spurious usage), the legal issue is settled immediately. We accept or reject the interpretation and move on. Thus, if the city and I disagree about whether my collie is a domestic "pet" subject to licensing, the city will simply win (at least on the grounds of plain meaning). Likewise, if the city contends that my station wagon is a domestic "pet," it will simply lose. If the proposed interpretation falls somewhere in the middle (a penumbral use) we must continue the analysis. Thus, if the city claims that the horse stabled in my garage is a domestic "pet," more argument will be needed. From the lawyer's perspective, the dynamics are easy to predict. As proponents of a particular interpretation, lawyers strive to show how their reading of a word or phrase lies as close to the core end of the spectrum as possible; as opponents, lawyers strive to show that the proposed interpretation is spurious.

DICTIONARY DEFINITIONS. How does one *demonstrate* or *prove* that a particular use of a word is core, penumbral, or spurious? We often resort to the dictionary, for it serves as a guide to usages. Thus, if the proposed usage does not appear at all in the dictionary definition of a word, we have evidence that the usage is spurious. Similarly, if the proposed usage appears in the first or second definition, we have some evidence that the usage is core. Beyond that, we work with the definitions themselves. Dictionary definitions are typically cast in a form that progressively narrows the range of a word's application. "Pet," for example, is defined by the dictionary on my desk as, "[a]n animal kept for amusement or companionship" — animals, but not all of them; only those "kept" [by humans], but not all of them; only those kept for "amusement or companionship." As lawyers and judges, we are likely to treat such definitions as generating necessary and sufficient conditions for the proper use of the term. The legal debate about my horse will then turn on establishing or denying the applicability of each element: "animal," "kept," and "amusement or companionship." This analysis may even send us back to the dictionary, as we debate the meaning of each element, but the point to see is how this shapes the *form* of our argument. Lawyers and judges typically debate the propriety of a usage by identifying an agreed set of definitional elements and then debating whether each of those elements has been satisfied.

STRICT AND LIBERAL CONSTRUCTION. As lawyers and judges, we reflexively seek a way of making decisions about word usage that appears more lawyerly than simple gestalt: "oh yes, that sounds right," or "oh no, that sounds funny." That is why we turn to definitions and their element-by-element analysis: it is a proxy for direct evidence on the acceptability of use, and its form has a nice syllogistic glow. But plain meaning analysis, with either gestalt or a dictionary, can often bring us up short. The proposed usage might be penumbral, neither clearly acceptable nor clearly not. It is here that we sometimes give plain meaning a nudge, using canons of construction to decide close cases. Criminal laws, for example, are subject to *strict construction,* their reach confined to what the legislature has plainly and unmistakably proscribed, and all ambiguities in a criminal statute are resolved in favor of the accused. Likewise, in private contracts, the language is often construed against the drafter, ambiguities resolved in favor of the nondrafting party. There are canons of *liberal construction* as well, such as the one applied to remedial legislation, that is, statutes that are aimed at providing new rights or benefits to a particular class of persons. In close cases, we provide the benefits.

There is, however, a sense of desperation in canons of construction: plain meaning analysis having not really settled the issue, we try to find a hook, any hook, to settle the matter. Close case? Throw it to the accused. But we might just as easily have said, criminal laws are important, protecting all of society against the predations of an unsavory few, so construe criminal laws liberally to pull in as much disreputable behavior as possible. For every canon of construction we can usually imagine an opposite one. Indeed, several years ago, Professor Karl Llewellyn collected dozens of well-accepted canons and for each one counterposed another one moving in the opposite direction.[3] His justly famous collection (it is astute and funny, rare commodities in legal writing) suggests the artificiality of relying on canons of construction to resolve close cases. For this reason, among others, we have sought alternative means for doing interpretive work — means that strike us as less subject to ridicule. We can turn to the drafters' intent.

Everett's Case

In determining the meaning of "moral turpitude" and "physical harm," two examples from the texts governing Everett's behavior, we might turn to the dictionary for guidance. "Moral turpitude" would likely require recourse to a dictionary in any event, since it is seldom used outside legal documents. The term "physical harm," because it appears in a criminal statute, may be construed narrowly (so that in a close case, Everett might escape liability). Suppose that Everett has indeed struck his co-worker, but that, except for a moment of pain, there was no physical manifestation of injury. Is this "physical harm"? In a close case, a narrow construction of the statute might lead us to say no.

What did the drafters intend? Until now, our search for word meaning has relied on public usage. That is, we have sought to determine how people normally use words in the course of their daily lives. But the meaning of a word or phrase can also be affected by the intent of the people who drafted it. The search for this intent has been described in different ways. In the context of private documents — contracts, wills, trusts, and so on — the difference is often described as a choice between *objective* and *subjective* approaches to textual interpretation. Either we look at what a reasonable person would think the terms of a document mean (the objective approach) or we look at what the parties themselves intended them to mean (the subjective approach). The debate between objective and subjective approaches to interpretation takes a different form in the context of public documents — that is, constitutions, statutes, ordinances, and regulations. Here the question usually presents itself as whether we should look beyond the plain meaning of a law and investigate its *legislative history* — what the legislators or constitutional drafters said about the language during its drafting, debate, and adoption.

---

[3]*See* Karl N. Llewellyn, "Remarks on the Theory of Appellate Decision and the Rules or Canons About How Statutes Are to Be Construed," 3 Vand. L. Rev. 395, 401–406 (1950), *reprinted in* Karl N. Llewellyn, *The Common Law Tradition: Deciding Appeals* 521–535 (1960).

CONTRACTS, DEEDS, AND OTHER PRIVATELY CREATED DOCUMENTS. Courts do not categorically reject or adopt a focus on the drafters' intent when they interpret private documents. When a court takes up the interpretation of a private document, it is likely to say that the intent of the parties will control, thus suggesting a subjective approach to interpretation. In the next judicial breath, however, the court will likely say that the primary source for ascertaining the parties' intent is *the language they actually used in the document,* thus suggesting an objective approach. In this way, both approaches are applied to the same case. The switch between subjective and objective approaches represents a dramatic shift in interpretive theory, but does not often result in dramatically different results. We all speak the same language, and drafters almost always use their words the same way we all use them.

As a practical matter, because of this commonality of language and usage, it is inevitable that the interpretation of private documents begins with public usages, the plain meaning of the words employed, departing from that meaning, however, when we are presented with good evidence that a different meaning was in fact intended. Such evidence can come in many forms. In the most obvious case, if the parties have *defined* the word or phrase at issue in the same document, we will follow that definition instead of the plain meaning. In other, subtler cases we may turn to drafters' intent when the plain meaning of a word or phrase renders the relevant obligation or right difficult to understand or makes it hard to square with other rights and obligations in the same document. We also look beyond plain meaning when confronted with *terms of art,* words and phrases that have developed special meanings in a particular field. Such terms can arise in agreements between specialists in the same field — between merchants, for example, or between stockbrokers or doctors. Terms of art also arise (and their special, nonpublic meanings applied) in highly stylized documents, like deeds, which have long history of use.

The drafters' intent can unsettle the plain meaning of a private document, but those who seek that result face several challenges. First, we generally place the burden of proof on the proponent of the special meaning. This burden can be easily met if the word or phrase has been explicitly defined in the document, but is harder to meet in other cases. Second, evidence of a special meaning can usually be gathered only from the document itself. If the document gives us a cue to look more deeply, then we are inclined to do so. When, however, the purported evidence comes from other documents, from the circumstances under which the language was produced, or from contemporaneous oral statements of the parties, our willingness to consider such evidence declines precipitously. This waning enthusiasm, this reflexive unwillingness to countenance special meanings unless forced upon us by the document itself, can be seen in the limits on the use of *extrinsic evidence* in the interpretation of deeds, wills, and trusts, and in the *parol evidence rule* in contract law. Third, proponents of special meaning must generally show that *both* parties intended and understood that meaning. Otherwise, the special meaning will smack of sharp practice, overreaching, or unfair dealing, and will seldom be enforced.

Everett's Case

In determining the meaning of "moral turpitude" we would check to see if the drafters themselves had defined the term in the contract; if not, we would want to know if it has developed into a term of art (and that both parties understood that special meaning); if neither is the case, the term's plain meaning would normally stand.

LEGISLATION AND OTHER PUBLICLY CREATED DOCUMENTS. Drafters' intent is relevant not only for private documents, but for public ones as well. As noted earlier, constitutions, statutes, and regulations are backed by *legislative history.* The materials behind statutes — statements of the legislators as they introduce bills for passage, testimony at committee hearings, final reports of committees recommending that the bill be passed, and statements of legislators made during the floor debates on the bill's passage — are available from the legislature itself and are often collected and printed by private law publishers. Portions of legislative history for important federal laws, for example, are reprinted in *United States Code, Congressional & Administrative News,* as well as in other privately published compilations. Constitutional conventions inspire similar collections of historical material.

The importance of all these materials, however, is subject to debate. As recently as 30 years ago, many courts and commentators took the position that legislative history should not be consulted unless there was a special reason to do so. Thus, one was foreclosed from examining legislative history unless the plain meaning of the relevant language was nonsensical, hard to understand, or difficult to square with other provisions of law. It is worth noting that the antipathy toward legislative history has been even stronger in England, where until quite recently records of parliamentary activity were never consulted by the courts.

The reasons for this antipathy, both English and American, are straightforward. First, constitutions, statutes, regulations, and ordinances are public acts and should be given a public meaning, that is, the plain meaning likely to be understood by the citizenry at large. Second, only the final language of a constitution, statute, regulation, or ordinance has been approved by the body concerned; the materials that constitute legislative history are generated by that body's individual members and committees, who by themselves have no power to legislate. Third, legislative materials have historically been much more difficult to locate than the resultant laws, their use as interpretive guides thus raising concerns over notice and fairness. Fourth, the proper use of legislative materials requires a sophisticated understanding of the legislative process that most citizens do not possess, thus intensifying our concerns over notice and fairness.

Despite these historical sentiments, the barriers against the use of legislative history have crumbled on both sides of the Atlantic. In current American practice, one generally needs no special showing to present a court with evidence of legislative history; committee reports and floor debates, for example, are raised and discussed as a matter of course in American courtrooms. English courts, for their part, now examine the parliamentary history of an act if there is a special reason to do so. The growing acceptability of legislative history is explained in part by the growing availability of legislative materials and a more widely dispersed sophistication about their use. This has helped to ameliorate, if not eradicate, our earlier concerns over notice and fairness. In addition, a serious, recurring objection to the old rules has finally begun to change hearts and minds: if one has evidence that the creators of a particular law intended a certain result, how can one properly ignore such evidence? Increasingly, our courts have answered that they cannot.

This does not mean that legislative history is always relevant or that a particular piece of that history will be given much weight. The argument against the use of legislative history retains vitality in those states and jurisdictions (especially counties and cities) where legislative materials are not reliably recorded or widely available. Recourse to legislative history is also less likely in certain areas of law, like criminal law, where notice and fairness concerns are particularly strong. Even if the use of legislative history is generally acceptable, there will inevitably be questions about what weight should be given to a particular floor debate, a particular legislator's remarks, or a particular committee report.

Everett's Case

In determining the meaning of "physical harm," we would review the statute's legislative history, to see if any legislative committee or individual legislators addressed the issue of whether pain without physical manifestations was meant to be included within the meaning of the phrase.

What is the purpose of the language at issue? We have just seen that the meaning of a word or phrase depends on its plain meaning and sometimes on the drafters' intent. The proper interpretation of a word or phrase can also be affected by the purposes behind it. In other words, the plain meaning of a word or phrase can be shunted aside or modified if we believe it will defeat the purpose for which the obligation or right was created in the first place. Thus, if the city ordinance on pet licensing is aimed at ensuring that all animals in the city are registered, so that health regulations can be enforced, then the horse stabled in my garage is likely to be considered a "pet," even if horses aren't normally called that. The plain meaning interpretation would create a loophole — animals that aren't usually considered pets would go unregulated — which would defeat the purpose behind the ordinance.

Recourse to purposes is eminently sensible, but raises two difficult problems: (1) determining what those purposes are; and (2) figuring out whether they are advanced or hindered by the interpretation at issue. The first problem can be easily resolved only when the relevant document explicitly states its purposes. Such statements are commonly included in newer statutes, but they are rarely found in constitutions, private documents, and older statutes. If there is no explicit statement of purposes, we must imply them, with all the difficulties such guesswork entails. Perhaps the greatest challenge is that legal documents have all sorts of purposes, more or less explicit, more or less plausible. In the face of this abundance, lawyers predictably argue about which purposes should be considered, and assuming there are several, which purposes should be considered paramount.

We are occasionally helped in this regard by presumptions and precedents. In willmaking, for example, we presume that the testator wanted to avoid intestacy, so that if one reading of a will leaves some of the testator's property unmentioned (thus to pass intestate) and another results in all the testator's property passing by the will, we presume that the second reading of the disputed language is correct. Failing a governing presumption on purposes, there may be some precedents, in which earlier judges have construed similar language and declared what they believed to be the relevant purposes. Presumptions, however, can be overturned and the persuasiveness of older cases can almost always be disputed. As a consequence, arguments about purposes are endemic to the interpretive enterprise and consume thousands of pages in the legal reporters. It is classic lawyers' work.

Assuming that the relevant purposes have been agreed, we next argue about whether a proposed interpretation advances or hinders those purposes. This analysis can be problematic even if only one relevant purpose has been identified, but the problem more frequently arises because the language at issue has several purposes and a particular reading advances some of them and spoils others. The only sensible way to proceed at this juncture is to argue about which purpose is paramount. Again, because there is seldom any decisive way to settle this issue, debates about the relative importance of purposes is a recurrent theme in interpretive debate.

Everett's Case

Both phrases "moral turpitude" and "physical harm" could be subjected to argument based on purposes. In representing Everett, we might suggest that the purpose of the moral turpitude clause — normally involving dishonesty, conniving, and stealing — is to permit the firing of persons with long term flaws of character, especially of an economic character, not to weed out a person who has suffered just one spur-of-the-moment loss of control. On the physical harm requirement of the assault statute, we might argue that its purpose is to distinguish and punish those actions resulting in longer term harm, and is not aimed at a transitory flash of pain. (Other statutes may indeed cover this lesser sort of injury, but we may still be able to avoid conviction on the statute cited.)

How has the language been construed in the past? Until now, we have treated interpretive issues as if we were meeting a word or phrase for the first time. To determine the proper application of a novel word or phrase we might examine its plain meaning, ascertain the drafters' intent, and determine its purposes. But sometimes we can sidestep all of this analysis. Sometimes the word or phrase has been interpreted in earlier cases and the power of *stare decisis,* the power of judicial precedent, changes our mode of analysis. Prior judicial cases can give us actual determinations of how a word or phrase should be applied. If we can find past decisions on whether a horse is a "domestic pet," those decisions will most certainly be cited and debated in deciding whether old Trigger back in my garage must be licensed. A court's holding that a particular interpretation is clearly acceptable (or clearly not) can settle the interpretive issue.

The problem, of course, is that prior cases are rarely directly on point. The word, though the same, may have come from a different constitution, statute, ordinance, or regulation. The difference of context will cause lawyers and judges to question whether the meaning given in the prior case can simply be imported into the current one. In addition, any differences in the facts of the current case will call the usefulness of prior decisions into question, and the territorial and hierarchical nature of precedent means that even if the facts of an earlier case are nearly identical, the earlier case will not be dispositive unless it was rendered by a higher court in the same jurisdiction. Despite these limits on precedential value, the lesson for lawyers is clear: in both planning and litigation, a search for prior judicial interpretations of a word or phrase is always desirable. If an earlier, binding case can be found, the results are generally dispositive; if the earlier cases are similar, the results are generally persuasive.

Everett's Case

Both phrases "moral turpitude" and "physical harm" have a great deal of case-law behind them. If any of those cases appears in our state, and more particularly in our state supreme court, we will have to take account of those decisions in seeking to interpret the terms.

Judicial Decisions. We now move to a different set of interpretive problems. Many rights and obligations are established in judicial decisions rather than authoritative texts. This changes the way we search for their meaning, the way we determine what actions (or restraints from action) those obligations and rights require. Judicially declared rights and obligations — rules from the *common law* — have no text. When a judge holds, for example, that "landlords must maintain residential units in a habitable condition," the obligation is not tied to the precise words the judge uses to describe it. The judge might have instead declared that "owners of all rental apartments and houses owe to their tenants a duty to keep the demised premises in a healthy and safe state of repair," or simply, "the implied warranty of habitability is recognized in this state." The same rule can be formulated in different ways.

As a consequence, the primary challenge of common-law adjudication is to determine the meaning of a *rule,* not the meaning of a particular word or phrase. This may seem an odd distinction, or one without content, but the difference has a profound effect on our methods of interpretation. Common-law adjudication must hit a moving target; those who work with common-law rules — both lawyers and judges alike — are not tethered to any particular form of words. Common-law interpretation does not begin with a *predetermined* word or phrase, against which any results must be justified or compared.

Everett's Case

If Everett is sued in a civil tort suit by his alleged victim, the basis for the claim will lie in the judge-made law of torts (civil wrongs). More specifically the relevant tort action would be one for *battery*. There is, however, no authoritative text for what constitutes battery, a text from which all lawyers and judges must begin their analysis.

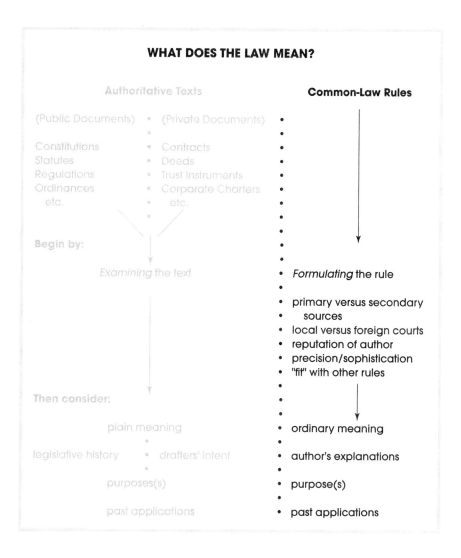

WHAT DOES THE LAW MEAN?

Authoritative Texts		Common-Law Rules
(Public Documents) • (Private Documents)	•	

Constitutions • Contracts
Statutes • Deeds
Regulations • Trust Instruments
Ordinances • Corporate Charters
  etc. • etc.

Begin by:

  Examining the text   • Formulating the rule

    • primary versus secondary
    •   sources
    • local versus foreign courts
    • reputation of author
    • precision/sophistication
    • "fit" with other rules

Then consider:

  plain meaning   • ordinary meaning

  legislative history • drafters' intent   • author's explanations

  purposes(s)   • purpose(s)

  past applications   • past applications

How do we characterize the common-law rule? In the interpretation of a common-law rule, one of the first jobs is to settle on an agreed form of words to describe it, an ironic but perfectly understandable state of affairs. Having just said that the distinguishing characteristic of common-law rights and obligations is the *absence* of a set form of words, we must now acknowledge that the first order of business is to come up with a set form of words anyway. We have no other choice. Common-law rules, like all rules, are linguistic phenomena and must be expressed in language. However we may describe the implied warranty of habitability, for example, we have to describe it *some* way in order to work with it.

A rule's precise formulation can be important. The exact words chosen can make a particular action (or restraint from action) seem clearly required, only dubiously required, or not required at all. Depending on how we describe the implied warranty of habitability, for example, we can make it more or less likely that my landlord is required to replace the broken lock on the front door of my apartment. Cases can be effectively won or lost at this stage of the analysis, and the dynamics of the debate are predictable. The plaintiff in a lawsuit will argue for a formulation that makes the defendant's actions seem as clearly as possible to violate the relevant right or obligation, and the defendant will argue for a formulation that makes his or her actions seem consistent with it. The lawyers must present arguments to push the description of the rule in one direction or the other.

In theory, interpreters of the common law (both lawyers and judges) enjoy a wide latitude in word choice, but in practice the choice may be limited. Some common-law rules have been described so often in exactly the same language that an interpreter is unlikely to depart from that language. Following a much-repeated formula from prior cases is easy and safe; departures from such a formula require effort and risk error. Only a brave, or a foolish, or an extraordinarily well-tutored lawyer or judge would dare to depart — in even the smallest detail — from Professor John Chipman Gray's formulation of the common-law rule against perpetuities. "No interest," we all repeat from Professor Gray, "is good unless it must vest, if at all, no later than twenty-one years after some life in being at the creation of the interest." In cases like the common-law rule against perpetuities, the exact verbal formulation of the rule has effectively been set. Lawyers will seek to modify it only when they have no other choice (that is, when the standard formulation makes the case an almost certain loser), and judges will agree to the change only when presented with extraordinary arguments. Different common-law rules display different levels of ossification and thus provide different ranges of latitude in their formulation.

For those common-law rules that have not fully ossified, the interpreter will have some latitude in choosing their precise formulations, and the lawyers will have some room for argumentative maneuver. Lawyers obviously argue for choices that best advance their client's interests, but they cannot argue for a choice simply on the ground that it helps their client win; nor, of course, will a judge make the decision on that basis. The search then commences for objective criteria. We do in fact have standards for choosing among different formulations of a common-law rule, although the standards are so numerous that it is difficult to predict the results in any particular case. As a general matter, however, our *primary* source for verbal formulas is prior judicial decisions. Because only judges can authoritatively declare the existence of common-law rules, we naturally turn to those declarations for examples of the form in which those rules are cast. But we can also turn to *secondary* sources, such as restatements, treatises, law review articles, annotations, and legal encyclopedias, where persons other than judges have described common-law rules. There is much to learn about the proper handling of these sources, and the first year of law school is in part aimed at building a sophisticated understanding of these sources' relative persuasiveness in different contexts. In summary, however:

- All else being equal (though it seldom is), formulations from primary sources will be preferred over those from secondary sources. Thus, if one formulation appears in a case and another in a law review article, the former will be preferred.
- Among formulations found in cases, those from the same jurisdiction will be preferred over those from "foreign" jurisdictions; formulations from a higher court will be preferred over those from courts at the same level or below; formulations from more recent cases will be preferred over formulations from older cases; and finally, formulations from cases whose facts are similar to the instant case will be preferred over formulations from cases whose facts are dissimilar.
- Formulations from legal writers who are generally well respected, or who are known for their expertise in a particular field, will be preferred over those from other writers. It never hurts to propose a formulation of a common-law rule by Oliver Wendell Holmes, Jr. or Benjamin Cardozo, acknowledged masters of common-law adjudication. Likewise, it never hurts to propose a formulation of a tort rule devised by William Prosser, even though he was only a law professor writing a treatise, because his work in torts is so well known and respected.
- Formulations that are clear, concise, elegant, or sophisticated will often be preferred over those that are convoluted, sloppy, or otherwise bear the marks of an amateur. Common-law adjudication is a craft and neatness counts.
- And finally, one formulation might be preferred over another because the latter does not "fit" as well with other rules, either common-law or statutory. We seek coherence in our legal system, remaining alert for inconsistencies and trying to minimize or eliminate them.

Everett's Case

Actions for battery have a long history in the courts, and many definitions of the action can be found in the case-law, as well as in treatises and other well-accepted sources of learning, such as the Restatement of Torts. As Everett's attorneys, we will seek to formulate the rule by emphasizing those past formulations that mention great violence and willfulness (opening the way for us to argue that the injury was slight and the striking accidental). We would try to distinguish those formulations holding that even a slight touching can be a battery.

What does the rule mean? Assuming that the verbal formulation of a common-law rule has been decided, we must then determine which actions (or restraints from action) are required by that formulation. This will depend, of course, on what the chosen words mean. And word meanings, in turn, will be determined in the first instance by what reasonable people of ordinary intelligence would think they mean. Thus does the plain meaning rule insert itself in common-law adjudication, much as it does in the interpretation of authoritative texts. The pull of plain meaning constrains what actions or restraints from action can properly be said to be required by the common-law rule. If the formulation we have chosen for the implied warranty of habitability, for example, requires that the landlord maintain the premises in a "safe and healthy condition," then we cannot require the landlord to change a lightbulb in the refrigerator or repaint the kitchen because the tenant doesn't like the color. We could only do so if we could show that those conditions rendered the apartment unsafe or unhealthy. As with authoritative texts, we might even turn to a dictionary to flesh out the meaning of the relevant terms in our verbal formulation.

Despite all of this, plain meaning has less power in common-law interpretation. To see this, we must return to first principles. We started this discussion by noting that in order to work with common-law rules, we must reduce them to a particular formulation. This is still true: we have to start *someplace.* And we also saw that we often choose between formulations, adopting one from an earlier case, for example, while rejecting another one from a treatise. Also true: we often make such choices. But none of this means that we are bound to the words of the formulation we have adopted. Once again, because common-law rules are not tied to any particular verbal formulation, we are not strictly tied *even to the formulation we have chosen to apply.* As a consequence, the plain meaning of that formulation is relevant but not dispositive. We might even choose more than one formulation. Every lawyer has worked with cases in which courts adopt one formulation of a common-law rule, only to suggest a different formulation a few paragraphs later. Though frustrating, the practice is perfectly plausible, because once again, common-law rules are not tied to any particular verbal formulation. Two or more formulations can co-exist simultaneously. In such a world, the plain meaning of any one formulation, even one we adopt, loses its dispositive power.

As plain-meaning analysis declines in importance, other interpretive approaches grow to fill the gap. In formulating common-law rules, authors tend to *explain themselves.* After judges announce a particular formulation of a common-law rule, for example, they are likely to explain what it means. Treatises, restatements, and other books that provide *black letter law* (that is, specific verbal formulations of common-law rules) always follow the black letter rules with commentary, explanations, and examples. In using a particular formulation of a common-law rule, one must also examine any such explanations and take account of them. We can see this as a rough analogue to the drafters' intent regarding statutes, but its importance in common-law interpretation is paramount. Common-law rules are habitually explained and those explanations cannot be ignored. Thus, for example, discussions of the implied warranty of habitability in cases and treatises might indicate that adequate interior lighting is an essential element of safety, and as a consequence a landlord is obliged to replace a burned-out lightbulb in the bathroom (even though the aquamarine paint in the kitchen can remain).

Common-law rules have purposes, too, and purposive interpretation takes on special importance in common-law adjudication. Common-law rules are often expanded beyond (or contracted inside) their plain meaning boundaries, if needed to fulfill the rules' purposes. If we decided that one of the primary purposes of the implied warranty of habitability was to shift all maintenance responsibilities to the landlord, on the theory that landlords are in a better position than tenants to undertake them, then we might be more inclined to force even a repainting of the kitchen whose color, we must admit, is in serious need of change.

Finally, because the meaning of common-law rules is less firmly tied to any particular formulation of words, the rules necessarily take a great deal of their meaning from their prior applications, from the kinds of actions or restraints from action they have previously been understood to require. And our major source for *that* knowledge, of course, is prior judicial decisions. As a consequence, common-law adjudication is obsessed with case-law — finding it, parsing it, and debating it. More particularly, we examine the precise actions called into question in earlier cases, along with the judges' determinations about whether those actions did or did not violate the relevant rule. The judges' determinations are usually quite easy to resolve: they either found liability to exist or they didn't, and this conclusion will be stated explicitly. As a consequence, the analysis of case-law centers around: (1) close readings of the *facts*, to determine exactly which actions were called into question; and (2) debates about whether those actions are sufficiently similar to those in the case at hand to warrant the same determination of liability. The facts become crucial, their examination indispensable. This is an appropriate time to review how such facts are found in the first place.

Everett's Case

In preparing grounds upon which to challenge a claim of battery, we would begin by arguing for the favorable version of the rule (see above), and then seek to interpret it in light of its purposes and with close attention to how the rule has been applied in the past: which defendants, under what circumstances, were found to have violated their obligation not to commit battery. We would seek to show how our case looks more like cases in which the defendant was not found to have committed the tort.

What Are the Facts?

As we noted earlier, legal determinations of liability are usually characterized as an application of the law to the facts. We have just considered the process of law finding, examining the questions we ask when trying to interpret the meaning of a legal obligation or right. We now turn to fact-finding, the second grand project in legal decisionmaking. Having decided what actions (or restraints from action) are required by an obligation or right, a person's legal liability turns on whether he or she took (or refrained from taking) those actions.

Anyone who makes judgments of legal liability (judges, of course, but also executive branch officials, arbitrators, and lawyers, among others) must find facts. Depending on the context, a lawyer might have to decide whether a client's shipment of dental floss arrived in good condition; a judge or jury might have to decide whether a criminal defendant stabbed the victim 27 times with a kitchen knife; or an official with the Internal Revenue Service might have to decide whether a taxpayer timely filed an income tax return for calendar year 1997. Legal fact-finding in all these cases follows the natural course of human inquiry into facts about the world, but with some highly stylized additions.

Primary Sources of Fact. In daily life, when we inquire into the facts of a matter, we have the most confidence in our own direct observations. If we want to know whether it is raining, we look outside and see. Legal fact-finding follows the same impulse. But direct observation is sometimes difficult, inconvenient, or expensive. We may be working in a windowless, interior office with so much work that we can't go outside, even for a minute, to check the weather. More commonly, direct observation is simply impossible because we want to know whether something happened in the past and we weren't there at the time to observe it. Whether it rained yesterday in Oslo cannot be answered by the direct observation of first-year associates then toiling away in the bowels of an office building in Cincinnati. Legal fact-finding habitually encounters this same problem: we seek to establish the occurrence of past events and the fact-finder (lawyer, arbitrator, judge, jury, etc.) was not there at the time to observe them.

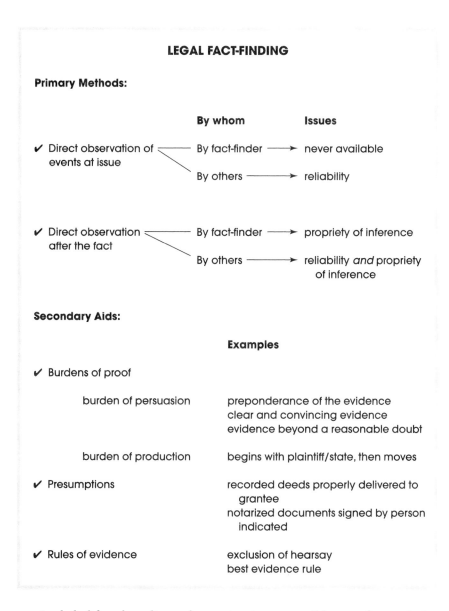

LEGAL FACT-FINDING

Primary Methods:

	By whom	Issues
✔ Direct observation of events at issue	By fact-finder	never available
	By others	reliability
✔ Direct observation after the fact	By fact-finder	propriety of inference
	By others	reliability *and* propriety of inference

Secondary Aids:

	Examples
✔ Burdens of proof	
burden of persuasion	preponderance of the evidence clear and convincing evidence evidence beyond a reasonable doubt
burden of production	begins with plaintiff/state, then moves
✔ Presumptions	recorded deeds properly delivered to grantee notarized documents signed by person indicated
✔ Rules of evidence	exclusion of hearsay best evidence rule

In daily life, when direct observation is not possible, we often seek the reports of others who *were* at the right place at the right time. We call our Norwegian classmate from law school, now practicing in the capital, and ask her about the weather. Or we pull the *Oslo Gazette* and read the weather report. The reports of others, however, introduce a new concern for reliability: we must ask whether our informants are good observers and whether there is any reason to suspect that they have not told the truth. Norwegian weather reports, from friends or weather reporters, do not typically raise serious concerns about reliability, but even here we can imagine some doubts.

Would our classmate, so very defensive about the appalling climate in Scandinavia, actually lie about whether it had rained? Was there a misprint or mistake in the *Oslo Gazette*? Legal fact-finding follows the same pattern. When direct observation by the fact-finder is difficult or impossible, we turn to the reports of others who have themselves made such observations. We also take special precautions to ensure the reliability of those reports. In the courtroom, we do this, among other ways, through the authentication of documents and the crossexamination of witnesses.

In daily life, when past events are at issue, we can also make direct observations after the fact and draw inferences from what we observe. Needing a vacation anyway, we race to Oslo to see whether the ground is wet. This form of investigation does not raise the reliability concerns that attend the reports of others, but raises new questions about what inferences can properly be drawn from what we have seen. Dry ground in Oslo does not necessarily establish the lack of rain on the day in question; that blazing Norwegian sun could have destroyed the evidence. Again, the legal inquiry into facts follows the same pattern. When direct, contemporaneous observation by the fact-finder is difficult or impossible, we can turn to the direct observation of *circumstantial evidence,* but with special concerns for the propriety of the inferences that can properly be drawn from that evidence.

These, then, are the major modes of fact-investigation, both in and out of law: direct, contemporaneous observation; reports of direct, contemporaneous observations by others (raising questions of reliability); and direct, *post-hoc* observation (raising questions about the propriety of the inferences that can be drawn). These methods and the questions they raise are often doubled or combined. A *New York Times* report of Norwegian weather is at best a report of someone else's report, doubling the questions about reliability. A police report that the defendant's fingerprints were found on a bloody knife in the bushes outside the victim's home is at best a report by others of circumstantial evidence, layering questions of reliability over questions about the propriety of inferences.

Fact-finding problems are further compounded by the nature of the facts we wish to ascertain. So far, we have discussed only those facts that might be called purely physical, such as the existence of rain in Oslo. Both in and out of law, however, we are often called upon to ascertain "mental" facts, and this raises special problems. In daily life, for example, we often make judgments about whether someone is angry or happy or friendly. In legal life, we are sometimes concerned with emotional or similar states, but also with questions of *intent.* In law, the character of a person's action and whether it results in legal liability often turns on the intent with which the person took that action. Did the testator intend to make a will? Did the plaintiff intend to make a gift? Did the defendant intend to kill the decedent? (Intent questions are also found in daily life, and can have important ramifications. The proper response to my daughter's bruised arm, for example, turns in part on whether my son *intended* to hit her with the baseball bat.) Questions of intent are so endemic to the law that they sneak into questions that on their face look purely physical. Whether a defendant signed the contract has not only the physical component (did she write her name or make some other mark at the end of the document?), but also an intent component (did she intend to sign a contract when she made the mark?) If she made the mark without the intent, she didn't sign it.

Questions about mental states raise special problems because, in the normal course, the best evidence of a person's mental state is that person's own report of the condition. If someone says he is angry that usually ends the inquiry. If someone says she meant to give the Picasso to the museum, that usually settles the question of her intent. In legal matters, however, self-reporting is often problematic, either because the subject is unavailable (the willmaker, sad to say, has died), the subject remains silent (the defendant does not take the stand), or the subject's truthfulness is called seriously into question. Because a finding of intent is often crucial, and because it turns so much on self-reporting, there is always the temptation to lie. "It was an accident, you see. I didn't *mean* to throw Mrs. Clayton into the vat of hydrochloric acid."

When self-reporting is either unavailable or of dubious accuracy, we are forced to turn to other evidence, about which there is often legitimate debate. To establish a particular mental state, we might inquire into the subject's facial expressions, body language, tone and level of voice, and so on — outward physical manifestations of the mental state at issue. This kind of evidence is sometimes helpful in determining emotional states, but is generally much less helpful in determining a person's intent, that mental state with which the law is so often concerned. Whether a person meant to take an action often cannot be answered satisfactorily by looking at his face.

Everett's Case

In determining what happened on that fateful day at the tire plant, the most obvious sources are the reports of our client, the co-worker, and any other persons who witnessed the events (all direct evidence). Our client and the alleged victim would raise obvious questions of reliability, but so would other witnesses, who may not have seen everything that went on. We might also turn to a physician's report on the victim's condition shortly after the altercation (circumstantial evidence). The mental state of our client (regarding knowledge for the criminal assault; intention and willfulness for the tort) could only be established directly by the self-reporting of our client (of dubious reliability) and others' testimony about his demeanor and actions before and after the alleged incident (also of dubious reliability and raising additional questions about the propriety of inferences).

Secondary Aids to Fact-Finding. In daily life, we can often be casual about our fact-finding. All else being equal, we would like to get things right, but so little turns on the matter that we can safely make a guess or leave the issue open. It does not really matter, after all, if it rained yesterday in Oslo, at least not to first-year associates in Cincinnati. Legal fact-finding, in contrast, almost always has a special intensity of purpose and we make special efforts to ensure the accuracy of our conclusions. We do not make people pay money, put things back the way they were, or send them to jail without being very sure of our conclusions. And unlike daily life, we seldom have the option of leaving the issue open. We *must* decide whether the defendant trespassed on another's property, paid the contract price, or is guilty of murder. The dual imperatives to: (1) decide and (2) decide *correctly* magnify the problems associated with fact-finding and have impelled us to create methods — patterned and often highly stylized methods — for dealing with those problems.

Who has the burden of proof? That we must decide questions of fact one way or the other has generated the institution of the *burden of proof.* Evidence of a particular fact may be nonexistent or unreliable, inferences from reliable evidence may be of dubious propriety, and mental states may be hard to determine. Faced with these uncertainties, but also with the imperative to decide the factual issue presented, we respond by deciding ahead of time who wins and who loses when we are not sure of our conclusions. Lawyers and judges engaged in the fact-finding process, therefore, will always ask, "Who has the burden of proof?" In criminal law matters, the state always has the burden of proof. In civil cases, the burden of proof is usually on the plaintiff. That is, the person who wants the court to act, i.e., to find criminal or civil liability, must prove every element of that liability in order to succeed. This is sometimes called the *burden of persuasion.*

Burdens of persuasion come in three basic types. Lawyers and judges must know which type to apply in each situation. The three basic burdens of persuasion (though terminology sometimes varies a little) are:

- a preponderance of the evidence;
- clear and convincing evidence; and
- evidence beyond a reasonable doubt

These burdens respond to the fact-finding imperative to decide correctly. At the very least, we require that the facts upon which we rely be more likely than not to exist — that is, by a preponderance of evidence. This is the most common burden of persuasion in noncriminal cases. We move to higher levels of proof when our perceived need for certainty increases. When a person seeks to controvert the veracity of a document that is valid on its face — a serious matter, because the ability to rely on facially valid documents is an important one — we often require clear and convincing evidence of facts that would invalidate it. Thus, if a deed to property appears to contain the seller's signature (and the seller wants to deny that she signed), the seller would have to show in a very clear way (not just "more likely than not") that the signature was forged. Finally, when we seek to hold a person criminally liable for an action — a *very* serious matter, because it threatens that person with a loss of liberty — we require evidence beyond a reasonable doubt.

At the end of the day, when all the evidence for both sides has been produced, the party with the burden of persuasion will lose if the evidence is close. That is, if the standard is a preponderance of the evidence, the party who has that burden will lose if the evidence is fairly equally weighted for both sides. If the standard is clear and convincing evidence or beyond a reasonable doubt, the party who has that burden will lose if the burden-holder's version of the facts is only more likely than not. The burden of persuasion generally stays with the same party throughout the fact-finding process, i.e., with the state in criminal proceedings and with the plaintiff in civil proceedings.

The burden of persuasion, however, must be distinguished from another burden of proof, the burden of going forward with the evidence, also called the *burden of production*. The party with the burden of production is the one who must introduce evidence in order to get or keep the case going. If the party does not come forward with such evidence, that party will lose. Generally speaking, both the burden of persuasion and the burden of production start with the same party. Thus, the plaintiff in a civil case such as a breach of contract action will have both the burden of persuasion (the plaintiff must show that it is more likely than not that the defendant breached their contract) and the burden of production (the plaintiff must be the first to introduce evidence of the breach). Once the plaintiff in a civil case has made a *prima facie* case, i.e., has presented evidence establishing each element of the defendant's liability, the burden of production shifts to the defendant to refute the plaintiff's evidence. If that is done successfully, the burden can shift back to the plaintiff again, who must present additional evidence of the defendant's breach. This shifting burden of production is important during the course of a trial, but less so outside of it. As planning lawyers, and even as lawyers and judges at the *end* of a trial (when all the evidence for both sides has been produced) our main concern is about the burden of persuasion.

How does one meet or defeat this burden of persuasion? Lawyers generally try to present as much evidence as possible, regardless of which burden of persuasion applies or who has it. One never knows in advance how much evidence will be enough, and it never hurts to provide more evidence than what, in retrospect, would have been necessary. One doesn't know in advance how much evidence is enough partly because one does

---

BURDENS OF PROOF

Burden of Persuasion	*Starts* with the plaintiff/state
	Stays with same party throughout litigation

V.

Burden of Production	*Starts* with person who has burden of persuasion
	Shifts to other party once *prima facie* case is made
	Could *shift again* once rebuttable evidence is produced

---

not know the extent and persuasiveness of the other side's evidence, and partly because the fact-finder's decision is cloaked in mystery. Fact-finders must determine just how sure they are of the facts sought to be proved, and this involves a judgment that defies analytical treatment. To be frank about it, the different levels of proof are simply patterned, sophisticated ways of saying that one must be "pretty sure," "very sure," or something in between. Lawyers can hardly anticipate what level of evidence will be necessary to satisfy these levels of certainty, except to note (vaguely and unhelpfully) that higher levels of proof require more evidence than lower levels. The fact-finders themselves can hardly say more than that they have taken all the evidence into consideration and have decided the facts in accordance with the relevant standard. At its base, fact-finding is characterized by "a unified psychological configuration having properties that cannot be derived from its parts" — in a word, a gestalt. From the lawyers' perspective, this makes fact-finding unpredictable and scary.

We are not, however, left completely in the dark. Fact-finding is literally a matter of common sense, governed by our common experience regarding the kinds and levels of proof necessary to establish particular facts. If the plaintiff must prove that her shipment of dental floss arrived at the defendant's warehouse by November 15, 1995, uncontroverted testimony of the defendant's shipping clerk that he saw the goods arrive on November 8 (a concession clearly against his employer's interest) will likely establish the arrival date under any level of proof. If, on the other hand, the relevant shipping documents are marked "received" on November 19, or if the shipping clerk keeps changing his story on the witness stand, we know that the plaintiff's ability to establish the arrival date will be seriously impaired. Because these matters are common sense, lawyers can consult their own judgment and predict with some confidence whether they will be able to establish the facts they need to win their cases.

Common sense is not our only recourse. Some kinds of evidence are proffered with such frequency, and some kinds of facts are sought to be established so often, that we have developed traditions about their proper treatment. Some of these traditions remain a matter of common law; others have been codified in statutes and court rules. These traditions can be found in *presumptions* and *rules of evidence*.

Are there any relevant presumptions? Because legal fact-finders are constantly faced with questions about what factual inferences can be drawn from other facts, and because certain factual issues arise frequently, certain presumptions have arisen around those cases. Here are just a few that arise from property disputes:

- Recorded deeds are presumed to have been delivered to the new owner by the old one.
- Notarized documents are presumed to have been signed by the person whose signature was notarized.
- The recipient of a gift is presumed to have accepted the gift if it is beneficial to that person.
- Owners of joint-tenancy bank accounts are presumed to intend a right-of-survivorship for the money in the account.

The law is full of such presumptions, and they tend to appear in just those places where direct evidence of the facts at issue are problematic. *Intent* questions, for example, are very often governed by presumptions. Lawyers and judges engaged in fact-finding should always ask, "Is there a relevant presumption?" They should also ask whether the presumption is rebuttable, and if rebuttable (as we spiral more deeply into fact-finding) what burden of proof is required to rebut it. Despite occasional complexities, presumptions ease the way in a world full of factual uncertainty, and the law makes heavy use of them.

Are there any relevant rules of evidence? Fact-finding is also heavily influenced by the rules of evidence. These rules respond — in complicated and sometimes preposterous ways — to concerns about the reliability of sources and the propriety of inferences in the fact-finding process. Witnesses can testify about what they themselves heard or saw, but they cannot testify about what others said they heard or saw (that is *hearsay*), except under certain (quite numerous) circumstances. If the content of a document is called into question, the original document must be offered (that is the *best evidence*), except under certain (again quite numerous) circumstances. The rules of evidence are so complicated and important that we have arranged an entire course around them with the singular and ominous title of "Evidence."

Rules of evidence reach their peak of significance in the courtroom, when a jury serves as the fact-finder. This is to be expected, since evidence rules evolved historically from the efforts of judges to shield juries from unreliable evidence and improper inferences. When a judge serves as fact-finder, the rules of evidence weaken both expressly (certain rules explicitly change in that context) and implicitly (judges tend to apply the remaining rules less fastidiously, believing themselves better equipped than juries to sift the probative from the spurious). Outside the courtroom, the formal power of these rules declines precipitously. Arbitration, for example, is often touted as a useful alternative to courtroom decisionmaking precisely because the rules of evidence are discarded or simplified. The rules of evidence have no formal power at all in the negotiation and settlement of disputes or in the planning of future transactions. Still, in all these contexts, the rules of evidence retain a subtle tyranny. We think ahead, anticipating what evidence can be introduced into court when deciding whether to settle a case or when planning what documents should be drafted to carry out an upcoming transaction. Lawyers and judges engaged in the fact-finding process (and lawyers who anticipate its eventual occurrence) therefore always ask, "Is there a relevant rule of evidence?"

Everett's Case

In a criminal prosecution of Everett, the state would have the burden of showing Everett guilty of assault beyond a reasonable doubt. In a tort case brought by his co-worker, the alleged victim would have the burden of showing the elements of battery by a preponderance of the evidence. In both cases, Everett's opponents would have the burden of going forward with the evidence, but if they did so, Everett would have to step forward with his own evidence or lose. The actual taking of testimony in court would be subject to the rules of evidence regarding relevance, hearsay, and other matters.

We conclude our discussion of fact-finding by noting that areas of the law outside the fact-finding process also respond to concerns about the reliability of evidence and the propriety of inferences. The statute of frauds, the statute of wills, and similar laws that require written documents for specified transactions, for example, are aimed primarily at encouraging the production and retention of reliable sources of evidence. Under the statute of wills in most states a will must be in writing and signed by the willmaker to be effective, even if there is ample evidence about what the decedent wished to do with his property. Such laws work differently from rules of evidence, because they deny the *existence* or *enforceability* of rights and obligations created in unapproved ways. These laws are controversial precisely because they attempt to address a fact-finding problem (wanting to make sure we know the decedent's wishes) with a law-finding or remedy-finding solution (denying that the decedent had any legally enforceable wishes at all). The solution is out of phase with the concerns that animate it. As a consequence, statutes and rules of this type cause controversy almost every time they are applied.

How Does the Law Apply to the Facts?

Legal liability is determined by applying the relevant law to the relevant facts. We have now reached the final stages of a lengthy analysis: starting with how legal rights and obligations are interpreted, and continuing with how facts are found. All that remains is to apply that law to those facts.

Application Generally. The final step of applying the law to the facts is almost always anticlimactic. All the hard work has already been done. If we have already determined (let's say) that a horse is a pet for purposes of my town's licensing ordinance and established that I am keeping a horse stabled in the back of my lot, the last step of application is hardly a step at all: I'm liable. In other words, legal argument almost never concerns the actual process of application. The fights show up earlier, about what action (or inaction) the law requires and whether that action (or inaction) has actually occurred. By the time we reach the final, formal stage of application, the case has already been won or lost.

This is true even in more complicated cases and more complicated planning situations. In the case of old Trigger, we could imagine that the city ordinance has exceptions to the licensing requirement for "beasts of burden" or "work animals," that I've only had the horse in the garage for ten days, and that it's not my horse at all but my friend Tom's. These changes add new questions of law and new questions of fact: Is the horse a "work animal"? Is there a grace period for applying for a license and has it expired? Does the obligation to obtain a license apply to the animal's owner or to the person in possession? Has the horse really been in the garage for only ten days and is it really Tom's? Once these questions are answered (the finding of law and facts), the work of application is again straightforward. Assume that a horse is *not* a "work animal" under the ordinance, that one has five days to apply for a license, and that the obligation to obtain a license falls on the owner, not the possessor. The application of law to the facts is still easy. I have not, in this new situation, incurred legal liability under the ordinance (though my friend Tom probably has). Cases can get complicated, and planning for clients is often filled with contingencies and questions, but the final application of the law to the facts is seldom the primary challenge.

Everett's Case

Once it is agreed (if it is) that the "physical harm" requirement of the criminal assault statute requires more than momentary pain, and that there was in fact no more than momentary pain in this case, the application of law to facts is fairly simply: Everett is not guilty of criminal assault. Once it is agreed (if it is) that "moral turpitude" requires a baseness or vileness of character, and that Everett's action resulted from a solitary, momentary loss of temper, then the application of the employment contract to the facts is fairly simple: Everett has not acted in a way that justifies dismissal from his job for cause. Once it is agreed (if it is) that battery requires an intentional act, and that Everett struck his co-worker by accident, then the application of law to the facts is fairly simple: Everett is not liable for battery.

Application in Special Cases. Having said all of that, there are occasions when we can be sure of both the law and the facts, but question their implications for liability. The final step of application is affected by issues of vicarious liability, substantial compliance, and excuses of various sorts. We discuss those complications now.

Is there vicarious liability? Sometimes a person's actions lead not to her own liability but to someone else's. Our generic term for describing this mechanism is *vicarious liability*. On these grounds, for example, children's actions can be attributed to their parents and employees' actions attributed to their employer. We have already seen the principle of attribution working in the *creation* of obligations and rights (there called agency), and now we see it again in the context of liability. Questions about vicarious liability are sometimes unavoidable. Juristic persons, for example, can *only* be held liable on this ground, for the simple reason that juristic persons can only *act* through others. A corporation, we recall, can only act through its officers, directors, and employees. Issues of vicarious liability can also arise whenever a person, natural or juristic, is claimed to have established an agency relationship with someone else.

One of the most common sources of vicarious liability is the *master-servant rule,* the rule that, within certain boundaries, employers are legally

SPECIAL CHALLENGES IN FINDING LIABILITY

Doctrine or Principle	Effect
✔ Vicarious Liability	Expands liability to new persons
✔ Substantial Compliance	Avoids a finding of breach
✔ Excuses incapacity coercion immunity impossibility	Even assuming a breach, blocks liability anyway
✔ Miscellaneous Blocks death of party release estoppel self-help	Post-breach situations that can make liability disappear

responsible for the actions of their employees. Because the employers of the world usually have more money than their employees, those who believe themselves harmed by someone's employee have an incentive to attribute that employee's actions to the more deeply pocketed employer. This dynamic is especially apparent in tort cases involving personal injuries, and issues of vicarious liability arise frequently in personal injury practice. If I am hit by a delivery truck, I am likely to sue not only the driver but the delivery company as well.

The ability to attribute one person's actions to another for liability purposes depends on whether there is in fact an agency or similar relationship between the persons concerned. As we saw in the previous chapter, the ability to attribute actions from agent to principal typically depends on the answers to a group of subsidiary questions: Did the purported agent have capacity? Was the agency relationship validly created? Was the agency relationship still in existence at the relevant time? Did the agent act within the scope of the agency? If all the questions are answered affirmatively, vicarious liability will likely attach. Master-servant law, because it is invoked so frequently, has developed its own special vocabulary and questions, all of which students are likely to encounter during their law school careers. Vicarious liability raises obvious questions of fairness (why should one person be liable for another's actions?) and social policy (is it not better to place liability on the person most capable of bearing it?), and legislatures often step in to modify the rules. As a result, the field of vicarious liability, and especially the master-servant rule, is full of unresolved tensions and often in flux.

Was there substantial compliance? Sometimes the actions taken by a person, even though not exactly the ones required by law, will be understood as sufficient to meet the law's requirements anyway. If the results are satisfactory, why quibble over minor variations in form? The desire to credit actions that almost suffice can be satisfied either formally or informally. In some areas of law, in some states, we recognize a formal *substantial compliance doctrine*. When the doctrine is recognized, the primary question in any particular case will be, of course, whether the compliance was substantial enough to be treated like full compliance. For this determination, we sometimes have case-law to guide us. Failing such guidance, we analyze whether the divergences between the actual and required actions are significant and whether ignoring those differences would advance or hinder the rule's purposes.

Despite its facial attractiveness, the formal doctrine of substantial compliance has not proved to be a particularly popular mode of analysis. First, implementation is a challenge. No matter how much we dress up the analysis, determining whether compliance is substantial has the troubling aura of gestalt: "yes, *that's* substantial; no, *that* isn't." Second, form *does* count and cannot be lightly cast aside. People rely on the actions of others, and we have all been taught since early childhood that meeting our obligations only halfway, or most of the way, is not enough. And finally, we have an informal alternative that does the same job.

We reach the same goal of the substantial compliance doctrine — giving credit to actions that are almost right — through *interpretation.* Suppose, for example, that a right or obligation appears on its face to require actions X, Y, and Z, and a person has instead done X, Y, and Q. Suppose further that Q is very much like Z, and that Z is much less important than X and Y in the original scheme. Instead of saying that the person has failed to meet the requirements, but is saved by the substantial compliance doctrine, a decisionmaker is likely to *interpret* the original right or obligation in such a way that X, Y, and Q are found to comply in the first place. We smuggle the decision to ignore one or more requirements into the broader work of interpretation, rather than treat the issue separately, where it calls attention to itself.

On the whole, judges would rather push an accepted form of analysis — interpretation — to the breaking point than risk a form of analysis that, despite its clarity and relative lack of hypocrisy, invites criticism and possible reversal. As a consequence, one tends to find substantial compliance doctrine only in those areas of law where the legislature or time-honored precedent has approved it. Thus the doctrine is used in some states' probate laws regarding the requirements for the proper execution of a will, and in other states, regarding the requirements for deeds of land. Illinois law, for example, provides that deeds may be "substantially" in the form given in the statute. The *interpretive* move, however, is much more common, and much legal debate is dedicated to deciding whether a set of actions not quite sufficient should be found sufficient anyway.

Is liability excused? Even after one determines that a particular action (or restraint from action) is required, and that a person has indeed failed to act (or refrain from acting) in the required way, the person may escape liability nonetheless. Legal liability can be *excused* for a number of reasons, primarily because of something about the person who was obligated to act, or because of something about the situation in which the action was taken. All told, there are at least four major excuses to liability:

- lack of capacity
- coercion
- immunity
- impossibility

We will discuss each briefly.

LACK OF CAPACITY. A person's action or failure to act can be excused because that person lacks capacity. As we saw in Chapter 2, minority and mental incompetence are the primary sources of incapacity for natural persons. If a mentally incompetent person kicks me, she will not incur legal liability for that action, even though battery is proscribed by tort law and she has battered me. If a minor agrees to sell me his bicycle for $25 and then refuses to hand it over when I tender the money, he will not incur legal liability for that refusal, even though such promises are binding under contract law and he has reneged on his promise. Criminal law provides some of the clearest examples of this principle, where minors are frequently excused from criminal liability and where insanity, temporary or otherwise, provides a well-known defense.

In Chapter 2, we reviewed the questions that typically arise when a minor or mental incompetent tries to create a legal right or obligation. Similar questions arise when violations of law are alleged. When minority is claimed as an excuse to liability, one can ask: What is the relevant age of majority? Has that age been reached? If not, exactly what is the nature of the age-related disability? Are the actions at issue within the scope of the disability? Similarly, when mental incompetence is claimed as an excuse to liability, one should ask: What is the relevant standard of mental competence? Does the person meet that standard? If not, from exactly which actions is the mental incompetent exonerated? Is the action at issue subject to exoneration?

Juristic persons can lack capacity, too, but their actions are seldom excused on that basis. Juristic persons, as we have seen, are incapacitated because they are not legally authorized to act in a particular way. Generally speaking, however, the sorts of things that juristic persons most often do to incur legal liability — breach contracts, violate property rights, commit torts, fail to file proper tax returns or other government reports — involve action or inaction that is typically within their authority in the relevant sense. And when they do overstep their bounds, they incur liability for that reason. At the end of the day, incapacity seldom exonerates juristic persons from liability.

It should be noted that a person's incapacity can also be addressed at earlier stages of the liability analysis. If, for example, a prohibited action requires a particular intent for its commission, we might find that a minor or incompetent person is unable, as a matter of law, to form that intent. The prohibited action having never been "taken" in the first place, there is no need to excuse it later. Thus, if the person who batters me is mentally incompetent, we can either use that incompetence as an excuse to liability or find no battery in the first place, on the theory that she could not have intended to hit me, as battery law requires. This intent-blocking way of handling incapacity is limited, of course, to those contexts in which a particular intent is required, such as in criminal law and intentional torts.

Questions of capacity can also be shifted to an even earlier stage of the analysis, by understanding a particular rule (or set of rules) as *not applying at all* to persons without capacity. Thus, we could think of criminal law as simply exempting minors from its proscriptions, rather than giving them a defense to liability that would otherwise obtain. Criminal laws are sometimes drafted in a way that makes this analysis a natural one, but other laws are not. We do not, for example, generally speak of exempting minors or mental incompetents from contract or property law. Regardless of its place in the analysis, however, the end result is the same: a claim of incapacity potentially blocks a finding of legal liability.

COERCION. Legal liability can also be excused on the ground that a person's actions were coerced. If a company's actions violate the antitrust laws of the United States, the company can sometimes avoid liability, for example, by showing that those actions were required by a foreign government (the *foreign sovereign compulsion doctrine*). Similarly, if someone steals my car, he will likely avoid liability under both criminal and property law if he was forced to do it at gunpoint. We are reluctant to hold persons responsible for actions they were forced to take.

In order to excuse liability, the alleged coercion must be clearly established. An immediate threat of direct physical harm can often exonerate a person from legal liability, but sometimes the threat of other harms (like legal liability in another country) will suffice. In any event, the threat must be immediate, the threatened harm must be serious, and there must be a clear connection between the threat and the taking of the (otherwise) prohibited action. Claims of coercion, therefore, typically raise the following questions: How immediate was the threat? How serious was the harm threatened? How close was the connection between the threat and the action?

Like incapacity, claims of coercion can also be addressed at an earlier stage of the analysis. Sometimes an action is deemed not to have occurred at all because it requires a particular intent, and the threat of harm vitiates that intent. Since the action was not "taken" in the first place, there is no need to excuse it later. The innocent bystander who is threatened at gunpoint to get in my car and drive it away will not have formed the proper intent (the *mens rea*) to commit a crime and thus will not have met all the requirements for criminal liability in the first place.

IMMUNITY. Liability can also be blocked because the person violating an obligation or right is *immune* from the liability created thereby. Even if it is clear, for example, that the Norwegian ambassador intended to strike — and did strike — another person at a diplomatic party in Washington (say, over an unfriendly remark concerning the weather in Oslo), the Norwegian ambassador will likely escape liability under U.S. tort and criminal law. The ambassador may be recalled by her own country, or declared a *persona non grata* and asked to leave the United States, but she will not owe damages, pay a fine, or serve any time in the D.C. jail. Immunities represent the clearest case of exoneration from liability: they are handled at this stage of the analysis and no other. They are never understood (like incapacity or coercion) to vitiate intent and thus prevent liability from arising in the first place.

Immunities can arise either from a person's status or from an *ad hoc* grant. There are many status-based immunities: diplomats, legislators, prosecutors, judges, and governments (both domestic and foreign) all enjoy certain immunities from liability. *Ad hoc* grants of immunity are perhaps most common in criminal law, where witnesses are often encouraged to testify by granting them immunity from liabilities arising either out of their testimony or the events described there.

An immunity based on status predictably raises the question of whether the claimant does in fact hold the status at issue. Although there are usually formal, easily verifiable criteria for deciding whether a person is a member of the legislature, a prosecutor, a judge, or a domestic or foreign government, status arguments sometimes arise. It could be asked, for example, whether the Palestine Liberation Organization is to be given those immunities accorded an international organization. Because status-based immunities are seldom absolute, in the sense that they shield the holder from legal liability in all circumstances, status-based immunity claims invariably raise the issue of whether the claimant is immune from the particular liability at issue. Under U.S. law, for example, a nation can be liable for failure to pay rent for the building where it keeps its consulate, but not for refusing to issue a visa to a particular applicant. In addition, most status-based immunities are available only when the claimant is acting within the scope of the duties associated with that status. When judges leave the courtroom, when legislators leave the statehouse, when prosecutors go on vacation, their immunities begin to fade. We generally ask, "Was the action at issue taken within the scope of that person's official duties?" If not, the immunity will not shield the claimant from liability.

Ad hoc grants of immunity raise a different, albeit predictable issue. There is almost never any question about whether a particular person is entitled to the immunity: either she is the person who received the grant or she is not. But the grant will specify, with more or less precision, the exact scope of the immunity, and this is where most questions arise: is the liability at issue included within the grant? Such an inquiry will in turn raise the same issues that one finds in the interpretation of any authoritative text.

IMPOSSIBILITY. Actions that violate a right or obligation are sometimes excused because the *situation* made no other action possible. If while driving, I swerve from the road to avoid a car that has entered my lane and, as I skid off the highway, hit a mailbox, I am likely to be excused from both civil and criminal liability for damaging someone else's property. I am excused because my action of hitting the mailbox was *unavoidable.* Conversely, failures to act can be excused because the required action was *impossible.* If, for example, I fail to paint your house as promised, but only because your house burned down two weeks ago, I will not incur liability for breach of contract. Situational excuses from liability can be found in many areas of law and go by many different names: act of God, *force majeure,* impossibility of performance, necessity, compulsion, and so on. The underlying concept is not particularly controversial — we don't usually hold people liable for actions (or inaction) that they had no ability to control.

Even so, the impossibility or unavoidability of an action does not always excuse liability. This is clearest in the context of privately created rights and obligations. Parties to a contract can anticipate that ships may be lost at sea, that factories may be shut down by strikes, and that houses may burn to the ground. As a consequence, they typically allocate the risk of loss when the shipped goods, the factory products, or the house designated in the contract cannot be delivered because of these events. In other words, parties to a contract often decide ahead of time which of them will incur liability when performance becomes impossible. If the risk has been allocated to a party by contract, he cannot escape liability by claiming impossibility of performance.

In the absence of the parties' agreement, the law often allocates such risks. In property law, for example, there is a rule in every state for who must bear the risk of loss if a house — under contract to be sold — burns down before the closing and thus becomes impossible to deliver. (Historically, states put the risk on the buyer, but many now put it on the seller.) If the risk is on the seller, the seller will not be excused from failing to deliver the promised house on the promised date and will incur liability to the buyer. Similarly, in tort law, the unavoidability of a particular accident may absolve an actor of liability for harm to others. Most torts can be excused in this way, but some are matters of *strict* or *absolute liability*. If, for example, the potentially liable person is engaged in an ultrahazardous activity, say the production of fireworks, strict liability is imposed and even unavoidable accidents will not be excused.

When claims based on impossibility or unavoidability are raised, we inevitably ask whether the required actions were truly impossible or the prohibited actions truly unavoidable. I don't have to paint your house if it burns down, but I might still be liable under the contract if I can't paint your house on time because my scaffolding equipment has been stolen. Impossibility is a judgment, not a self-evident fact, and we often struggle to distinguish the impossible from the merely inconvenient and difficult. Likewise, I am not liable to the owner of the mailbox if I really had no choice when I swerved off the road to avoid another car, but if I had been speeding right before the accident, questions can be raised about whether my action was truly unavoidable.

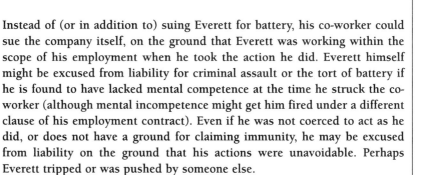

Everett's Case

Instead of (or in addition to) suing Everett for battery, his co-worker could sue the company itself, on the ground that Everett was working within the scope of his employment when he took the action he did. Everett himself might be excused from liability for criminal assault or the tort of battery if he is found to have lacked mental competence at the time he struck the co-worker (although mental incompetence might get him fired under a different clause of his employment contract). Even if he was not coerced to act as he did, or does not have a ground for claiming immunity, he may be excused from liability on the ground that his actions were unavoidable. Perhaps Everett tripped or was pushed by someone else.

Is liability otherwise blocked? Sometimes legal liability is not exactly excused, but disappears nonetheless. In this class of cases, liability comes to an end not so much because of something about the person who incurred the obligation (incapacity, coercion, immunity) or something about the situation (impossibility), but because of something about the person who was harmed. Four primary examples of this phenomenon are:

- death
- release
- estoppel
- self-help

Again, we discuss each ground briefly.

DEATH. Historically, the law viewed legal rights and obligations in a highly personal manner. When a man died, his rights and obligations died, too. A corollary was this: liabilities owed to a person were often extinguished at that person's death. Assume that in 1602 James trespasses on Elizabeth's property. In the sense that we have been using the term, he has already incurred legal liability for this action, because he has violated Elizabeth's right to exclude him. Elizabeth, for her part, has a cause of action against James — a ground upon which to take James to court and obtain a remedy. When Elizabeth dies, however, the cause of action may come to an end. Historically, the question was commonly formulated as whether a particular cause of action survived the decedent. In the past, a great many causes of action did not survive the decedent, and thus the liable person (James) was relieved of liability when the person harmed (Elizabeth) died.

Nowadays, most causes of action do survive the decedent, generally because we deem them to have passed automatically to the decedent's estate, heirs, or devisees. In addition, for those actions that do not survive, we sometimes create a special cause of action that substitutes for the one that expired. In earlier days, for example, if someone wrongfully caused the death of another, no civil suit against the wrongdoer could be brought because the person with the cause of action (the victim) had died and the cause of action did not pass to the decedent's estate or relatives. It is still true in most states today that the decedent's cause of action does not pass to the decedent's estate or relatives, but *wrongful death statutes* typically create in the decedent's spouse and descendants *their own* cause of action against the person who wrongfully caused the decedent's death. Despite these historical trends, some causes of action, in some states, do not survive the decedent or result in the creation of substituted action. In these remaining cases, the death of the person harmed has the effect of extinguishing liability.

RELEASE. It is always possible that a person harmed by another's action or inaction will *release* the other from liability, or, as it is sometimes put, *hold* him *harmless*. A release can be given before or after liability has arisen, and different issues arise depending on the timing of the release.

Anticipatory releases from liability can be found everywhere. They are common features of leases and contracts of all sorts — between banks and customers, shippers and carriers, buyers and sellers of goods, lawyers and their clients, and so on. In all leases and contracts there is likely to be a hold harmless clause, specifying which actions by which parties will *not* give rise to liability. Such anticipatory releases commonly raise two questions: whether the terms of the release cover the liability at issue and whether those terms are enforceable. The first question is generally settled by interpreting the language of the release and involves an analysis we addressed earlier in this chapter. The second question, however, raises a new issue worth exploring. Historically, courts and legislatures have been concerned to limit the ability of persons to release each other from liability, especially when the parties are perceived to be in an unequal bargaining position. The Carriage of Goods by Sea Act, for example, strictly limits the ability of carriers to limit their potential liability to shippers. Landlords are typically prohibited, usually as a matter of judge-made law, from limiting certain kinds of liability to their tenants. Attempts to limit liability for intentional torts, in many contexts, are frequently called into question. As a consequence, one cannot assume that a release of liability will be enforced, and consultation with the statute books and prior judicial decisions is necessary when anticipatory releases are invoked.

Releases of liability can also be made after the liability has arisen. In the negotiation and settlement of a legal dispute, for example, the final settlement will almost always release one or both of the parties from any liability arising out of that dispute. Those convicted of crimes can be pardoned, thus releasing them from criminal liability for the pardoned crimes. Like anticipatory releases, those made after liability has arisen can raise interpretive questions. This is less common, however, since the parties already know what liability is to be released, and presumably will have described it properly in the relevant documents. Likewise, enforcement questions are raised less frequently, generally because post-violation releases are negotiated on a case-by-case basis, which lessens (though it does not preclude) worries about overreaching and sharp practice.

Releases should be contrasted with waivers, which work in a different way. A *waiver* is a voluntary relinquishment of a known legal right. Rights that are waived cannot be enforced, and so the practical result — no liability — is the same. But a waiver extinguishes the relevant *right*. As such, waivers are relevant to the earlier question in our analysis, "Is there a law?" (If there is a waiver, the answer to that question is no.) Releases, in contrast, do not extinguish the relevant right or obligation or deny its violation. Releases assume the existence both of the right and its violation, but terminate liability nonetheless.

ESTOPPEL. Sometimes liability is extinguished by a different sort of action by the person harmed, much subtler than death or an explicit release.

Sometimes the person harmed is *estopped* from holding another liable because of actions the harmed person has taken. Under normal circumstances, for example, you cannot enter my property without my permission; if you do so, you incur legal liability to me for the entry. But I can be estopped from asserting that liability if I have taken certain actions (or refrained from certain actions) beforehand. If you cross my property again and again to build a house on the lot behind mine, and I watch you in silence until your half-million dollar house is completed, and *then* complain, a court will likely hold that I am precluded (i.e., estopped) from suing you in trespass, effectively exonerating you from liability.

The rule regarding *estoppel* is difficult to state in general form, but runs roughly as follows: (1) if a person acts in such a way that invites action by another; (2) if the second person does in fact act in the invited way; (3) if it is reasonable to do so; and (4) if denying the propriety of the second person's action would cause the second person substantial harm; then the first person will be precluded from — estopped from — challenging the second person's action. In shorthand, we often say that a person is estopped from asserting liability against another if that second person has reasonably relied to his detriment on the acts of the first. This is the doctrine of *equitable estoppel* and it has the effect of extinguishing liability that would otherwise be imposed. In the trespass case above, if I seemed to acquiesce in your use of my land during the construction of your home, if you reasonably relied on that acquiescence, and if denying it now would cause you substantial harm (you have no other way to reach your expensive new home), a court might preclude me from holding you liable in trespass. If so, your past and future crossings of my property will not give rise to legal liability. (A related doctrine, often called *promissory estoppel,* has similar elements — a promise by one person, followed by detrimental reliance on the promise by another — but has the effect of *creating* a legal obligation in the first person, rather than *excusing* some liability of the second.)

Another doctrine, the *clean hands doctrine,* can arise in similar circumstances and have similar effects. Under this doctrine, one who has acted fraudulently or questionably with respect to a matter will not be heard to complain about the actions of others concerning the same matter. It is a looser, more amorphous doctrine than equitable estoppel, and is invoked less frequently. Even so, cases are still won and lost on this ground. When, for example, an ex-husband wants to reopen and change the property settlement from a divorce on the ground that his ex-wife understated her assets, he might be denied that relief if he himself had been uncooperative in revealing his own assets during the original settlement negotiations. His ex-wife's liability for being untruthful is effectively terminated.

SELF-HELP PRIVILEGES. Finally, some actions, normally improper, can be made proper because they are in response to a previous wrong. Thus, if I pick you up and throw you out the door, I will ordinarily be liable to you for battery. But if I take that action because I have just caught you robbing my house, I might be excused from liability, because my actions were taken in response to your having violated one of *my* rights. Similarly, if I fail to deliver the last shipment of dental floss to your warehouse, in clear violation of our contract, I might be excused from liability because my failure to ship the goods was in response to your earlier refusal to pay the required contract price at the required time.

This exoneration from liability is founded on the possibility of self-help and the privileges it generates. Self-help is a kind of *remedy* — and will be discussed more fully in the next chapter — but it has important ramifications in determining *liability*. Some actions, which on their face would generate liability, are excused because they are the proper self-help remedy for previous wrongs. As we will see in the next chapter, self-help is not always permitted, and when permitted, its modes of exercise are often strictly limited. Consequently, this ground for blocking liability raises the following questions: Was there a previous wrong? Was this action a response to it? Is that form of response permissible? The answer to the last question depends on the law of self-help and the law of remedies more generally, to which we now turn.

Everett's Case

If the co-worker dies, his cause of action against Everett will not survive unless it is deemed to pass to the co-worker's estate. If Everett dies, the tort action may fail as well, unless Everett's estate can be substituted as the new defendant. In the normal course, any criminal action against Everett would not survive his death. It is unlikely that Everett's co-worker will release him from liability (except in the context of a settlement), nor does it appear that an estoppel is possible. The state can never be estopped, as a general matter, and there is nothing in the facts to suggest that either his company or his co-worker invited Everett to act the way he did. It could be, however, that Everett acted in self-defense, to deflect an initial blow from the co-worker. If that were true, Everett would likely be found not to have violated any obligation discussed in this chapter, not under criminal law, not under tort law, and not under the employment contract.

IN S U M M A R Y

- Individuals can make liability decisions without recourse to courts or other government officials.

- All methods of private (nongovernmental) decisionmaking — *negotiation, mediation, conciliation,* and *arbitration* — require the consent of the parties to the dispute. Most legal debate about these methods centers, in one sense or another, on whether they have been consented to by the parties concerned.

- Governmental decisionmaking occurs not only in the courts, but also in the executive branch.

- Decisions by both executive and judicial officers raise questions of authority (the *jurisdiction to adjudicate*): whether a particular bureaucrat or judge is the right one to hear a case. There are many grounds upon which such jurisdiction can be questioned.

- Even after jurisdictional issues are resolved, the parties may debate what *procedures* are to be followed, and if not followed, whether this invalidates the final decision.

- Deciding whether an obligation or right has been violated requires the application of the law to the facts. As a consequence, the two major challenges facing any decisionmaker are to:
  - *interpret the law;* and
  - *find the facts*

- The proper methods of legal interpretation depend on whether the law at issue comes from:
  - statutes and other authoritative texts; or
  - judicial decisions

- The interpretation of *statutes* and other authoritative texts (like *contracts* and *deeds*) must begin with the precise words used in the text and no others. Those words are then interpreted by examining:
  - the *plain meaning* of the words;
  - the *drafters' intent;* and
  - the *purpose* behind the language

- Unlike statutes and other authoritative texts, *common-law rules* derived from judicial decisions have no set formulation of words, but the analysis of such rules must begin by choosing *some* formulation.

- Legal *fact-finding* involves some of the same procedures as investigating facts in everyday life, but there are some major differences, including highly stylized traditions regarding:
  - burdens of proof
  - presumptions
  - rules of evidence

- Once the law has been interpreted and the facts found, *applying the law to the facts* is generally straightforward. Most legal debate centers on the earlier stages of the analysis.

- Even so, several doctrines and principles can change the results that would normally obtain when the law is applied to the facts. These doctrines and principles include:
  - vicarious liability
  - substantial compliance
  - excuses (lack of capacity, coercion, immunity, impossibility)
  - other grounds upon which liability disappears (death, release, estoppel, self-help)

What Will Be Done About a Violation of Law?
(Questions of Remedy)

THIS CHAPTER

- Takes up the third great question of legal analysis: What will be done about a violation of law?

- Explains how remedies work: the theories behind the major options and how those options can be invoked and enforced by the parties to a dispute

---

- Shows what remedies are available against the state (e.g., federal, state, and local governments) and by the state against others (e.g., individuals in criminal and regulatory law)

- Shows what remedies are available in purely private transactions between individuals, with special attention to the law of damages

We began in Chapter 2 with the first great question of legal analysis, "Is there a law?" If an obligation or right has been validly created (and not later terminated) we can then ask the second great question, "Has the law been violated?" We now address the last great question in legal analysis: assuming that a legal right or obligation exists and that it has been violated, *what will be done about it?* This is the question of remedies.

From the perspective of an aggrieved person, remedies are vital. Someone has been hurt, maligned, or put in a difficult position, and that person wants action. That person wants things fixed and fixed now! Whether any fixing can be done, and who can do it, are the subjects of this chapter. Remedies are also important for clients in the planning stages, for remedies relate to the risks involved. We may not know ahead of time whether a particular course of action violates the law or not. The law may be unclear or there may be some special features in the client's plan of action that render a clear assessment impossible. But if we know that the remedies for potential liability are mild, we will be less concerned about those uncertainties. If, on the other hand, the penalties for missteps are severe, we will be much more conservative in deciding whether to forge ahead anyway.

THE WORLD OF REMEDIES

How Remedies Work

A remedy is a response to liability. Remedies usually follow liability in time; an obligation or right has been violated and the remedy is aimed at rectifying the situation. But remedies can also anticipate or prevent liability by seeking to restrain action that, if taken, would generate liability. This second kind of remedy stops people in their tracks, preventing them from taking action that would violate a right or obligation. The clearest examples of this kind of remedy are the judicially imposed *temporary restraining order* and *preliminary injunction*. Generally speaking, these anticipatory and preventive remedies are rarely applied. They require a special showing by the proponent of the remedy, such as a high likelihood of success on the merits (i.e., that liability will eventually be found) and a risk of irreparable harm to the proponent if the anticipatory remedy is not imposed. These difficult showings and the consequent rarity of anticipatory relief reflect the understandable reluctance of judges to interfere in situations where no one has yet violated an obligation or right. The remainder of this chapter will focus on the more common remedies that arise after someone has in fact violated an obligation or right.

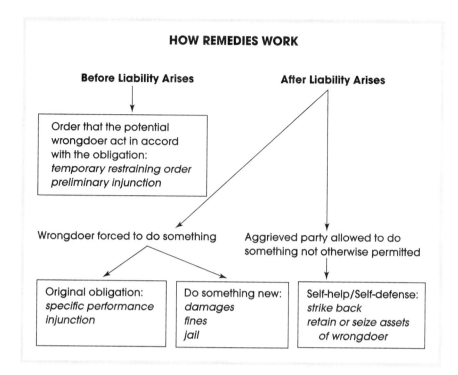

HOW REMEDIES WORK

Before Liability Arises | After Liability Arises

Order that the potential wrongdoer act in accord with the obligation:
temporary restraining order
preliminary injunction

Wrongdoer forced to do something | Aggrieved party allowed to do something not otherwise permitted

| Original obligation: *specific performance* *injunction* | Do something new: *damages* *fines* *jail* | Self-help/Self-defense: *strike back* *retain or seize assets of wrongdoer* |

Remedies of all types presuppose the existence of at least two persons: a liable party and an aggrieved party. Someone did (or will do) the harm; someone else has been (or will be) hurt. As a consequence, remedies can respond to liability in one of two ways: (1) by requiring the liable party to act in a certain way; or (2) by permitting the aggrieved party to act in a way not otherwise permitted. What can a liable party be required to do? Most obviously, the liable party can be required to act as originally required. If a used-car dealer wrongfully refuses to deliver possession of a car after the buyer has paid the purchase price, the dealer can be required to turn the car over. If someone has been crossing my land without my permission, that person can be required to stop. In one sense, this remedy is nothing more than a reaffirmation of the original obligation. What is added, however, is the aggrieved party's ability to *engage the assistance of others,* often a court, to compel compliance — a point to which we will return in a moment.

But remedies are not confined to new demands to comply with the same old obligations. The liable party can also be required to act in *new* ways, different in kind from the action originally required. Parties who have violated a legal right or obligation might be required to pay a fine to the state, pay money to the aggrieved party, leave the country, or go to jail.

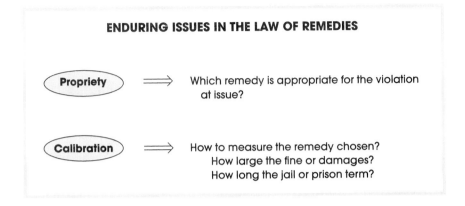

This feature of remedies is so deeply entrenched in our law that we are likely to miss its significance. If a person fails to perform an obligation, we can immediately see the sense in demanding the required performance. To demand *something else entirely* is both peculiar and nonintuitive, even though we do it all the time. Because of this, arguments about remedies are riddled with concerns about propriety and calibration: *which* curious, nonintuitive responses are appropriate? (incarceration? money?) and how should they be measured? (how *long* a sentence? how *much* money?).

Most remedies set forth explicitly what action the liable party is required to take. If a defective toaster injures someone, a standard remedy is to require the manufacturer to pay money damages to the injured party. Sometimes, however, remedies work indirectly, changing the liable party's rights and obligations, which in turn necessitates a particular course of action. Thus, for example, the Securities and Exchange Commission can suspend a stockbroker's license for violations of the securities laws. The suspension of the license does not demand, on its face, that particular actions be taken, but the stockbroker risks new liability if she continues to deal in securities during the period of the suspension.

As noted at the outset, an entirely different class of remedies focuses not on the liable party, but on the aggrieved one. That is, some remedies respond to liability by permitting the aggrieved party to act in ways that would not otherwise be permitted. When, for example, a tenant falls behind in the rent, the landlord in many states is permitted to seize some of the tenant's personal property and retain it until the rent has been paid. Had the rent not been in arrears, of course, such action would be a violation of the tenant's property rights. The remedy makes the seizure lawful. In this case, the remedy (called "distress") is cast in direct terms, setting out the new actions the aggrieved party (the landlord) can take. But as before, these new permissions can also be achieved indirectly, by changing the aggrieved party's rights and obligations. When someone breaches a contract the other party (the nonbreaching, aggrieved party) is sometimes permitted to consider the contract at an end. The obligations having come to an end, the aggrieved party is no longer bound to complete the contract.

In sum, remedies can respond to liability by rectifying the wrong or seeking to prevent it. When applied after the fact, remedies can require the liable party to act as he should, or instead require that he pay money, put things back the way they were, pay a fine to the state, or go to jail. In the alternative, after-the-fact remedies can give the aggrieved party permission to act in a new way not otherwise permitted: seize personal belongings, stop performing a contract, or return gunfire. And all of this can be accomplished directly or indirectly, by either explicitly requiring or authorizing specific actions (the direct method) or by changing the rights and obligations of the liable or aggrieved parties, which in turn requires or authorizes them to act in specific ways (the indirect method). The world of remedies, in short, is full of options and possibilities, and requires some sorting out.

Everett's Case

Because Everett has come to us *after* he allegedly struck his co-worker, anticipatory forms of relief (temporary restraining orders or preliminary injunctions) will not be an issue. Anticipatory relief from physical violence is rare in any event, although some options do exist. In family and child law matters, for example, threatened family members can seek an order of protection against an aggressive or threatening relative, ordering that person to stay away from the family home.

The Two Great Questions of Remedy

Different kinds of liabilities generate different remedies. Violations of criminal law give rise to a range of remedies different from those that follow a breach of contract. The precise set of remedies available for a breach of contract, in turn, depend on who breached the contract and how. Even after we know the range of available remedies in a particular situation, it is often necessary to choose among them. A nonbreaching party in a contract, for example, cannot both demand performance from the breaching party *and* rescind the contract (thus releasing both parties from their obligations under it). As a consequence, the first question lawyers usually ask is: *Exactly which remedies are available* in this situation?

TYPES OF REMEDIES

Most private law remedies: (contract, property, tort, debtor/creditor)

Self-executing ➔ Parties can demand/impose ➔ Courts can enforce

Most public law remedies: (criminal law, regulatory law)

Non-self-executing ➔ Courts must impose ➔ Court must enforce

The second question has to do with implementation and enforcement. Many remedies, especially in the context of civil law, are *self-executing* and do not require official court action to be implemented. The law is filled with rules providing that when certain kinds of liabilities arise, the liable party is obliged, then and there, to take certain rectifying actions, or the aggrieved party, then and there, is permitted to take certain responsive actions. When the seller of a home refuses to complete the sale pursuant to the sales contract, the buyer can immediately demand that the seller complete the sale and deliver a deed, demand damages from the seller for the breach, or rescind the contract and demand a return of any down payment the buyer has already provided. Recourse to courts or other decisionmaking bodies is needed only when the liable party resists the aggrieved party's demands. In this context, the courts do not so much impose the remedies as *enforce* them.

Other remedies must be *imposed*. Remedies of this sort are often found in criminal and administrative law. Only a court can sentence someone to prison or impose a criminal fine. Only the Supreme Court of Illinois can suspend or revoke an Illinois attorney's license to practice law. Only the executive branch of the federal government can ban a particular company from exporting its goods to countries outside the United States. As a consequence, the second major question of remedy is: *How can the available remedies be enforced?*

Remedies, Courts, and Others

Before addressing these two great questions of remedy, we pause to review the relation between remedies and courts. Courts are crucial actors in the field of remedies. As we have just seen, certain remedies, such as criminal sentences, can be imposed by courts and no one else. Even when a remedy is self-executing, the aggrieved party must often go to court anyway to force compliance. What courts will do, and not do, in imposing or enforcing remedies shapes the entire field. The law of remedies never operates very far from the shadow of the courthouse.

Having said that, it bears emphasis that remedial issues arise all the time and everywhere, not just in the courtroom after a judge has found a criminal defendant guilty or given judgment for the plaintiff in a civil suit. Remedial issues arise whenever liability is determined, asserted, or contemplated, and as we saw in the last chapter, liability is determined, asserted, and contemplated by all sorts of people in all sorts of places. Lawyers, of course, are constantly concerned with liability and remedies:

- A client asks her lawyer whether she can evict some unruly tenants by changing the locks on their apartment door, and her lawyer determines that lock-outs are prohibited in their state. The lawyer will likely suggest alternatives.
- A client engaged in the production of dental floss has a dispute with a supplier, because its last three shipments of wax were substandard and unusable. After the lawyer satisfies herself that the relevant supply contract has been breached, the lawyer might suggest that all payments be stopped.
- A state district attorney reviews a case file and decides that a plea bargain is desirable. What she offers the defendant depends in part on the range of sentences that might be imposed if the defendant were eventually convicted at trial.

Indeed, all persons — not just lawyers — ask and answer remedy questions. The decision of whether to pay a parking ticket, fight it in traffic court, or ignore it completely will be influenced by what sanctions might be imposed in the wake of each course of action. Indeed, the decision of whether to risk a parking ticket in the first place is informed by the consequences of violating the parking ordinance. How (and whether) a purchaser of shoddy merchandise pursues the seller depends in part on the range and effectiveness of available responses to merchants of substandard goods. Indeed, whether the merchant cares very much about the quality of goods in the first place depends in part on the remedies available to buyers. We even expect drug dealers to make calculations about remedies, for we hope the promise of longer sentences will influence them to ply their trade at least 1000 feet from any school. All of us, lawyers and laity, sinners and saints, examine questions of remedy.

We have just seen that many persons, not just courts, deal with questions of remedy. Conversely, not every action taken by courts involves a remedy. Sometimes parties go to court or appear before other decision-making bodies to seek declarations regarding liability and nothing more. These actions are known as requests for *declaratory relief*. Generally speaking, parties seek declaratory relief when they want to work out the

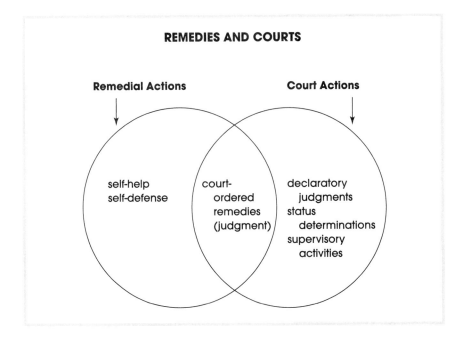

remedies for themselves, or, in a defensive maneuver, when they want to clarify the legality of actions taken in the past or contemplated for the future. Thus, parties to a commercial dispute might arbitrate the question of liability only, leaving to later negotiation or another tribunal the consequences of that liability. Likewise, trustees might seek judicial confirmation of their power to make a particular investment of trust assets, that is, their ability to make such an investment without incurring liability to the trust's beneficiaries or others. In both cases, the legal response to liability — the remedy — is irrelevant.

Similarly, people sometimes go to court or appear before other decisionmaking bodies to request action even when no particular liability has arisen or is contemplated. This is most common in *status determinations,* where parties seek to determine the status of persons or things. Thus, courts and other bodies regularly make orders and declarations of heirship, incompetence, citizenship, paternity, and property ownership, for example, without determining that anyone has violated some obligation or right, much less imposing or enforcing a remedy.

Finally, courts and other decisionmaking bodies often work in a supervisory capacity, and in that capacity issue orders and declarations that involve no remedies. Courts, for example, supervise their own operations and those of the practicing bar. They also supervise the administration of trusts and estates. As a consequence, courts can issue orders adopting new rules of evidence, changing standards for admission to the bar, approving the final distributions of estates, and changing the language of trusts that can no longer be carried out because of changes in circumstances — none of which involves anyone's liability or what to do about it. Supervisory work of this kind *can* involve determinations of liability and remedy (as when a court disbars a lawyer for misconduct) but it need not. In short, although courts lie at the center of remedial work, not everything they do involves remedies.

WHAT REMEDIES ARE AVAILABLE?

As we saw at the beginning of this chapter, remedies respond to liability by: (1) requiring the liable party to act in a particular way; or (2) permitting the aggrieved party to act in a way not otherwise permitted. This opens a wide range of possibilities: civil fines; criminal fines; money damages; the suspension or revocation of a license; ejection from real property; the seizure or forced return of personal property; the forced sale of real or personal property; the garnishment of wages; probation; home detention; jail time; and death by injection, among others. No single liability opens up all these options, and determining which responses are available for which liabilities is a major concern of judges, lawyers, and their clients. The range of legal responses available for a particular liability can be affected by a number of factors: the kind of obligation violated; the powers of the decisionmaker who is called upon to act; the status of the aggrieved and liable parties; the actual circumstances of the parties when the liability arises or when the remedy is sought; and prior agreements between the parties, among others. Typically, these factors conspire so that only two or three possible responses will be available in any particular situation.

The single greatest determinant of available responses is the nature of the right or obligation violated. International rights and obligations, for example, have a set of remedies distinct from domestic rights and obligations. Remedies in domestic law, in turn, are affected by whether the right or obligation is part of public or private law. (*Public law* governs the relations between states and individuals, and includes constitutional, criminal, and regulatory law, while *private law* governs relations between individuals, and includes property, tort, and contract law.) Within the two broad categories of public and private law, one can draw meaningful distinctions between fields, as between criminal and regulatory law, and between contract and tort law. Remedies in one field are often not available in another. We will begin by examining the remedies in public law, followed by those in private law. Inside each broad category we will often distinguish between areas or fields, but also emphasize the commonalities so that the larger picture is kept in view.

Everett's Case

Because Everett faces three kinds of actions, we will have to work with three very different sets of remedies, based on criminal law, tort law, and contract law, respectively.

The Remedies of Public Law

In public law all obligations are owed to or by the state. This makes the remedies of public law quite different from those in private law.

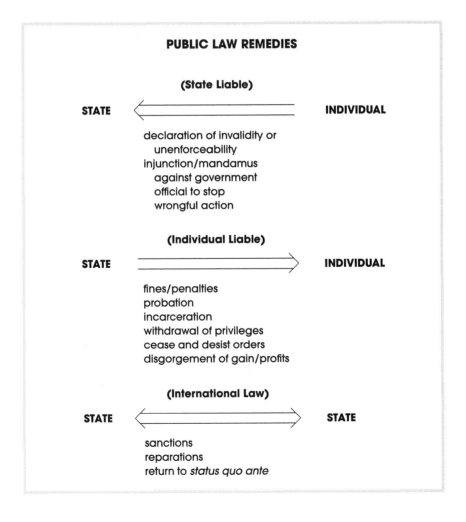

PUBLIC LAW REMEDIES

(State Liable)

STATE ⟵─────────────── INDIVIDUAL

declaration of invalidity or
unenforceability
injunction/mandamus
against government
official to stop
wrongful action

(Individual Liable)

STATE ───────────────⟶ INDIVIDUAL

fines/penalties
probation
incarceration
withdrawal of privileges
cease and desist orders
disgorgement of gain/profits

(International Law)

STATE ⟵───────────────⟶ STATE

sanctions
reparations
return to *status quo ante*

Remedies Against the State. States, their organs, and officials are often obliged to act (or refrain from acting) in particular ways by constitutions, statutes, ordinances, and other laws, including international law. But states are different from you and me, and when they violate a legal obligation the consequences are different. First, the state is a juristic person and can't be treated as if it has a physical body. The state can never be confined to quarters, jailed, imprisoned, or electrocuted. (States can be terminated, but invading armies, not legal process, often play the decisive role.) Second, at least domestically, the state has a monopoly on punishment: it can punish, but not be punished. The state cannot be fined or penalized by withdrawing rights or privileges against its will. Third, the state (including its organs and officials) is often immune from liability. With liability blocked, no remedy can be had.

Because of these peculiar characteristics of the state, remedies *against* the state, when permitted at all, are generally confined to requiring that the state perform its obligations in accord with their original tenor. This can be accomplished in two ways. First, because the state acts through its government — its branches, departments, bureaus, offices, and ultimately particular officials — one can demand that particular organs or officials act in the required ways. Thus, one could demand that state prison officials improve the conditions of the prisons, so that confinement there does not violate the constitutional prohibition against cruel and unusual punishment. If the Federal Communications Commission improperly withdrew a television license, one could demand that the license be reinstated. The second option when governments violate law is to deny legal effect to the nonconforming actions. This is most common when laws or regulations violate constitutional or statutory restrictions. Thus, if the Illinois General Assembly were to authorize the coinage of money (a power the federal constitution gives exclusively to the federal government), or the Food and Drug Administration were to regulate tobacco as a drug (in contravention of congressional statute), these actions would likely be handled by deeming them void.

Although state liabilities are usually remedied by requiring government organs or officials to act in conformity with the state's obligations or by considering the nonconforming actions a nullity, for certain kinds of domestic liability the state can be treated like a private party. It can be required to pay money damages to those harmed by its actions. This usually occurs in the context of *waived immunity*. Historically, the English king "could do no wrong," that is, he could not be sued in his own courts. Over time, this concept developed into the idea that governments — even kingless ones — were immune from liability and remedy. American governments, however, have progressively waived their traditional immunities regarding actions that are not intrinsically governmental. Governments do many different things: they make laws, administer social programs, regulate businesses, adjudicate disputes between private parties, collect taxes, raise armies, declare war, investigate and prosecute crime, build roads, and buy pencils. Some of these actions are intrinsically governmental and some are not. That line is not always easy to draw, but some things are clear: only governments can impose taxes; anyone can buy a pencil. When governments waive their traditional immunity for actions not intrinsically governmental, they commonly specify the appropriate remedies, remedies that are patterned on those available against private persons. The Federal Tort Claims Act, for example, allows for the recovery of damages against the federal government when its employees injure persons or property while acting within the scope of their office, or when the federal government violates certain contractual obligations.

When states violate their international obligations, an entirely different set of remedies is invoked. Unlike the situation domestically, states *can* be punished for violating international law and they are not immune from whole classes of liability. When states violate their international obligations, offended states are permitted, depending on the facts, to take a series of unilateral, essentially punitive actions against the offending state: diplomatic sanctions, economic sanctions, and (in very limited circumstances) military sanctions. Reparations (money payments) are also a traditional remedy in international law, as is the requirement that the offended state return the parties to the *status quo ante.*

It bears emphasis that we are concentrating on the *nature* of available responses to government violations of law, leaving aside questions of *enforcement,* questions about *who* can demand that prison conditions be improved, declare a bad law void, or seek international reparations. The enforcement of remedies against the state is often problematic and will be discussed later in this chapter, when we treat enforcement issues systematically. For now, we remain focused on the *types* of responses available. To summarize, when governments violate legal obligations and rights, the most common remedies are to demand conforming action or to consider the nonconforming actions void. The range of remedies changes and expands when governments act like private individuals and when they violate international law.

Remedies Against Individuals. When states violate their obligations to others, the remedial responses are limited because of the special nature of the state. Those who violate their obligations *to* the state, on the other hand, are not so special. They are usually just you and me (natural persons) and the corporations, partnerships, trusts, and other bodies (juristic persons) we create, the kinds of persons for whom all sorts of remedies — from burning at the stake to a license revocation — have been devised. Even so, the range of remedies applied to private persons who violate public law is highly circumscribed. From the earliest times in American history we have been preoccupied, not to say obsessed, with limiting the power of the state. This obsession has led us to insist, among other things, that one's obligations to the state be made as clear as possible and that the remedies for those violations be made explicit. As a consequence, obligations to the state are almost always defined in statutory or regulatory language that also specifies the appropriate remedies. In those areas of law where obligations to the state are found — primarily in criminal and administrative law — the question of *which* remedies are available (the question that so animated us in the context of the *state's* obligations) is almost never an issue. We simply look and see. If a client is charged with assault with a deadly weapon or a violation of particular regulations of the Federal Communications Commission, we simply look up the relevant provisions in the state criminal code or the Code of Federal Regulations, respectively, and find what remedies are specified for those particular violations. This does not settle the matter, of course, for there is still a great deal of room for lawyerly maneuver. Our attention now turns to: (1) the choice between specified remedies; and (2) for any particular remedy, its proper measure.

In criminal law, the remedial choices are typically confined to probation, fines, incarceration, and sometimes death, with the forfeiture of property becoming more common for drug offenses. To the extent that the choice of remedies lies in the discretion of the judge (and sometimes jury), defense attorneys will predictably argue for the milder forms of response; prosecutors for the more severe. In addition, criminal statutes typically give ranges of penalties within each type: imprisonment for not less than ten years, jail for not more than six months, a fine of not less than $500, and so on. A great deal of predictable debate then concerns the proper level of the penalty imposed.

Although punishment of the liable party is the primary form of remedial action in criminal law, other options are sometimes available. Community service, for example, is sometimes imposed in lieu of jail time or other penalty. In addition, compensation to victims and their families is increasingly ordered when permitted by statute, and protective orders, aimed at preventing persons from acting in ways that would generate criminal liability, are becoming more common. These latter options are interesting departures from traditional public law remedies, mimicking the private law remedies of damages and injunctions.

Regulatory laws — securities laws, food and drug laws, environmental laws, health and sanitation laws, zoning laws, and so on — generate a wider range of remedies. Violations of regulatory legislation can invoke the possibility of civil fines and penalties; cease and desist orders; the disgorgement of profits; seizures or forced sales of property; garnishments of wages; and the denial, revocation, or suspension of licenses and permits, among other responses. One cannot, however, be jailed or executed for the violation of regulatory laws, for the tautological reason that the threat of such penalties makes the relevant law *criminal*. (This is not to say, however, that death might not be preferable to a 12-year battle with the Internal Revenue Service.)

Perhaps the most interesting twist in remedies for violations of regulatory law lies in the possibility of private enforcement. Regulatory law is public law, concerning obligations owed to the state. This suggests that the state, and only the state, is in the position to respond to violations of those obligations. But sometimes the state authorizes private parties, generally those who have been harmed by the offending action, to seek damages or injunctions against the offending party. The feature of private enforcement can be found, for example, in antitrust law, securities law, and civil rights law. Each area of law typically invites private action by promising plaintiffs treble damages, the payment of their lawyers' fees, or other inducements.

Despite the wide range of *potential* remedies in regulatory law, the precise remedies for any particular violation are, like criminal law, specified in the statutes, regulations, or ordinances that create the obligation in the first place. As a result, the basic question of *which* remedies are available is seldom a live issue. One simply looks and sees. Likewise, the remaining remedial questions are much the same as those that characterize criminal law: which of the specified modes of response are most appropriate (civil fine? license suspension?) and within each mode, what should be the proper level of response (how large the civil fine? how long the suspension of the license? and so on).

International law, which frequently obliges *nations* to act in particular ways, has far less pertinence here. First, international law simply does not impose many obligations on individuals. Such obligations are essentially limited to proscriptions against genocide, piracy, hijacking, and the commission of war crimes. Second, even when violations of those obligations are found, international law does not generally provide a special remedial regime. Apart from the formation of *ad hoc* tribunals, international law generally confines itself to requiring that *nations* engage in the relevant prosecutions. When that occurs, the individuals are generally prosecuted under domestic criminal law, raising questions of domestic remedies that we have already discussed.

Everett's Case

Everett's case does not involve any actions against the state, but does involve a potential action by the state against him. As in all such cases of state action against individuals, his potential punishment (here, under the criminal statute governing assault) will be set out in explicit detail, including the range of possible jail time and fines, eligibility for probation, and so on. If we were criminal lawyers practicing in the jurisdiction, we would likely have some ability to predict how the local prosecutors and judges would use the discretion that remains, and stand ready to argue for the mildest punishment possible.

The Remedies of Private Law

Remedies Generally Available. In public law, obligations run to or from the state; the state is always a principal participant. In private law — tort, contract, property, and commercial law, for example — the obligations run between private, non-state actors, and the state typically becomes involved only to resolve disputes. As a consequence, private law remedies focus on the parties themselves. These remedies are aimed at either punishing the liable person or making the aggrieved party whole.

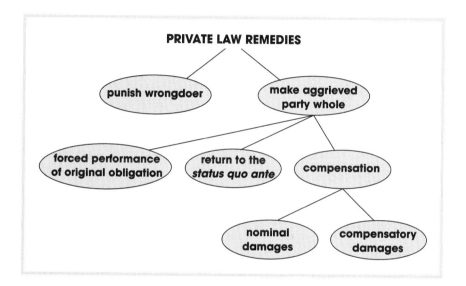

The aversion to punishment. Punishment, which dominates the remedial structure of public law, especially criminal law, plays a much smaller role in private law. One can never be put to death, jailed, or even fined for violations of private law. This is trivially true in the sense that the threat of such punishment would, by definition, make the relevant law public rather than private, but it reflects a deeper substantive judgment. The state has the exclusive power to punish, and we are reluctant to invoke this exclusive power in areas of law where the state serves not as a primary participant, but only as the referee between others.

This does not mean the impulse to punish has been banished from private law remedies, but it does mean that remedies of such character require a special justification. Punitive damages (money awards designed not to make the injured party whole, but to punish the wrongdoer) are traditionally unavailable for violations of contract obligations and can be imposed in tort cases only upon a showing of particularly egregious conduct by the liable party. In addition, private law remedies that aim to punish can only arise when they are *imposed*, and in the normal course, they can be imposed only by *courts*. Thus a *tortfeasor* can properly be said to owe the injured party compensation (and the injured party can properly demand it at any time, in or out of litigation), but the tortfeasor is not in any sense obliged to pay punitive damages until ordered to do so by a court.

Forced performance, return to the status quo ante *and compensation.* With an impulse to punish at a low ebb, the remedies of private law concentrate on making the aggrieved party whole. An aggrieved party can be satisfied in at least three ways. First, we can simply require the liable party to act in conformance with the relevant right or obligation, that is, to *demand the performance* originally owed to the aggrieved party. In a contract breach, for example, we can require the breaching party to perform its contract obligations as they were originally set forth in the agreement (the contract remedy of *specific performance*). Second, we can try to put things back the way they were before liability arose, by requiring the liable party to return the situation to the *status quo ante*. If a contract has been breached, we can try to put the parties back in the same position as they were before the contract was made (the contract remedy of *rescission*). Finally, we can make the liable party pay money to the aggrieved party for the losses suffered on account of the liable party's violation, that is, to compel *compensation*. In a contract breach, we can require a breaching seller to cover any additional expenses a buyer incurred in securing the promised goods from someone else (a call for *damages*). In contract law, the basic forms of "whole-making" remedies present themselves as specific performance, rescission, and damages, but the options of forced performance, a return to the *status quo ante* and compensation to the aggrieved party appear throughout private law.

The preference for damages. Among the favored remedies of forced performance, a return to the *status quo ante,* and compensation to the aggrieved party, compensation is the most highly favored of all. Compensation — the payment of money damages — is almost always available; the other modes of relief often require a special showing. Indeed, the law of damages so dominates our concept of remedy that lawyers often think of the options available to their clients as divided between damages and everything else. This is a curious state of affairs. When persons fail to do what they are obliged to do, the most natural reaction is to demand that they take the required actions (forced performance) or that they put things back the way they were (a return to the *status quo ante*), not to demand that they pay money instead. Yet, for historical and practical reasons, the payment of money is usually the law's first choice.

The historical preference for damages began in England, where the Law Courts developed a remedial system for private law that relied primarily on the payment of money. Over the years, the kinds of actions that could be brought in those courts became progressively stylized, narrow, and technical. As a consequence, many persons who felt themselves aggrieved by the actions of others could find no relief in the Law Courts and began to turn elsewhere for assistance. They increasingly turned to the Chancellor, the "keeper of the King's conscience," and the Chancellor soon responded by establishing his own set of tribunals to handle the new business. Over time, the Chancellor and the Chancery Courts developed their own unique causes of action, procedures, and remedies. One of their major innovations in the field of remedies was their willingness to force liable parties to act in particular ways, to demand performance rather than the payment of money.

As a practical matter, one turned to the Chancery Courts when relief in the Law Courts was unavailable or inadequate, but this practical aspect of the situation soon become a substantive requirement. The Law Courts, for their part, had become increasingly jealous of the Chancellor's new, roughly parallel system of justice, which drained away their business and fees. Partly to assuage the Law Courts, and partly to stem the growing flood of business in his own tribunals, the Chancellor soon took the position that one could seek relief in Chancery only if the remedy at law was inadequate. When we in America later borrowed these English ideas and traditions, we quickly discarded (and many states never adopted) a dual system of law courts and equity courts, but the old distinction between legal remedies (damages) and equitable remedies (specific performance and rescission) lived on. And today, because of an old fight between jealous English judges, and a purely accidental difference in the remedies they provided, a request for specific performance or rescission must often be accompanied by the assertion or demonstration that money damages would be inadequate.

The precise situation is a little more complicated, and turns on the distinction between legal and equitable causes of action, that is, between the kinds of lawsuits that English Law Courts traditionally entertained (legal actions) and those that Chancery Courts entertained (equitable actions). (The distinction, by the way, is important for reasons other than remedy: there is a constitutional right to a jury trial in legal actions, but not in equitable actions.) Historically, even in unified court systems that heard both legal and equitable causes of action, American plaintiffs who brought a legal cause of action were entitled *only* to the legal remedy, damages. But judges in these unified court systems, who regularly exercised both legal and equitable jurisdiction, soon began to break down the barriers between the two types of action and their associated remedies. That is, judges began to consider equitable responses to legal causes of action when the circumstances warranted. This is what appears to us today as the preference for damages: in *legal* causes of action, damages are preferred, but specific performance and other equitable relief can be granted if damages would be inadequate. If, on the other hand, the cause of action is equitable, an injunction (or similar order requiring action of some sort) is the appropriate remedy and the plaintiff need not show that damages at law are inadequate. Indeed, damages may not even be available for equitable actions. Even today, if one seeks to enforce an equitable servitude on land — a promise by a neighbor, for example, that he will build and maintain a fence on his own property — a court might not award damages even if the plaintiff wants them, but instead order specific performance.

The breakdown on the legal side of the equation (i.e., providing equitable remedies such as injunctions for legal causes of action) continues to this day. If a plaintiff wants an injunction, courts are increasingly willing to find, in that particular case, that damages are inadequate. An allegation of this sort, with the thinnest supporting argument, is often enough to move a court to issue an injunction. In addition, for whole *classes* of cases, judges have decided that damages are inadequate, so that the plaintiff can have an injunction instead of damages without any special showing at all. In real estate contracts, for example, sellers who later balk at the sale are regularly required (if that is what the buyer wants) to go through with the sale, rather than pay the buyer damages for breaching the contract. The theory is that money simply cannot compensate for the unique loss of the precise property the buyer thought he was getting. If one has contracted to purchase the house at 1316 Lake Street, the house at 385 Pine Street (even with damages) will not do. In sum, the purely historical distinction between legal and equitable causes of action informs the remedial debate — telling us at the very least whether a special showing is needed for one kind of remedy or another — and thus it retains importance for both lawyers and judges.

Apart from this historical distinction, the availability of damages or other relief often depends on the practical concern of what it makes sense to do. If someone *refuses to act* as he is obliged to, it makes sense to require his performance. Thus, if a person refuses to proceed with a contract, we can straightforwardly require that the contract be completed. But if someone *takes an action* that harms another, damages may be the only sensible recourse. If a person hits his neighbor over the head with a garden hose (raising, along with a lump, liability for the intentional tort of battery), what should we demand that the hose-toting tortfeasor do? The deed cannot be undone, so a return to the *status quo ante* is impossible. Is there, then, some other performance that can be required? Should we require that the tortfeasor nurse the victim's wounds? Substitute at the victim's job during recovery? Promise that he won't do it again? Such possibilities seem unusual, unwanted, or inadequate. Better to make the tortfeasor compensate the victim — pay him money — for the losses he has caused: the hospital bills, lost wages, rehabilitation expenses, and so on. As a general rule, damages are more likely to make sense as a response to *action* that creates liability, and more particularly, to action that cannot be reversed. For this reason, damages are the most common response in areas of law, such as tort law, that deal with actions that cause physical harm to others. Conversely, non-damage remedies are more likely to be found in areas of law, such as property and contract law, where *inaction* creates liability, or where actions result in no physical harm and a return to the *status quo ante* is therefore plausible.

Everett's Case

As a general matter, Everett cannot be punished for violating his obligations under tort law or his employment contract, in the sense of being incarcerated or forced to pay a fine to the government. He might, however, be subject to punitive damages under tort law. In the context of an alleged battery, it makes no sense to demand future performance in accord with the obligation, or to demand a return to the *status quo ante*. As a consequence, the only remedy for the tort violation would have to be some form of damages.

For the historical and practical reasons we have just reviewed, damages are almost always available, whether or not they are the preferred remedy. And damages can also be added to other forms of remedy. Thus, for example, if you overstay the end of your lease, I can both evict you from the premises *and* get damages for the period during which you overstayed. If you fail to perform a contract obligation in a timely manner, I might be able to demand both specific performance of your remaining obligations *and* damages for your delay in performance. Damages thus constitute the brooding omnipresence in private law remedies. The question then turns to their measure.

The measure of damages. Lawyers and judges are obsessed with the proper measure of damages. How much a case is "worth" affects whether a lawyer will take it on at all. Once they are involved in a case, plaintiffs' lawyers will seek the highest amount they possibly can and defendants' lawyers will resist the payment of anything at all. Once liability is established, the level of damages is often the last major battle to fight, and victories and defeats at this stage can dramatically affect the parties' ultimate satisfaction. Judges must often make the final determination. And even when juries set the damage award, judges can often raise or lower the amount by granting motions for *additur* (to raise the award) or *remittitur* (to lower it). The law of damages is wide and vast; we will only scratch the surface. Money damages come in three basic forms: nominal, punitive, and compensatory. We will briefly discuss the measure of each.

NOMINAL DAMAGES. Nominal damages — judgment for the plaintiff in the amount of $1.00, for example — are awarded when liability is found, but punitive and compensatory damages are unavailable. They are damages in name only, hence their appellation, and are awarded for the sole purpose of avoiding the unseemly result of liability without remedy. As such, the *measure* of nominal damages is seldom debated. No one really cares whether they are set at one dollar, ten dollars, or twenty-five cents. The fights concern the availability of the other forms.

Everett's Case

A judge or jury might award Everett's co-worker nominal damages if they decided that Everett's actions, while technically constituting a battery, resulted in no physical manifestation of harm and thus caused no compensable injury to the plaintiff.

PUNITIVE DAMAGES. Punitive damages, those awarded to punish the liable party and to deter similar conduct in the future, are limited to certain kinds of wrongdoing, primarily tortious conduct of a particularly egregious character. They are disfavored, as we have seen, because they call upon the state's prerogative to punish someone in cases where the state is acting merely as a referee. They are controversial because, though extracted for a public purpose, they result in private gain — the plaintiffs (and the plaintiffs' lawyers) keep the money. Punitive damages are also controversial because they are very difficult to measure. What dollar amount will punish and deter? Just how much is enough? The answers are seldom straightforward. Punitive damage awards have in fact varied so much, and sometimes reached such astounding amounts, that calls for statutory reform are heard with great frequency.

Everett's Case

If, despite Everett's claims that striking his co-worker was an accident, a judge or jury believes that Everett's action was not only willful, but wanton or malicious, they might award the co-worker punitive damages against Everett. As Everett's lawyers we might move for *remittitur,* seeking to reduce the amount of the damage award.

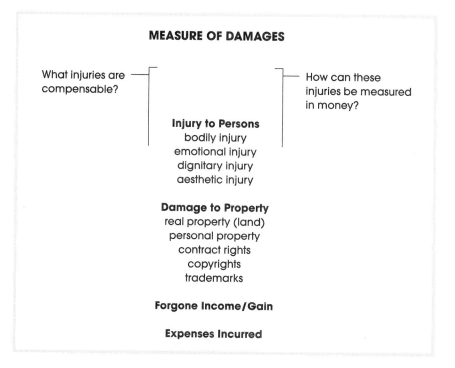

MEASURE OF DAMAGES

What injuries are compensable?

How can these injuries be measured in money?

Injury to Persons
bodily injury
emotional injury
dignitary injury
aesthetic injury

Damage to Property
real property (land)
personal property
contract rights
copyrights
trademarks

Forgone Income/Gain

Expenses Incurred

COMPENSATORY DAMAGES. Compensatory damages are less controversial, but not much easier to measure. Exactly which harms are compensable? Physical harms to persons and property are generally considered compensable, as are financial losses that have been incurred as a result of the breached obligation. We start with physical harms. Usually it is clear whether property has been physically damaged: either the car is dented or it isn't. But there are sometimes close cases. Does the mere presence of pollutants in the air above one's property constitute harm to that property, or must there be a more obvious physical manifestation, such as a blackening of the ground and buildings? Likewise, it is usually clear whether a person has been physically injured: either the victim has a broken arm or she doesn't. But again, there are close cases. Physical *discomfort* is a primary source of concern. Is it enough that one's stomach churns at the thought of the defendant's actions, or must there be more obvious physical manifestations of the discomfort? Sometimes the compensability of physical discomfort turns on the nature of the liability at issue. In tort actions, for example, damages for pain and suffering are generally allowable, but not in contract and property cases. Psychic damages are more problematic still. Emotional distress can be an item for damages in tort cases, if accompanied by outward physical manifestations of that distress, but not in most contract and property cases. Injury to one's sensibilities (aesthetic damages) are not compensable in any field of law. In sum, the fewer the outward physical manifestations of an injury, the less likely it is to be compensated.

Besides physical harm to persons and property, the expenses or other financial costs incurred by the aggrieved party on account of the liable party's action (or inaction) are generally compensable: hospital bills, the cost of obtaining promised goods from a different seller, the loss of future income, and so on. Aggrieved parties have an incentive to imagine all sorts of financial losses or expenses they have incurred on account of the liable party's action, and the primary question here centers on the closeness of the connection between the losses and the wrongful act. In contract law, this concern manifests itself as the distinction between *direct* and *consequential damages,* but the same kind of issue is raised in property and tort cases.

For injuries that are compensable, the question becomes how much compensation is appropriate. The answer is rarely obvious. If a seller refuses to deliver promised goods, and the buyer obtains goods from someone else, we can see that the cost of the substitute goods (less the contract price *not* paid to the breaching seller) could be a perfectly quantifiable amount. Likewise, hospital bills that a tort victim paid to recuperate from a battery can also be perfectly quantifiable. Even in clear cases, however, questions can be raised. Were the substitute goods exactly like the contract goods? If not, how should the numbers be adjusted? Can the battery victim who suffered a bruised leg admit himself to a very expensive private clinic in Gstaad, Switzerland and rightfully expect that the entire bill will be paid? If not, what is a reasonable cost of treatment?

More to the point, whole categories of compensable injuries are either difficult or impossible to quantify. How can lost income be calculated, when the aggrieved party might have lost his job within the next month anyway? How can one measure the loss I incur when my neighbor crosses my property without my permission? How can the pain and suffering one endures possibly be reduced to a sum certain? In an extraordinary number of cases, we are forced to guess and prognosticate, measure the unmeasurable and calculate sums that defy calculation. In the face of these difficulties, we do the best we can, guided partly by common sense and partly by what has been done in the past. We see how lawyers and judges have calculated damages in the past and we do it again. This learning is passed on from lawyer to lawyer by the examples of decided cases and by a growing number of books, monographs, and practice guides. Thick books, for example, have been written on the measurement of damages in securities litigation.

It is easy to make fun of workers' compensation statutes, which reduce the value of particular injuries to a sum certain — loss of finger ($10,000), loss of sight in one eye ($20,000), loss of sight in both eyes ($100,000) —

but all of us in the legal profession do essentially the same thing all the time. The rest of us avoid derision by the simple expedient of acting even more preposterously. Lawyers argue either for huge sums of money (if working for the plaintiff) or for nothing at all (if working for the defendant) and then turn the matter over to someone else. Juries and judges, for their part, work case by case, awarding amounts in splendid isolation from other cases and releasing their results in a form — individual opinions and awards — that are difficult to compare with others — all together an irresistible invitation for wildly disparate results in similar cases.

Everett's Case

If Everett were found to have committed a battery, the question of compensatory damages would lead to many issues and arguments: whether the co-worker sustained any physical injury at all, and if so, how to measure that injury in dollars and cents; whether the co-worker's psychic injuries, if any, were accompanied by sufficient physical manifestations to permit a recovery for pain and suffering, and if so, exactly how to measure that injury in dollars and cents.

Remedies Available in Specific Fields of Law. Certain liabilities arise so frequently that the law responds to them in patterned ways, giving standard sets of remedial options. It is these standard options, not the principles and preferences we have just reviewed, that lawyers and judges most frequently invoke. (The principles and preferences just reviewed helped to create these standard options in the first place and are still used today whenever an obligation or its breach is so unusual that no patterned responses have been developed.) The standardization of remedial options is most pronounced in the grand old categories of the common-law — contracts, property, and tort — as well as in the field of commercial debt. We will spend a few moments on each field.

Contracts. As we have seen before, the standard remedies for contract breaches are specific performance, rescission, and damages. There are standard rules for their availability: damages are always available; rescission requires a material breach; and specific performance can be had only if money damages would be inadequate. Furthermore, particular kinds of contracts and breaches are so common that we have developed more specifically tailored options. Contracts for the sale of goods, for example, are breached in predictable ways and our responses to them fall into standard patterns. Article 2 of the Uniform Commercial Code, legislation enacted in every state, anticipates most breaches of such contracts and specifies the remedial options. Likewise, contracts for the purchase and sale of real property are breached in predictable ways, for which standard responses have been developed, though in this area mainly through judicial decisions rather than legislation.

Property. Property law is brimming with standard remedies, many with unusual names. If one wrongly possesses personal property belonging to another, the owner can respond with an action for *replevin* (for a return of the property) or for *trover* (for damages). If one wrongly possesses real property belonging to another, the owner can respond by bringing an action for *ejectment* (the old common-law remedy) or *unlawful entry and detainer* (a streamlined, statutory remedy) to regain possession. Improper uses of another's real or personal property give rise to the torts of *trespass* and *conversion,* respectively. Improper uses of one's own land give rise to the tort of *nuisance.* Breaches of promise regarding the use of land are usually handled either as the violation of a *real covenant* (damages only) or an *equitable servitude* (injunction only). Landlord/tenant law provides a wealth of standard options, some of which are unexpected. When a tenant falls behind in the rent, for example, the landlord can not only sue for the rent, which we would expect, but is sometimes permitted (as we saw earlier) to seize the tenant's personal property and hold it as security for payment of the rent — *distress* — or to *terminate the tenancy* entirely and begin eviction. When a tenant overstays the end of a lease, the landlord can not only sue to evict or get damages, which we would expect, but can instead choose to hold the tenant to an entirely new tenancy. Tenants, too, have special remedies. When landlords violate their obligations to keep the premises habitable, the tenant can not only sue for damages or specific performance, which we would expect, but can also withhold part of the rent, or repair the condition and deduct the cost of repair from future rent payments. The precise conditions under which these special remedies can be invoked is a major preoccupation of landlord/tenant law.

Torts. Tort remedies are simple by comparison. Because most tort liability involves injury to persons or property, the wrongdoer cannot, practically speaking, put things back the way they were (return to the *status quo ante*) or do something useful (forced performance) except pay for the damage she caused. As a consequence, most tort liability is remedied by the award of damages. Assault, battery, libel, slander, conversion, trespass, nuisance, negligence, and the intentional infliction of emotional distress are most often handled in this way, although performances of certain types are sometimes required. In a libel case, for example, the plaintiff might receive not only damages for the injury to her reputation, but also the defendant's public retraction of the harmful statements. Tort law is also home to many self-help remedies, especially for those torts that threaten harm to persons or property. One can defend oneself against a battery or physically remove a trespasser. These options, however, are tightly controlled, and a review of those controls is a standard part of the first-year course in torts. In most states, for example, one cannot protect property (i.e., prevent or stop the tort of trespass) by shooting the trespasser.

Debt. Debt and its repayment have long animated the work of lawyers and judges, and debtor/creditor law has spawned a number of remedies both obvious and arcane. The dominant, recurring problem is sadly predictable: the debtor can't or won't repay the money owed the creditor at the time it is due. When that occurs, creditors can sue for the payment of the debt, as we would expect. But this *action for debt* is often insufficient because the debtor simply hasn't got the money. Creditors want more and the law has given it to them: the ability to force the sale of some of the debtor's property and use the proceeds to satisfy the debt, a process known as *levy, execution, and sale.* Creditors have found even these additional facilities inadequate or undesirable, and therefore frequently seek to arrange security for the debt at the time it is incurred. That is, they seek to secure repayment of the debt by taking an interest in particular items of the debtor's property, actually holding that property as a *pawn* or *pledge,* or leaving it in the debtor's possession and taking a *secured interest* (in goods) or a *mortgage* (for land). The law of secured transactions and mortgages has been developed in elaborate detail, setting out when and how creditors can take such interests in the first place, and, in the event of nonpayment, when and how they can force the sale of the subject property and make use of the proceeds. We also respond to debt with the entirely different regime of *bankruptcy,* with its own special processes and remedies.

We have reviewed the standard remedial options in contract, property, tort, and debtor/creditor law because they are basic, because they illustrate what standard options can look like, and because students are likely to meet them early in their careers. All fields of private law, however, have tended to develop at least a few standard options, and most law school courses in these fields — usually upper-division electives — spend some time on remedial questions. Admiralty law and corporate law, for example, have developed standard responses to oft-recurring liabilities. For our purposes, however, it is enough to review the principles and preferences underlying all private law remedies and to see how they are applied in a few major fields.

Changes by the Parties' Agreement. Private parties can agree to limit or expand the remedies available to them when liabilities arise. Such agreements are a common feature of leases, lending documents, and contracts of all sorts. They are common whenever parties voluntarily establish a legal relationship. As a consequence, they play a large role in contract law, debtor/creditor law, and some areas of property law. They are less important in tort law, simply because tortfeasors and their victims are less likely to have established a special legal relationship before the tort occurs. I've usually never even met the guy who scrapes my fender in the parking lot, much less have reached a prior agreement with him about how to handle the tort liability arising out of auto accidents.

Remedial changes by agreement are so varied that they are hard to summarize. Typical changes, however, include limitations on the *type* of damages allowable. Many contracts disallow *consequential* damages, i.e., money payments for injuries not caused directly by the breach, but which follow from it in some way. Thus, in a contract to supply parts to an automobile manufacturer, the contract may permit the recovery of direct damages (the automaker's cost, say, of obtaining the parts from a different supplier if the original one fails to deliver), but deny consequential damages (the costs, say, of down time and lost production while the manufacturer scrambles to find an alternative source). Another common remedial change is a provision for *liquidated* damages. Leases and contracts often provide that, upon the breach of a particular obligation, the breaching party will pay a specified amount of money to the nonbreaching party. The level of damages is thus reduced to a sum certain. Such a provision is almost always combined with a waiver of other remedies, so that the cost of a breach is firmly fixed. Leases of real estate typically contain a number of remedy-changing clauses, the most important of which is probably the landlord's ability to terminate the lease if the tenant violates any of its obligations. This is often important to landlords, because under the common-law in most states, a tenant's breach of a lease does *not* give the landlord the right to bring the tenancy to an end and evict the tenant.

Remedial agreements, when they appear, generally raise issues of *interpretation* and *validity*. The interpretive issues — determining exactly how the standard remedial options have been modified — are handled like those regarding any authoritative text. This makes the analysis predictable, but not easy, as several pages in the previous chapter demonstrate. As before, we are concerned about plain meaning, drafters' intent, and purposes. In addition, we are concerned with a particular type of clarity. The law is jealous of its remedies, and the *waiver* of a standard option must generally be made explicit. If the waiver is not explicit, we are likely to find that all of the standard options remain.

When clearly stated, remedial changes are generally enforced according to their terms. Within a wide range, we simply let people do what they want. Yet there are limits, and two such limits are commonly encountered. First, the parties must agree to the changes, which makes those changes *contractual*. As such, they can be denied effect on the same grounds as any contractual provision: for lack of consideration, fraud, overreaching, and unconscionability, among others. Second, remedial changes can be denied on the ground of public policy, a ground that can take several forms. As we saw in the last chapter, certain kinds of *liability* cannot be waived. As a consequence, we will not enforce an agreement that retains such a liability, but waives all remedies when it occurs. Thus, if a landlord cannot exonerate himself from liability for failing to maintain the demised premises in a habitable condition, we would not enforce a lease provision that, instead of waiving the liability, denies the tenant any recourse when the premises become uninhabitable. In addition, an agreed-upon remedy that *penalizes* one of the parties will often be denied effect. Liquidated damage provisions, for example, will not be enforced if the agreed-upon sum bears no relation, or only a tenuous relation, to the actual damages one could reasonably anticipate. If a contract for the purchase of an $80,000 house fixed liquidated damages for the buyer's breach at $40,000, the provision would probably be considered a penalty, and the seller's attempts to demand such a sum would be futile. Finally, experience has taught us that certain private relationships — landlord/tenant, creditor/debtor, merchant/consumer — often arise in circumstances of inequality, and remedial changes in those relationships receive special scrutiny as a matter of public policy. When a tenant, debtor, or consumer agrees to waive a remedy, or any time a landlord, creditor, or merchant has by agreement obtained a new one, such changes will often be scrutinized for fairness, and if found wanting, denied effect.

Everett's Case

Everett's employment contract can be understood as imposing a particular remedy for a particular breach of duty. That is, Everett's contractual duty of good conduct, if breached by acts of "moral turpitude," can be remedied by termination from employment (and not, for example, by an award of damages or specific performance). Such an agreement is usually upheld by the courts, unless (unlikely here) it is found to contravene an overriding public policy.

HOW CAN THE AVAILABLE REMEDIES BE ENFORCED?

We have seen that remedies respond to liability in many ways. They can require the wrongdoer to act in a particular way (either as originally required or in some new way entirely) or permit the aggrieved party to act in ways not otherwise permitted. Further details, as we have also seen, depend on whether public or private obligations are involved. We reviewed the remedies typically associated with international, criminal, and regulatory law, on the public side; and contract, property, tort, and debtor/creditor law, on the private side. Throughout all of this analysis, however, we did not worry very much about how these remedies could be implemented or enforced. But remedies, so crucial to the parties involved, remain abstract until someone takes action. And that someone, as a practical matter, is always the aggrieved party — the state in criminal law, the nonbreaching party in contract law, and so on. Our focus therefore shifts to the perspective of the aggrieved party as we explore the question, "How can the available remedies be effected?"

As a general matter, remedies are implemented and enforced in the following ways:

- the aggrieved party demands that the liable party act in accordance with the law of remedies (perform as originally required, pay damages, make restitution, and so on);
- the aggrieved party takes unilateral action made available by the law of remedies (lock the tenant out of the apartment, sell the debtor's pawned watch, and so on);
- the aggrieved and liable parties negotiate a solution, occasionally with the help of a mediator or conciliator, and reach a settlement on what actions must be taken (a plea bargain for six months jail time, a return of half the security deposit at the end of a lease, and so on); and
- the aggrieved party brings a lawsuit.

The first three responses are both common and important. In most cases, the actual response to civil liability is a demand for action and negotiation and settlement. Only when those methods fail does litigation come into play. As a consequence, good lawyers are almost always skilled negotiators, and law students are well advised to develop their skills early.

The list above is only a rough guide. Some of the listed options are not available in all cases, and other options, sometimes available, are not on the list at all. The precise means for effecting remedies (like the remedies themselves) depend primarily on the nature of the underlying obligation that has been violated. Is it public or private? Is it criminal or regulatory? Is it a matter of contract, property, tort, or debt? We will divide the following discussion along similar lines.

The Enforcement of Public Law Remedies

Remedies Against the State. The implementation of remedies against the state depends in part on what sort of obligation the state has violated and who precisely has been harmed. It will be useful, therefore, to divide the discussion between international and domestic obligations.

HOW REMEDIES ARE ENFORCED

Public Law

Area of Law	Nature of Obligation	Modes of Implementing Remedies

✔ International	State to State	• Unilateral demands for
		  ∘ correct action
		  ∘ reparations
		  ∘ return to *status quo ante*
		
		• Unilateral sanctions
		  ∘ diplomatic
		  ∘ economic
		  ∘ military
		
		• International arbitration
		• International and regional courts
		• National courts

	State to Individual	• Regional human rights courts • UN reporting • Humanitarian intervention
✔ Domestic	State to Individual	• Call for reconsideration • Appeal to superiors • Appeal to courts
	Individual to State	• Police action/detention • Public prosecution • Court conviction and sentencing

International obligations. As we have seen before, international law obliges states to act in particular ways — protect ambassadors, trade fairly, prosecute international hijackers, and so on. When states violate their international obligations, a special remedial regime is called into play. When a state violates obligations owed to *another state,* the offended state can: demand the performance of the obligations in accord with their original tenor, demand new actions (a formal apology, reparations) and take responsive actions of its own (sever diplomatic ties, impose trade sanctions, threaten and employ military force). Offended states are much less likely to invoke the aid of third parties in their efforts at implementation and enforcement. National courts are often not available because states accord each other immunity, with some exceptions, from domestic judicial action. This leaves international institutions and bodies, of which there are few. International arbitration is sometimes invoked, either *ad hoc* or as a result of a prior agreement between the parties, and recourse to the International Court of Justice is sometimes made, though its jurisdiction and powers are extremely limited. Sometimes the United Nations or similar regional organizations are called upon to act, but their jurisdictions and powers are limited as well. Indeed, the lack of third-party enforcement constitutes the most prominent difference between international and domestic legal systems. As a result, the international remedies for many interstate liabilities begin and end with negotiation and settlement, aided (or hindered) by threats of unilateral retaliation. Some of these options bear a family resemblance to domestic methods of enforcement (domestic and international negotiation, domestic damages and international reparations, to cite two examples), but the details are quite different and many options (the recalling of ambassadors) have no domestic equivalent at all.

When states violate their international obligations to *individuals,* a different remedial regime comes into play. Special international courts, of various levels of effectiveness, have been created in Europe, the Americas, and Africa to handle such matters, for both violations of human rights law and economic law. In Europe, for example, there is a European Court of Human Rights (which handles violations of European human rights treaties) as well as a European Court of Justice (which handles violations of European Community law, primarily economic in nature). In addition, the United Nations has developed an elaborate system for monitoring and reporting human rights conditions in member states and new forms of unilateral state action, such as humanitarian intervention, are being developed and debated. Enforcement in domestic courts is also a possibility, although each state is generally free to determine for itself the extent to which it will open its courts for the hearing of international human rights violations. U.S. courts, for a variety of reasons, are generally closed. Again, there are some family resemblances between international and domestic remedial schemes, but the implementation of international human rights law (and a little economic law) has its own unique methods and forums.

Domestic obligations. States can violate their domestic obligations law in many ways — courts can overstep their jurisdictional boundaries, executive branch officials can misapply a statutory requirement, legislatures can pass laws that violate constitutional guarantees, and so on. Whenever this occurs (or is alleged to have occurred) the first step is usually to request the errant governmental body or official to reconsider its action — the standard remedy of demanding that the liable party act in accord with its original obligation. Judges can be moved to reconsider a judgment or ruling, executive branch officials can usually be asked to reverse an earlier action, and legislatures can always be petitioned to repeal or replace offending laws. None of these responses, however, forces a change in any sense, and the likelihood of success is often low. No one likes to admit to mistakes.

If reconsideration is denied, or if the action is reconsidered and reaffirmed, the next step is usually an appeal to superiors. Governments are hierarchical, and any decision, except those made by persons at the top of the hierarchy, is subject to reversal by superiors. What constitutes an appeal to superiors depends on the branch of government involved. In the courts, higher courts review the work of lower courts, and only the federal Supreme Court is entirely immune from such appeal. In the executive branch — in departments, agencies, and bureaus — lines of authority are usually clear and publicly known, with well-developed patterns of appeal. The legislative branch, in contrast, has no relevant hierarchy. When the legislature violates an obligation of the state, as when it passes an unconstitutional law, there is no superior (within the legislative branch) to whom to turn.

Court action is the final option. For *judicial* violations of law, this is the same as an appeal to superiors — a lower court's action is appealed to a higher court. This kind of appeal is both common and well-accepted. For *executive* and *legislative* violations of law, however, an appeal to courts is much more contentious, because it pits one branch of government against another. Although we accept judicial review of government action in principle, our courts proceed cautiously, deferring in several ways to the work of the other branches. First, courts will not usually hear appeals from executive branch action unless the complainant has exhausted the appeal process of the offending agency, department, or bureau (the *exhaustion of remedies* requirement). There is no similar requirement for legislative action, because legislatures have no relevant hierarchy and thus no internal appeal. Second, courts are generally unwilling to intervene in disputes *between* the executive and legislative branches. When the propriety of an action is disputed, and the disputants are members of the legislative and executive branches, judges are likely to demur and refuse action, invoking the *political question doctrine*. The doctrine is often raised, for example, whenever members of Congress question the legality of U.S. military actions not backed by a congressional declaration of war. Finally, courts give those charged with executing and enforcing laws a measure of appreciation in their efforts, and are likely to act only when the impropriety is clear. Thus, for example, when an administrative agency acts on the basis of a statute it is charged with executing, the agency's interpretation of the statute is normally given great weight.

Though not driven by judicial deference to the other branches of government, *standing* is also a recurring concern in court actions against the government. Judges will dismiss a case — any case — on the ground of standing if the plaintiff does not have an individual stake in the outcome of the lawsuit. To invoke judicial enforcement of state obligations, the plaintiff must show that the state's nonconforming actions are of particular importance to it. Standing, though a general requirement, frequently becomes an issue in litigation against the government, when watchdog groups or associations seek to vindicate the rights of their constituencies. The members of a taxpayers' organization, for example, may be harmed by a governmental action, but not the organization representing them. The problem becomes acute when the organization seeking to reverse government action represents interests, like a clean environment, rather than natural or juristic persons. Because trees have no standing, the Sierra Club may have no standing either, when it seeks to reverse government decisions on national forests.

When we go to court, we may seek one of two things: a change in the government's course of action or a declaration that the questioned act is a nullity. When the judicial branch goes awry, we can in principle seek either result, that is, a simple *reversal* of the prior decision (forcing a change of course) or a *reversal and remand* (making the original judgment a nullity, but calling for another lower court hearing and decision). Similarly, when executive branch officials go awry, we can in principle seek either to have the decision declared invalid (making it a nullity) or to get a *mandamus* order against an official, a court order demanding that the official take a particular action (forcing a change of course). In both contexts, courts are more likely to nullify actions rather than require new ones, because this gives the governmental decisionmaker a second chance to get things right, rather than imposing a new solution. When *legislative* action is called into question, as when a law's constitutionality is challenged, there is only one choice of remedy. We can only seek to have the law declared invalid. Generally speaking, a legislature cannot be *forced* to act in a particular way (that is, to pass a law of a particular kind) and any attempt to do so generates a firestorm of controversy. We have seen this, for example, in recent attempts by federal judges to require state legislatures to redraw their electoral districts in particular ways.

In theory, any illegal governmental action is a nullity *from the start* and need not be countenanced by anyone. In theory, one need not take any of the actions we have discussed, but instead simply ignore the offending act. Practically speaking, however, many government actions are impossible to ignore. One risks financial peril and sometimes physical harm by insisting that government action is void and need not be taken into account. It may be true, for example, that a state's attorney licensing board cannot constitutionally ask about one's prior political affiliations, but one risks the ability to practice law if one refuses to answer. It may be true that the police cannot stop citizens on the street without an articulable suspicion about them, but one resists a stop-and-frisk at the risk of physical harm and an unwanted trip to the police station. Formal requests for reconsideration, appeals to superiors, and finally, appeals to courts are usually required.

Everett's Case

Nothing in Everett's situation raises questions about the state's breach of an obligation, international or domestic, so questions about the enforcement of remedies against the state are not germane.

Remedies Against Individuals. When the roles are reversed, that is, when individuals violate their obligations *to* the state, the remedial regime takes on a different cast. As we saw before, the remedies for violations of criminal and regulatory law are in the nature of punishment — the suspension or revocation of licenses, the imposition of fines, incarceration, and sometimes death. But only the state can punish, and thus, when an individual violates an obligation owed to the state, the state is both the aggrieved party and the enforcing body. This duality of function has been a source of great concern, for it makes the state the judge of its own cause. We have reacted to this problem in at least three ways.

First, the Constitution of the United States places a series of limits on public law remedies and how they are enforced. Similar restrictions appear in state constitutions. The Fifth Amendment to the Constitution, for example, requires the use of a *grand jury* to initiate proceedings in particularly serious crimes, protects against *double jeopardy* (being tried for the same offense twice) and *self-incrimination* (being forced to testify against oneself), and generally guarantees *due process of law.* The Sixth Amendment, aimed especially at criminal proceedings, requires a *speedy, public trial* by jury and guarantees the *assistance of counsel.* The Eighth Amendment prohibits the setting of *excessive bail or fines,* along with *cruel and unusual punishment.* Each of these constitutional guarantees has been subject to intensive judicial interpretation over the years and a large body of interpretive doctrine has been developed. As a consequence, the enforcement of public law remedies against individuals provides a rich mine of constitutional questions and argument.

Second, we respond to the state's dual role in criminal and regulatory law by dividing the pursuit and enforcement of remedies between different government organs and officials, often between different branches of government. The pursuit of remedies is usually given to the executive branch and the enforcement of remedies to the courts. The most serious of penalties — prison and death sentences — can *only* be imposed through courts, and *any* loss of liberty initiated by the executive branch — arrest and detention pending trial, for example — must eventually be approved by the courts. When members of the executive branch are given both pursuit and enforcement functions, as is more common in regulatory law, we often divide those functions between different officials, giving the pursuit of remedies to one and their enforcement to another. Thus, many government agencies employ one group of officials to pursue regulatory violations and another group of quasi-judicial officials, *administrative law judges,* to impose remedies or review their imposition by others. In addition, almost all regulatory actions are ultimately appealable to the courts.

Third and finally, we react to the state's dual role in criminal and regulatory law by carefully defining the procedures to be followed. The enforcement of remedies in criminal law, for example, is characterized by a formal prosecution: the filing of an official complaint (an information or indictment) followed by a trial and sentencing, each replete with a series of constitutionally and statutorily required procedures. Legal debate often centers around these procedures: Were grand jury proceedings necessary to initiate the prosecution? If so, was an indictment returned? Was the trial speedy? Was the evidence introduced at trial properly admitted? and so on. Procedure is crucial in regulatory enforcement as well. Whether remedies are imposed by administrative officials or the courts, the required procedures are set out, usually in great detail, in legislative enactments, regulations, and ordinances. As in criminal proceedings, the legal questions center around these procedures: Were they followed? Were they constitutional? Was there any abuse of discretion? and so on.

Everett's Case

Any criminal sanctions against Everett for assault can only come through a court determination; even a plea bargain (and its consequences) must be approved by the court. Judicial proceedings themselves would be hedged in with a series of protections regarding double jeopardy, a speedy public trial by jury, and prohibitions against excessive bail and fines, and cruel and unusual punishment. If the offense charged is serious enough, Everett would be guaranteed assistance of counsel.

The Enforcement of Private Law Remedies

The issues are different in private law. The state leaves center stage, no longer a principal participant, but rather an umpire or referee. When private liability arises and private remedies come into play, the two parties involved — liable and aggrieved — can take many actions that do not involve the state. It therefore makes sense to begin by asking what remedies can be invoked before either side repairs to the courts or other officials for vindication.

HOW REMEDIES ARE ENFORCED

Private Law

Liability Arises

⇓

Self-help/Self-defense
Unilateral Demand for Satisfaction

⇓

Court-Ordered Remedy (Judgment)

⇓

Enforcement of Judgment

⇓

Recognition and Enforcement of Foreign Judgments

Remedies Outside of Court. When liability under private law arises, the aggrieved party can almost always take some remedial actions immediately. For example, the standard remedies for material breach of contract include damages, specific performance, and rescission. When there is such a breach of contract, the aggrieved, nonbreaching party can therefore choose among several courses of action. One can invoke the remedy of damages by ceasing performance and demanding compensation for the losses sustained; the remedy of specific performance by continuing performance and demanding that the breaching party complete the contract as originally agreed; or the remedy of rescission by declaring the contract a nullity (releasing both parties from any obligations under it) and demanding that the breaching party take whatever actions are required to return the situation to the *status quo ante*. Likewise, if a tenant stays past the expiration of a lease, the landlord can invoke the available remedies by choosing to: (1) demand possession and damages; or (2) declare the tenant bound to a new tenancy. Court actions need not be filed to implement any of the contract and property remedies just described, and if the liable party responds as demanded, the remedial work has come to an end. It is therefore crucial to ask, in any particular case, how the available remedies can be pursued outside of court.

Some remedies can be pursued so effectively outside of court that the second step of court enforcement may never be necessary. Thus, if a house buyer breaches the contract by failing to tender the purchase price when promised, the seller can declare the contract at an end and retain the buyer's earnest money as damages: the contract has been terminated and damages have been obtained just as effectively and forcefully as if the seller had gone to court and received a judgment on similar terms. Likewise, if a tenant falls behind in the rent, and (in states that permit it) the landlord removes the tenant's belongings and changes the locks, the tenant will have been denied possession of the premises just as effectively and forcefully as if the sheriff had physically removed the tenant. If a pawned watch is not redeemed, the pawnbroker can retain the watch, resell it, and keep the proceeds, recovering its loan to the original owner just as effectively as if the pawnbroker had gone to court and received a judgment on the debt. This does not mean, however, that courts will never become involved. The *liable* party (the breaching home-buyer, the tenant with rent in arrears, the person who pawned the watch) might litigate the propriety of the aggrieved party's actions. But this shifts the burden of court action to the liable party, and the aggrieved party has already received immediate satisfaction. If the court case never comes, the satisfaction remains permanent.

In still other cases, *arbitration* can be the primary mode of enforcement. Agreements to arbitrate can be made ahead of time, as in the context of a long-term commercial contract, or *ad hoc,* after an alleged liability has arisen. Such agreements can specify whether arbitration is exclusive or nonexclusive (that is, required or optional) and whether it is binding or nonbinding (that is, whether the arbitral award constitutes a final decision on the merits or merely a recommendation to the parties). Arbitration agreements are common in international contracts and several kinds of domestic ones, including brokerage contracts between stockbrokers and customers.

Agreements to arbitrate raise questions of interpretation and enforcement. The interpretive questions are handled as they always are, with potential recourse to the plain meaning of the agreement's words, the intent of the parties, and the purposes for which the arbitral agreement was made. The enforceability of such agreements is a bit less predictable. Federal and state courts vary in their willingness to require exclusive, binding arbitration, even when the parties have agreed to it. The federal courts are the most willing to uphold such agreements, though some states remain hostile, permitting parties to avoid agreed-upon arbitration and repair to the courts whenever they wish to do so. Even hospitable courts can deny the enforcement of arbitration agreements if they are marked by fraud, overreaching, or unconscionability. If the agreement to arbitrate is not enforceable, or if there has been no agreement at all, the aggrieved party must turn to the courts.

Everett's Case

If Everett's employer believes that Everett violated his duties under his contract of employment, it could invoke the contractual (and nonjudicial) remedy of firing him. If Everett's co-worker believes that Everett committed a battery, the co-worker could (outside of court) demand the payment of damages. In either case, the proper remedy might be settled by arbitration (a particularly common mode of remedial settlement in labor disputes).

Remedies in Court. Despite the power of remedial action outside of court, it often happens that the liable party balks, refusing to take the actions demanded by the aggrieved party. (The liable party may even believe that the *other* party is the wrongdoer.) In such cases, the party who feels itself aggrieved must proceed to governmental enforcement. Who can be asked to help, and how they can help, are the questions to which we now turn.

First stage enforcement: complaint to judgment. When an aggrieved party seeks the judicial enforcement of a remedy, the court will not order that remedy without first confirming the underlying liability. Thus, for example, a court will not order you to return my Airstream trailer without first determining that you are holding it in violation of my ownership rights. Similarly, a court will not require Susan to make the final delivery of dental floss to Joe's Steak House without first determining that she is contractually obliged to do so. Because of this need to inquire into liability first, remedy-granting courts must have *jurisdiction to adjudicate.* Aggrieved parties who wish to enforce a remedy must therefore find a court that has it. We recall from the last chapter that a court may lack jurisdiction to adjudicate for many reasons: because the parties have insufficient contacts with the territory in which the court sits; because the case is not amenable to judicial resolution; because an action or agreement of the parties has precluded judicial action; because resolution of the issues in that court would be inefficient; because judicial proceedings in that forum would be unfair to one of the parties; or because other courts or other branches of government are constitutionally or legislatively charged with hearing the kind of dispute at issue. It could be that *no* court has jurisdiction to adjudicate. If not, then no court will provide a remedy.

Assuming there are courts with jurisdiction to adjudicate, the question turns to finding the right one. Litigants may be required to turn to the federal system exclusively, state systems exclusively, or may have the option of proceeding in either. Within each system there will be several options. Federal trial courts are divided between district courts (courts of general jurisdiction) and more specialized courts, like the Tax Court, the Court of International Trade, and bankruptcy courts. State courts, in like manner, are typically divided between courts of general jurisdiction and special jurisdiction — municipal courts, traffic courts, small-claims courts, probate courts, justice-of-the-peace courts, and so on. At both the federal and state levels, there are usually several courts of each type, geographically dispersed, and the challenge will be to find the right courthouse. In all cases, the overriding questions will be: does the chosen court have authority over the parties (personal jurisdiction), does it have authority to hear the type of case at issue (subject matter jurisdiction), and is it in the right place (venue)? If the aggrieved party gets to the right court (and is correct about liability), she will get a judgment that imposes a remedy: "judgment for the plaintiff for $100,000," "judgment for the plaintiff: defendant is hereby ordered to return the Airstream trailer to the plaintiff," and so on.

   Second-stage enforcement: post-judgment relief. A court judgment or arbitral award may be enough to persuade the liable party to comply. But what if it isn't? What if, despite the judgment or award, the defendant digs in her heels and refuses to meet the remedial demands? In that case, a second round of enforcement begins. The holder of the judgment or award must go to court and seek enforcement of the judgment or award itself.

   There is a large body of law on the enforcement of judgments, specifying what can be done when a defendant refuses to satisfy a court's judgment. When a defendant refuses to pay a damage award, the plaintiff (with or without a court's help) might be able to: force the sale of the defendant's assets; require a bank to turn over money held in the defendant's accounts; and garnish the defendant's wages. Exactly what can be done to enforce a judgment varies between federal and state judicial systems and from state to state. Generally speaking, however, a plaintiff who receives a damage award from a court becomes a *judgment creditor,* and is entitled to the same remedies as any other creditor with unpaid debts. (In some cases, judgment creditors get an even better deal — taking precedence over regular creditors when there isn't enough of the debtor's money to go around, or getting special ways to collect their debts not available to other creditors.) Alternatively, when a defendant refuses a court's demand that she take a particular action (say, return the Airstream trailer to the plaintiff), the plaintiff can usually return to court and ask that the defendant be held in *contempt,* thereby subjecting the defendant to fines and possible jail time until she complies.

   Likewise, there is a body of law on the recognition and enforcement of arbitral awards. In many states and in the federal system, this law provides that arbitral awards can be enforced just like court judgments if the original arbitral agreement and the subsequent arbitral proceedings meet certain standards concerning fairness and due process. In other states, arbitral awards are not treated so kindly and the ability to enforce them through the courts is less certain. When one seeks to enforce an arbitral award, the first step is to show that it qualifies for treatment like a court judgment. If it does, then the analysis switches to how the award (like any court judgment) can be enforced.

This second stage of remedial action — the enforcement of judgments and arbitral awards — requires a court with power over people and property, a court with the authority to bring the defendant into custody, for example, or to force the sale of land and personal goods. This authority is known as the *jurisdiction to enforce*. It is different from and narrower than the jurisdiction to adjudicate that sustains an original lawsuit. As a consequence, the court that *issues* a judgment may not be able to *enforce* it. Thus, I might bring a contract action against you in a Texas state court and receive a judgment against you along with an award of damages, but if you leave the state and take all your assets with you, the Texas courts cannot force you to pay. I must instead proceed to a court in whose territory you or your assets *can* be found, and seek further assistance. Generally speaking, the jurisdiction to enforce is highly territorial. Courts simply cannot compel persons to act, or deal effectively with their property, when those persons or property are located outside their territory.

As a practical matter, the distinction between the jurisdiction to adjudicate and the jurisdiction to enforce often requires plaintiffs to go to one court for determinations of liability and remedy, and to another court for enforcement of the judgment. Plaintiffs may be required to take action in two steps because they guessed wrong about the availability of the defendant or the defendant's assets in the original forum, or because the defendant or the defendant's assets moved after the commencement of the suit. Plaintiffs might even *choose* to proceed in two steps, despite the additional effort and expense, because they seek the friendliest or most convenient forum for the initial determinations of liability and remedy, and then hope to use the favorable judgment as the basis for enforcement action elsewhere.

This two-step process is addressed in a body of law concerning the *recognition and enforcement of foreign judgments*. (This body of law must be carefully distinguished from the earlier — and similarly named — body of law regarding the enforcement of judgments. That first body of law tells a court how to force a recalcitrant litigant to comply with the court's original judgment.) This second body of law tells a court when it is obliged to respond to the actions of courts in other jurisdictions, describing when it can or must recognize a foreign court's liability and remedy determination and help in its enforcement. Some of this law is constitutional, some statutory, and some a matter of common law developed by the courts themselves. At the constitutional level, the full faith and credit clause of the federal constitution requires that each state *recognize* the judgments of sister states. That is, each state is obliged to treat such judgments as if they issued out of its own courts (though it is not generally required to *enforce* those judgments in exactly the same way as the original court would). In contrast, neither federal nor state courts are constitutionally obliged to recognize or enforce the judgments of courts outside the United States, but they often do so when certain statutory or common-law requirements are met. This recognition and enforcement of non-U.S. judgments is often labeled a matter of *comity.*

When a plaintiff takes action in two steps, seeking a judgment of liability and remedy in one court and the enforcement of the judgment in another, questions regarding the recognition and enforcement of foreign judgments and the enforcement of judgments simply pile on top of each other. Thus, when one marches into court with the judgment of another court, the first issue is whether the original court's judgment will be recognized. If it is, the second issue centers on how the second court will enforce that judgment. The courts of Indiana, for example, are constitutionally required to recognize my Texas judgment against you, but exactly *how* they will enforce that judgment depends on Indiana's own statutory and common-law rules. Indiana might order the sale of your home and apply the net proceeds to my judgment, even though a Texas court would not.

Everett's Case

If Everett wants to sue his employer for wrongful discharge, or if Everett's co-worker wants to sue Everett for battery, each must, at a minimum, find a court with jurisdiction to adjudicate (because no court will apply a remedy unless it has determined the existence of liability). Even if that court finds liability and imposes a remedy — Everett's reinstatement with back pay; the payment by Everett of compensatory damages to his co-worker — the plaintiffs may well need to enforce their judgment against a recalcitrant defendant. The enforcing court could be the same or a different court from the one used originally.

The Problem of Delay

The great impediment to all remedial action is *delay.* All of the things that aggrieved parties want — initial determinations of liability and remedy, and the enforcement of judgments by the same or different courts — can be blocked by the passage of time. Courts otherwise willing and able to help will refuse to do so if the relevant *statute of limitations* has run. Court action of any kind, both criminal and civil, can only be commenced within a certain period after the liability has arisen. Once that period has passed, the court will grant no remedy nor even decide the case at all. In equitable actions, even lawsuits brought within the statutory time limit can be blocked by *laches,* which blocks the pursuit of equitable actions after an unreasonable time has passed.

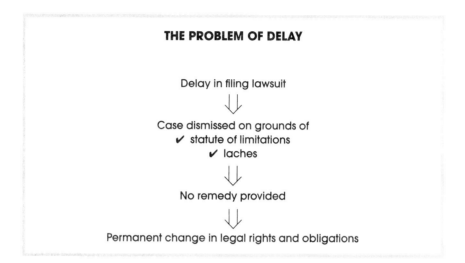

THE PROBLEM OF DELAY

Delay in filing lawsuit

⇓

Case dismissed on grounds of
✔ statute of limitations
✔ laches

⇓

No remedy provided

⇓

Permanent change in legal rights and obligations

Statutes of limitations raise questions of two predictable types: Which time limit applies? Has that time limit expired? The relevant period of time within which an action must be brought depends on the nature of the obligation violated. Actions for the possession of real estate are often permitted for 20 years (or sometimes longer) after the cause of action arises; actions in response to contract and tort liabilities must usually be brought sooner, within 5, 3, or even 1 year after the cause of action arises. The precise time limits are set out in each state and many distinctions are made. For property causes of action in Illinois, for example, there are (among others) 75, 40, 20, 10, 7, 5 and 4 year statutory periods, the applicability of each depending on the precise nature of the cause of action, what the plaintiff wants, and other circumstances.

Finding the right period is just the beginning of the analysis. Whether that limit has passed depends on when the cause of action arose. This usually refers to the time when the defendant first violated his obligations by taking or failing to take the required action, what we have called the creation of liability. But there are some surprises. Sometimes we do not consider a cause of action to have arisen until the plaintiff knew or should have known that the defendant violated an obligation, instead of when the violation actually occurred. This *discovery rule* delays the commencement of the statute's running (giving the plaintiff more time to sue) because one can only know, or reasonably be expected to know, about a liability sometime *after* it has come into existence.

Debate about the discovery rule centers on whether it is available for the particular statute of limitations at issue (it often is not); whether it is available for the particular case at hand (it often is not); and when the plaintiff in fact knew or (now guessing) should have known that the cause of action arose.

The statutory time limit can also be lengthened by *tolling*. Statutes of limitations commonly provide that their commencement will be delayed or their running suspended for reasons ranging from the minority or other disability of the plaintiff, the plaintiff's military service abroad, or the defendant's physical absence from the state or country. The precise grounds for tolling vary state by state and statute by statute. Once one determines that a ground for tolling has arisen, the issues are mainly factual: Was the plaintiff a minor when the cause of action arose? Was the defendant in fact absent from the state or the country at that time? and so on.

The doctrine of *laches,* sometimes applied in equitable causes of action, is juristically simpler than statutes of limitations, but much less predictable in its application. The doctrine of laches provides, in a general way, that a plaintiff may not pursue a lawsuit if that plaintiff's delay has been unreasonable, even if the relevant statute of limitations has not yet expired. What makes a delay too long is the mystery. It often has something to do with the reasons for the plaintiff's delay (were they unscrupulous or unsavory?), in combination with some special harm to the defendant that could have been avoided had the plaintiff acted more quickly. Its mystery, and its effect of reducing the time limits otherwise set by the legislature, has largely consigned the doctrine of *laches* to the trash bin of legal history, but when an action is equitable, one never knows when the doctrine might be pulled out of the trash, dusted off, and applied.

Everett's Case

Both the state's criminal action and the co-worker's civil tort action are subject to (different) statutes of limitation. If the statutory periods expire without the relevant lawsuits having been filed, all remedial action against Everett will be blocked. Because neither action is based on an equitable cause of action, the doctrine of laches would not apply in this case.

Statutes of limitations are remedial in form, often cast in terms such as: "No suit may be brought unless within five (5) years after the cause of action arose." So close, however, are the links between legal rights and judicial remedies, that the denial of a judicial remedy because of the passage of time often results in the extinction of the underlying right. When someone wrongfully possesses another's property for a sufficient number of years, for example, the statute of limitations by its terms simply denies the original owner *judicial* enforcement of his claim against the trespasser. If that were all it did, the original owner could still engage in self-help to retrieve the property or regain possession, since self-help does not, by definition, require court action to implement. But we have long held that extinguishing the possibility of a *lawsuit* extinguishes the *underlying property right*. Once the statute has run, the erstwhile owner can do *nothing at all* to vindicate his claim. Without any judicial remedy, he is found to have no right, and the adverse possessor becomes the owner. "No remedy in the courts" becomes "no right at all" — an astonishing display of legal magic and a suitable place to conclude our discussion of remedies.

SUMMARY

- Remedies can respond to liability *before* or *after* that liability has arisen.

- *Anticipatory* or *preventive* remedies (e.g., temporary restraining orders and preliminary injunctions) are relatively rare and require a special showing by the person who seeks to have them imposed.

- Remedies respond to liability by:
  - requiring the *wrongdoer* to act in a particular way; or
  - permitting the *aggrieved party* to act in a special way not normally available

- The remedies available in any particular situation depend on:
  - whether the obligation violated is *public* or *private*
  - if public, whether the wrongdoer is the *state* or an *individual*
  - if private, whether the cause of action is *legal* or *equitable,* the *nature* of the breach, and the *current situation* of the parties

- Although courts are important players in the world of remedies, a great deal of remedial decisionmaking goes on outside of courts, and much of the work inside of courts does not involve remedies (e.g., declaratory judgments, status determinations, & supervisory work over trusts and estates).

- Each major area of law has developed a standard set of remedial options, and the study of those options is covered thoroughly in most law school courses.

- The main remedies *against the state* are:
  - a refusal to recognize the legal validity of the offending action
  - forcing the state (or its officials) to reverse course and act in accord with the state's obligations

- The main remedies *by the state* against individuals involve punishment of various sorts, including fines and incarceration. Individuals are protected from an overzealous state by:
  - constitutional limitations on prosecution and punishment
  - dividing the power to prosecute from the power to convict among different governmental bodies or actors
  - adherence to procedural requirements

- *Private law remedies* include:
  - forcing performance of the original obligation
  - returning the situation to the *status quo ante*
  - compensating the aggrieved party

- *Damages* are the preferred remedy in most private civil actions, and come in three types:
  - nominal
  - punitive
  - compensatory

- *Compensatory damages* raise predictable issues about
  - which kinds of injury are compensable at all (physical harm to persons and property, emotional and other psychic harm, etc.)
  - how the compensable injuries can be quantified in money

- In private transactions, the parties can generally agree on which remedies will be available, although there are public policy limits on such agreements.

- Many remedies can be implemented and enforced *without recourse to the courts.*

- When asked to provide a legal remedy, the court must have both *jurisdiction to adjudicate* (to find liability) and *jurisdiction to enforce* (to impose a remedy).

- After a judgment is given in a particular case, *further remedial action* may be required because the losing party refuses to pay the judgment.

- In such a case, the owner of the judgment (the winner of the case) can seek to *enforce the judgment* by selling the loser's property, garnishing the loser's wages, or similar action. If the loser's assets are in a jurisdiction other than the original court, the owner of the judgment must go to the court where the assets are and seek *recognition and enforcement of the foreign judgment.*

- *Delay* in bringing a lawsuit can be one of the greatest obstacles to obtaining a judicial remedy for liability; and lawyers must be careful to meet the filing deadlines provided in *statutes of limitations.*

From Questions to Answers

(On Legal Argument)

THIS CHAPTER

- Leaves behind the three great questions of legal analysis and concentrates on the answers

- Explains how legal arguments, like legal questions, fall into predictable patterns, and why some arguments are better than others

- Describes each of the primary virtues in legal argument, with special emphasis on those virtues not commonly found in everyday argument

We have finished our survey of legal questions: Is there a law? Has it been violated? What can be done about it? We have seen that each question breaks down into several subsidiary ones, and each of those subsidiary questions into more questions still. Questions, questions, and more questions. If we deal with these questions only as we meet them, typical in both legal study and practice, they can overwhelm and confuse us. But when pulled together and put in their places, they make sense. They fit. The law may be a jungle, but not a jumble.

Pulled together and organized, this mass of questions provides the *structure* of legal analysis. This structure gives us some confidence that we understand what we are doing when we tackle legal problems. It helps us to know where we are and where we might go next. But this structure, for all its virtues, is not enough. As lawyers and judges, we work with real people with real problems, giving advice, helping to solve problems, marshaling arguments on their behalf and deciding cases. For all of this work, knowing the questions is not enough. We have to give answers, too.

How we give those answers depends on the role we are playing, as litigators, transactional lawyers, or judges, and limited by the ethical and professional obligations we owe to our clients and society more generally. Once litigators know the right questions to raise, they already know the answers they want — the ones that will help their client win the lawsuit. Is there a law? Yes! Has it been violated? Indeed it has! What should be done about it? A damage award of at least $6,000,000! The defendant's lawyer, of course, will have other answers in mind. Each must try to convince the other that she is right, hoping to discourage further proceedings or provoke an early settlement in her client's favor. If neither side is convinced, each will bring her arguments to court.

Transactional lawyers proceed differently. Clients walk into the office with plans, more or less well-defined, on what they want to accomplish — provide care for an elderly father, make a will, buy a house, file a corporate tax return, merge two businesses. The transactional lawyer wants her client to succeed. Like the litigator, therefore, once she knows the questions to ask, she also knows the answers she would like, and thinks about the arguments she would deploy to sustain them. But planning allows more room for adjustments. A client's objective can often be attained in more than one way. As a consequence, the planning lawyer often has the luxury of taking a more objective view of the situation, evaluating the strength of her various arguments and answers, and recommending the course of action about which she is most confident.

Judges must decide which answers are correct. Their role, unlike that of litigators and transactional lawyers, does not predispose them to a particular answer. They serve no client with a problem or objective to reach. This absence of predispositions, this impartiality, makes legal questions harder to answer. Judges cannot rely on the "push" from a client's interests. Instead they must review the arguments for and against the answers proposed to them, choosing the answers that seem best supported. They work without a net.

Despite their differences, all three roles involve *advocacy* and *decision-making*. Transactional lawyers, as we noted above, see a regular mix of both. Litigators, though primarily advocates, must decide matters as well. They must evaluate the strength of the opposing side's arguments to decide whether to settle. They must evaluate the strength of their own arguments to decide which points to press in negotiation, which to present in court, and which make on appeal. Judges, although primarily decisionmakers, must also advocate, marshaling arguments for their position in the public decisions they render. In other words, all of the roles require an ability to *make* and *evaluate* legal argument.

Some arguments are more effective than others. All lawyers and judges sense this and the good ones know exactly why. Legal arguments are more effective when they display certain values, when they invoke certain principles traditionally revered in legal debate. This chapter reviews these influential values and principles. Some of them are obvious, some less so, and many run at cross-purposes. Knowing the questions to ask is not enough. We must also know what makes some answers better than others.

IN THE TRENCHES

Most legal battles are fought in the trenches, with fairly straightforward arguments about the state of the facts and the state of the law. It is easy to see why this should be so. Most judges have a large docket of cases to handle; most lawyers are busy. The last thing that appeals to a presiding judge or to fellow lawyers in planning and negotiation is the attempt to characterize every issue as a clash of titanic principles. Just tell us whether the decedent signed the will; leave Patrick Henry out of it. Most legal business is routine and correctly treated as such. Any administrative system — like the administration of justice — comes to treat common cases routinely. It would be strange, and too expensive for clients and litigants, if this were not the case. Routine, however, doesn't mean that details are ignored and that everyone is sleepwalking; it just means that molehills remain molehills. A case that can be decided by the simple application of a city ordinance is settled in exactly that way.

Lawyers first argue facts and law, trying to persuade a judge (or the party across the table in negotiation) that the relevant facts and the applicable law require a holding (or agreement) in their favor. Lawyers introduce into evidence those facts most favorable to their client's cause. They present the facts

WHAT MAKES A GOOD LEGAL ARGUMENT?

The Virtues	Relevant Questions
Truth	✔ Are the facts faithfully represented? ✔ Are statutes quoted accurately? ✔ Are prior decisions characterized fairly?
Precision	✔ Are there extraneous details in the facts? ✔ Are any important facts left out? ✔ Do the discussions of the law draw all the necessary distinctions?
Coherence	✔ Do the facts make sense? ✔ Are any unusual facts explained? ✔ Have past cases been pulled together in a sensible or plausible way?
Logic	✔ Are there unproven assumptions? ✔ Do the conclusions follow from the premises?

that are introduced in as flattering a way as possible. On the law, they argue about the meaning of statutes and prior court decisions, seeking broader or narrower interpretations of the words that were used, distinguishing away harmful cases, and showing similarities with helpful ones. They seek to show how the facts and law as they have described them require a decision in their client's favor. In these very basic arguments about the facts and the law, the vital ingredients are truth, precision, coherence, and logic.

Truth

We always, ultimately, seek the truth in law or else the whole enterprise loses its value and moral foundation. Lawyers are obliged to tell the truth about the law. They are required by rules of ethics to reveal to courts even harmful precedents that neither the judge nor their opponents have discovered. They are obliged not to lie about the facts. They need not, under all circumstances, reveal everything they know, but *when* they speak, they must tell the truth. As a practical matter, truth-telling inspires trust, and lawyers with reputations for truth-telling enjoy a decided advantage in persuasive ability when dealing with adversaries and judges.

None of this means, of course, that lawyers never lie when they present the facts or the law, but we recognize it as a problem — both moral and professional — when they do. Nor does it mean that truth is a simple thing, that we can always tell the difference between truth and falsehood, for sometimes the truth can never be known, as when clients hide documents and lie about their actions. Nor does it mean that the truth is not sometimes compromised, even necessarily compromised, by other goals like the lawyerly need to preserve a client's secrets. Still, truth remains the imperative by which all other principles and strategies are judged.

Precision

In recitations of both law and facts, precision is highly regarded. Sloppy arguments are bad arguments, even when they are truthfully made. Lawyers and judges are obsessed with precision, an obsession that students confront (often unhappily) from the first day of law school training:

> *Speaker 1:* A person was walking down the street one morning . . .
> *Speaker 2:* An adult or a child?
> *Speaker 1:* A man was walking down the street one morning . . .
> *Speaker 2:* Wait! Was it important that the person was a man? Would anything have been different if it was a woman?
> *Speaker 1:* Okay, okay. An adult was walking down the street one morning . . .
> *Speaker 2:* In the street or on the sidewalk?
> *Speaker 1:* As I was saying, an adult was walking down the sidewalk one morning, when he fell into a hole . . .
> *Speaker 2:* Wait! What kind of a hole? Big? Little? Was it easy to see?

Despite its maddening aspects, there is a point to precision. As we have seen in earlier chapters, questions of liability can turn on the ages of the parties, the location of an incident (telling us *who* might have the relevant obligation or right), and the relative culpability of the parties involved. We have also seen that gender is seldom important.

The law makes all kinds of distinctions between persons and events. One's recitation of law and facts must take account of those distinctions. Otherwise, we do not know all we need to in order to analyze a problem. Conversely, some distinctions are *not* important, and to recite them can be misleading or at least a waste of time. Precision generally forces us to give more details than we would in daily conversation, but also involves knowing when to stop.

Coherence

When presenting the facts of a case — to a colleague, an opposing attorney, or a judge — a lawyer must tell a story. And a good story is infinitely preferable to a bad one. Stories in law, however, are obviously different from stories by Balzac, Hans Christian Anderson, or the Brothers Grimm. Because the primary requisite is truth, fiction — at least obvious fiction — dooms a legal story from the start, even when it improves the plot. So lawyers must start with the facts, the facts they know and the facts they have the interest, will, and investigative skill to discover. Once collected — always imperfectly, always contingently — deciding which facts to recite and which to ignore, which to emphasize and which to slight, deciding how everything shall be connected and explained, requires discernment, judgment, and sometimes art.

Despite the intellectual prejudices of our postmodern world, the law still assumes that the truth is coherent. A good legal story is a coherent story. It has to make sense. In law, things happen in order, motivations are understandable, and what we expect to happen usually happens; the unusual, the unique, and the unexpected must be carefully explained. The legal storyteller, speaking and writing within the bounds of factual truth and expository coherence, labors within a more constricted range of mobility than novelists and poets. For all of that, there is still some play in the joints and room for lawyers to develop storytelling abilities ranging from the merely serviceable to the exceptional.

Coherence is also important when the discussion turns from the facts to the law. As we saw in Chapter 3, we try to make sense of previous judicial decisions, make them fit together, understanding them as reiterations or justifiable modifications of each other. We try to make sense of statutes as well, fitting the current statute in with others, fitting the exact phrase at issue with the sentence and paragraph in the statute where it appears. We tell stories here, too, and the more coherent the better.

Logic

When we come to apply the law to the facts, logic becomes paramount. Again, despite the intellectual prejudices of our postmodern world, legal debate presupposes that logic in law is both possible and desirable. In the kingdom of law, the syllogism reigns supreme: all Greek food is delicious; mousaka is Greek food; mousaka is delicious. The defendant is not guilty of first-degree murder because it requires premeditation, and the defendant did not go to the bar intending to harm the victim. The plaintiff cannot rescind the contract because rescission requires a material breach, and the defendant's breach was not material. Lawyers constantly work under the restraints of syllogistic logic, more or less formally applied, and the training starts early. In law school, we spend a great deal of time parsing cases, asking whether the conclusions follow from the premises. We always hope that they do.

Everett's Case

As Everett's counselors and advocates we will be guided by the imperatives of truth, precision, coherence, and logic, as we discuss his case with public prosecutors, his co-worker's lawyers, and the tire company, and in presentations before courts. Zeal, in the representation of clients, is a professional responsibility, but so too are truth and fair dealing.

In the trenches, in the daily work of lawyers and judges, truth, precision, coherence, and formal logic are the primary standards by which legal work is appraised. We object to our opponents' arguments about the state of the law and the state of the facts mainly on the grounds that: (1) they are false or misleading; (2) they blur important distinctions; (3) they don't hang together or don't make sense; and (4) they don't prove what they claim to prove. Arguments that don't founder on these grounds are pretty good arguments. But they may not be enough. Both parties in a legal dispute may have true, precise, coherent, and logically impeccable positions.

BIG ARGUMENT

A second kind of legal argument tends to appear in close cases — when standard, first-level arguments seem evenly divided. We then move from the nuts and bolts of interpreting law and presenting facts to broader arguments sounding in public policy and legal philosophy. Because lawyers never know whether they are beating their opponents badly enough, this second kind of argument — "big" argument — shows up in many cases anyway, whether they are close or not. Big argument can also be employed for a different purpose — to make easy cases hard ones. Thus, a lawyer might employ such arguments to call for the rejection of an old line of cases, whose wisdom and precedential value had not seriously been questioned before.

Big arguments involve big subjects — justice, morality, democracy, and freedom — subjects that dwarf the problems lawyers and judges handle most of the time. As a consequence, most lawyers are reluctant — wisely — to argue grandly in every case they handle. Not every parking ticket is a threat to democracy, and pretending that it is provokes justifiable scorn among colleagues, opponents, and judges. Clients may see a clash of monumental importance in every legal matter that concerns them, but their lawyers must

---

BIG ARGUMENT

✔ Law and Morality ➜ arguments about justice, fairness, right and wrong

✔ Public Policy ➜ arguments about what policies the law is seeking to achieve

✔ Deference ➜ arguments that a judge should defer to other branches (legislative or executive), other judges, other governments, or the parties themselves

✔ Sanctity of Rules ➜ arguments that the relevant rule must be followed literally or strictly, to preserve the rule and rules generally

---

exercise greater discernment. Even so, there are times when fundamental principles of law and morality *are* at stake and big argument is appropriate.

Law and Morality

We sometimes argue for a particular result because it is *right*, right in the moral sense of the term. The force of this claim, as well as our ability to make it at all, depends on the relationship between law and morality. To what extent, if any, does the law take account of moral concepts and teaching? The relationship between law and morality has occupied thinkers for thousands of years. So much has been written, so much has been said, that only the ignorant or the foolish would raise the issue at all, much less try to handle it in a couple of paragraphs. Yet we proceed.

At the time of America's independence from England, our country's founders were steeped in the traditions of natural law: law that existed independently of human will; law whose contours were defined by the will of God, or, for non-believers, by the very nature of human beings; and that could often be discovered by human reason. Persons with such beliefs could assent to a Declaration of Independence calling for "the separate and equal station to which the Laws of Nature and of Nature's God entitle them," and could believe all men "endowed by their Creator with certain unalienable Rights." Natural law, it can hardly be missed, looked and acted a lot like morality — proceeding from similar sources and aimed toward similar ends. To those immersed in the tenets of natural law, there was an intimate connection between what is lawful and what is morally right.

But times change. The nineteenth century saw the rise of positivism, a view that law is best understood as the commands of the sovereign, or in more modern terms, the authoritative pronouncements of the properly constituted government of a state. Law, from the positivist perspective, is contingent, essentially political, and properly separated from morality. Law is what the government declares and what judges do about disputes. From such a perspective, it is much easier to believe that an immoral law — or a demonstrably immoral legal outcome — can be a proper one. The claim of moral rightness or wrongness packs less punch.

In recent years, no other theory on the nature and sources of law has gained wide acceptance. Legal philosophy has instead dissolved into several theories or approaches to law, each with its own set of working assumptions and methods of analysis — the most recent approaches including critical legal studies, feminist jurisprudence, critical race studies, and the law as literary text. There is now no simple story to tell, since each theory or approach tends to have its own position on the relationship between law and morality. In addition, most of the new stream of legal scholarship rejects the possibility of moral absolutes, good for all time and people, arguing instead that moral principles are contingent upon the particular time and place in which they are held. As a result, even the approaches that keep a close connection between law and morality end up keeping a close connection between law and nothing very much at all.

Despite variations, one trend is clear. In American jurisprudence, the link between law and morality has been deteriorating since the middle of the nineteenth century. Back in the law offices and courtrooms, the deterioration finds a parallel in the hesitancy with which lawyers and judges approach moral claims. Lawyers rarely make arguments based solely and boldly on moral principles, and when they do, they are perceived as being at the end of their argumentative rope. Judges almost never take an action just because it's right. The trait is learned early. By the third week of law school, students know that the surest way to provoke derisive laughter from their classmates is to criticize a legal decision because it is "unfair."

Jurisprudential theory probably doesn't have much to do with this state of affairs, except that it feeds into and helps to foster a general climate of moral cynicism — the vaguely held, almost reflexive distrust of moral claims that permeates contemporary social and political discussion. And law school doesn't help. By emphasizing that we are teaching something new and different, by staring blankly when someone argues about the fairness of a case, waiting instead for an analysis of how it changes the law of torts, we inevitably, if unwittingly, teach that fairness is irrelevant. And if law school didn't breed contempt for moral argument, law practice and judging surely would. Every client and litigant thinks he is right, that justice is on his side, that the moral answer is his answer. In case after case, parties swear up and down that it is they who seek justice and truth, while their opponents seek only venal, self-interested gain. Who, after watching this particular parade of human behavior, can walk away without a healthy suspicion of moral claims in the courtroom?

In any event, to say that a particular result is right or just or fair is simply to state a conclusion. The morality of a situation is judged by reference to more specific standards of behavior. The award of money damages to a plaintiff, for example, might be right because the defendant took the plaintiff's goods without paying for them. The concrete standard of behavior — honesty in commercial dealings — justifies the grander moral judgment. These more detailed standards of moral behavior can come to us from many sources. They can be revealed to us (as in the Torah, the New Testament, and the Koran), come down to us as received traditions of proper behavior (the things we learned in kindergarten), or be produced by reasoning, often within particular schools of thought founded by thinkers as wide-ranging as Confucius, Aristotle, and Immanuel Kant.

Among the sources of behavioral standards, lawyers and judges rely most often on received tradition. The peculiarly American concern for the separation of church and state makes explicit references to religious texts a relative rarity in briefs and judicial decisions, although citations to the Bible can sometimes be found. An ignorance of philosophy, along with a commendable reluctance — even among the cognoscenti — to impose a particular "man-made" ethical system on others, make explicit references to systematic moral philosophers even rarer. Religious and philosophical support is generally recruited only when it reinforces a standard of behavior already grounded in custom.

Deriving standards of conduct from custom, however, is a difficult business. There is obviously great variation in human behavior and a great many views about which of it is good. One can only be sure — and then, only relatively sure — of the least problematic, most fundamental standards of conduct. As a consequence, when judges and lawyers turn to custom for argument and decision, they generally limit themselves to the simplest virtues — honesty, moderation, promise-keeping — and similarly undisputed traits of good character.

There is nothing wrong with simple virtues, but simple virtues derived from custom lack "supporting material," a deficiency that limits their usefulness to lawyers and judges. Virtues derived from religious and philosophical traditions appear in contexts where more has been said and explained. Buddha and Jesus and Jean Paul Sartre said quite a lot, and so have their followers. Arguments about morality in religious and philosophical traditions can call upon these broader sets of materials. Virtues derived from custom, in contrast, come to us only with their names and a few basic examples of their application. Be honest, keep your word, help others. There is simply not much for advocates and decisionmakers to work with.

As a consequence, moral arguments in legal briefs and judicial decisions have a rough-hewn, perfunctory character. There isn't much more to be said, for example, than that the opposing party's actions have been duplicitous and that one's client should therefore prevail. In the legal version of moral reasoning, the virtues are simple and the arguments rudimentary.

Everett's Case

Rudimentary or not, we might argue that Everett had worked for years at the tire plant without incident, that he was under a great deal of stress at the time of the altercation, and that the co-worker had made a threatening gesture right before Everett acted. For all these reasons, firing Everett or finding him liable criminally or in tort would be unfair. Such arguments would only supplement more standard doctrinal arguments on self-defense, the required mental state for criminal assault, and so on, but would help to show why the doctrines *should* be applied as we suggest.

Law and Policy

Though often ambivalent about the use of moral reasoning, lawyers and judges are unreservedly devoted to public policy, always searching for the policy that makes one legal position better than another. Public policies are identified and applied both in the interpretation of statutes (deciding, for example, whether to read a particular phrase broadly or narrowly) and in the application of judge-made rules (deciding, for example, whether to extend an old rule to a new situation). In common-law adjudication especially, public policy can have more radical effects, sometimes being used to carve out new exceptions to well-established rules or to abandon those rules entirely. The love of policy, and the assurance of its worth in legal argument, are taught from the beginning of law school, where classroom discussions return again and again to the policies *behind* the statutes and cases under review.

It was not always so easy to refer to policy in legal briefs and American courtrooms, at least not so explicitly, so often, and so much as a matter of course. The turning point came in the late nineteenth and early twentieth centuries, with a growing acceptance of an *instrumental* or *functional* view of law. Law, according to this view, is purposive, a matter of means and ends, and the ends must always be kept in mind. A law's application is only justified to the extent that it furthers the ends, the purposes, the policies that animate it. In 1897, for example, Oliver Wendell Holmes could write that "a body of law is more rational and more civilized when every rule it contains is referred articulately and definitely to an end which it subserves."[4] The instrumental view of law is largely unquestioned today and invites "policy talk" in every memo, brief, and decision in American legal practice.

Instrumentalism is so well accepted that it is hard to imagine an alternative. If law doesn't serve some social purpose, then what in the world does it do? But life before legal instrumentalism was neither ignorant nor absurd. We have always known that laws serve social purposes, that particular laws are aimed at remedying public problems or furthering public goods. But we have also thought that law does other things, too. In the world of the nation's founders, for example, where law was closely tied to "nature and Nature's God" and where God had already revealed a great many laws in the Bible, an analysis of means and ends was not so pressing. That which God has proclaimed as law (and human laws that looked like them) did not have to be justified by some exterior purpose or social advantage. We could guess at that advantage, that policy, but we might be wrong and God's purposes were sometimes a mystery. We risked error if we strayed from the words of the law and inquired into its underlying social ends. Instrumentalism shifted the emphasis, taking the awareness that law serves social purposes and making that awareness paramount, insisting again and again that all law, as well as any particular law, be justified by the social ends it seeks to attain. Policy analysis became indispensable.

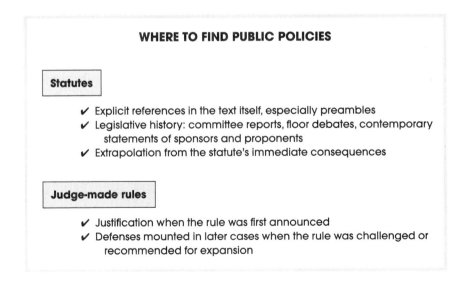

WHERE TO FIND PUBLIC POLICIES

Statutes

- ✔ Explicit references in the text itself, especially preambles
- ✔ Legislative history: committee reports, floor debates, contemporary statements of sponsors and proponents
- ✔ Extrapolation from the statute's immediate consequences

Judge-made rules

- ✔ Justification when the rule was first announced
- ✔ Defenses mounted in later cases when the rule was challenged or recommended for expansion

---

[4]O. W. Holmes, "The Path of the Law," 10 Harv. L. Rev. 457, 469 (1897).

Where do we find the policies behind the laws, the ends for which the laws are means? For statutes, the legislature often tells us directly, enacting bills that feature a set of "whereas" clauses describing what the legislature sought to achieve. Legislative committee reports and floor debates often discuss the purposes for which a piece of legislation was proposed and thus presumably why it was passed. And finally, the policy behind a statute is sometimes determined from the words of the statute itself, advocates and judges generalizing a policy from the statute's more immediate consequences. A statute increasing the amount of the homestead exemption on property taxes might, for example, be understood to express a public policy favoring home ownership.

Sometimes finding the policy behind a statute involves nothing more than a change of labels. In a recent case, a statute requiring that motorists maintain at least $25,000 of liability insurance was said to express the public policy (this is a true story) that motorists maintain at least $25,000 in liability insurance. Taking a perfectly serviceable statutory requirement and calling it a public policy may seem an odd and useless rhetorical move, but it has important consequences. Lawyers and judges often add the public policy label to strengthen a statute: either to brace it against efforts to interpret it narrowly or carve out exceptions, or to expand its reach, pressing it into service in ways not originally contemplated. In the insurance example above, the statute's point was to impose an obligation on motorists, but the question before the court concerned the interpretation of an automobile insurance policy that appeared to exclude the required coverage. Calling the statutory amount a matter of public policy, the court used the statute for the expanded purpose of contract interpretation, reading the policy in a way that provided coverage up to the minimum statutory amount.

For judge-made rules, the underlying public policy is usually made explicit . . . somewhere. If one can find the case in which a rule originated (often more difficult than it seems), the reasons then given for the rule's adoption can usually be translated into a description of its policy goals. More commonly, however, lawyers and judges turn to prior cases in which an established rule was being pressured — either attacked or recommended for expansion. In such circumstances, judges usually discuss the reasons behind the rule and thus the policies that animate it.

The translation from judicial reasoning to public policy is often straightforward, but not always. First, as with statutes, there is play in the joints. The same judicial statement of reasons, for example, can generate wider and narrower interpretations of the public policy involved. A judge might say that a rule in debtor/creditor law has been fashioned to protect the debtor. But is the public policy to protect the debtor at all costs, or only in the precise circumstances addressed by the rule? Lawyers and judges have room to maneuver and they use it. Second, the reasons for many judge-made rules have changed over the years. A great many property rules, for example, were initially justified by their usefulness in maintaining (or constraining) the landed gentry of England, but the retention of those rules is often justified today by the need for stability in land titles, which depends, it is argued, on the continued vitality of the ancient rules. This means that advocates and judges are not confined to reporting previously announced reasons and policies, but can suggest new ones, an invitation to creativity that is often hard to resist. Third, in translating from judicial reasons to public policy, it is something of a challenge to say why the policies are *public*. In the analysis of statutory policies, it is at least nominally clear why they are public: they have been announced by bodies that *represent* the public, a majority of whose members have agreed to them. But judges are not representative in the same way. In the federal system and one-third of the states they are not even elected. What, then, makes judicial reasons "public" ones, judicial policies "public policies"? If we say it is because the rules have been developed for the public good, we have only begged the question, for it is seldom clear that one rule rather than another will advance that good. This explains why, in determining what public policies underlie common-law rules, both lawyers and judges tend to confine themselves to those policies that either (1) find support in constitutional and statutory texts as well; or (2) have been repeated so often — without legislative challenge — that their status as public policies seems assured.

In arguing about public policy, lawyers and judges are not limited to the policies that can be gleaned from the precise statute or common-law rule at issue, but can also refer to the *field* of law in which it appears. Securities law, for example, is animated by public policies (among others) promoting truth-telling between buyers and sellers of stocks and bonds, along with the prompt, public dissemination of information that could affect market prices. Property law is marked by a special concern for the stability of land titles, contract law by a deference to private decisionmaking, and criminal law by an abhorrence of wrongful conviction. At even higher levels of abstraction, public policies are sometimes derived from whole *classes* or *branches* of law: public law, private law, statutory law, and common law. In any case involving public law (i.e., criminal and regulatory law), for example, one's attention might be drawn to a special concern for openness and transparency of procedures. At the highest levels of abstraction, some policies can even be found by examining the special nature of American law (as opposed to other national systems) or the special nature of law (as opposed to other social institutions). At this point, the term *public policy* often gives way to other terms such as *fundamental principles* or *foundations* of American law, but the mode of analysis is the same. And finally, if law-related policies aren't enough, lawyers and judges also divine public polices from our political system (democracy, our particular structure of government), our economic system (capitalist, free market), and other aspects of our society and culture.

WHAT CAN GO WRONG WITH POLICY ANALYSIS

✔ Policies are often hard to divine from available sources

✔ Two or more policies are often plausible, and those multiple policies run at cross-purposes

✔ Policies can change over time. As a consequence:
  • old policies can always be discarded as outdated
  • new policies can always be suggested for old rules

✔ Policies operate at different levels. Policies can underlie:
  • a rule
  • an area of law
  • a branch of law (public versus private law)
  • American law
  • the law generally

✔ When policies do clash, it is often impossible to choose sensibly between them

---

It is easy to make fun of public policy arguments. They are shamelessly manipulable and promise a clarity of analysis they cannot deliver. Public policies lurk behind every statute, rule, branch, class, and system of law, and good lawyers can always find a policy — often several — to support their position. So can their opponents. As such, policy arguments frequently do no more than substitute a clash of competing policies for a clash of competing rules. And the policies we cite are often so general (freedom of contract, protection of the tenant) that choosing among them — deciding which shall prevail — is no easier than answering the original question. And yet, courts and legislatures *do* take a special interest in some problems and try to handle them in particular ways. We have made *choices* about how markets should work, how property should be protected, how law-breaking should be discovered and punished — real choices among real options, choices that differ from those made by peoples in other countries and other generations. That is public policy, and although we can make fun of the reckless and pompous way it is often debated and applied, the subject itself is no joke. An analysis of public policy, purged of bombast and brought back to size, approached in good faith and applied with discernment, can make one legal answer better than another.

Everett's Case

In searching for public policies to use in defending a criminal action against Everett, we would look first to the criminal statutes themselves and then to what judges and others have said about them. We are likely to find many policies, often working at cross-purposes and at different levels of generality: the need to keep our streets safe, the desire not to punish anyone under a criminal law unless its requirements are clear, and so on. In connection with any tort suit against Everett, we would look to see what judges have said about the policies lying behind (at ever-greater levels of abstraction) the tort of battery specifically, intentional torts (as opposed to negligence) more generally, and the tort system.

Deference

The two kinds of "big" argument that we have just reviewed — those relying on morality and public policy — have an argumentative appeal that everyone can appreciate. All of us, lawyers and non-lawyers alike, want legal answers that are morally right and that advance the public good. There are other kinds of "big" argument, however, that appeal more directly to lawyers and judges, arguments that are employed much more frequently and that, in daily legal practice, are much more important. One of these obscure but potent arguments is the call for *deference*.

We often think of the law as a powerful, coercive force, pushing people around this way and that. But the law is actually timid and full of self-restraint. We see this primarily in the principle of legality, the principle that all actions are legal unless made illegal. The law will not intervene without an explicit warrant to do so. This timidity, this self-restraint, is driven by powerful ideals regarding personal autonomy and freedom of action, firmly held views that people ought to be left alone to do as they wish. Judges, as the final arbiters of law, are subject to similar pressures. Although we think of judges as powerful officials (and in some ways, of course, they are), they are steeped in an ethos of self-abnegation and restraint. As a consequence, judges are often asked — and often agree — to defer to the will, the decisions, the judgment of others.

The most obvious aspect of this deference is the binding nature of constitutions and statutes. Judges are constantly reminded of their duty to apply constitutional and statutory language in preference to other sources of guidance and to apply it as it is written, bowing in two senses to the will of constitution-makers and legislatures. This does not mean, of course, that the duty is always heeded, but it does mean that a flat refusal is not permissible. A judge cannot say (without certain reversal and probable impeachment), "the constitutional [or statutory] provision cited to me clearly covers the case at hand, but I refuse to apply it."

Equally obvious and almost as powerful is the call for deference to earlier judges — the doctrine of *stare decisis*. Judges are asked again and again to put aside their own convictions and instead handle a matter like a colleague, often long since dead, handled it before. As we know, binding precedent need not always be followed, but reasons must be given — changed social conditions, changing statutory policy in related fields, and so on. We also know that unwanted precedents can also be distinguished away on their facts, more or less credibly, more or less hypocritically. But these weaknesses or exceptions to the doctrine of *stare decisis* should not blind us to the power of the call. We are all taught from the beginning of law school, judges and lawyers alike, that precedent matters, that precedent binds.

Judges are asked to defer to the work of the coordinate branches of government. The separation of powers doctrine cautions judges not to tread on executive and legislative prerogatives. The political question doctrine even more pointedly warns judges away from dealing with matters better handled by the executive and legislative branches. Deference to the legislative branch is secured, as we have already seen, by the binding nature of statutes. Deference to the executive branch is secured by doctrines that give officials and agencies a wide margin of error before courts will step in. Many administrative actions will be overturned only if they constitute an abuse of discretion; agencies charged with administering a particular statute enjoy a strong presumption that they have interpreted it correctly; and judicial review of any matter touching on foreign affairs is extremely rare.

Judges are frequently asked to defer, not only to coordinate branches in the same government, but to other governments as well. State judges are asked to defer to the federal government by way of the Supremacy Clause; federal judges are asked to defer to state governments under the banner of federalism, bolstered with occasional success by the Tenth Amendment to the Constitution, which provides that "powers not delegated to the United States by the Constitution, or prohibited by it to the States, are reserved to the States respectively, or to the people." Judges are also asked to refrain from interfering with the prerogatives of foreign governments. The immunities granted to foreign sovereigns, diplomats, and consular officials keep the courts from reviewing many of their actions, and the act of state doctrine cautions courts not to sit in judgment of the acts of foreign governments taken within their own territories.

Quite apart from the doctrine of precedent, judges are also asked to defer to other courts, both foreign and domestic. They are asked to refrain from hearing a case at all because, among other reasons, the parties do not have

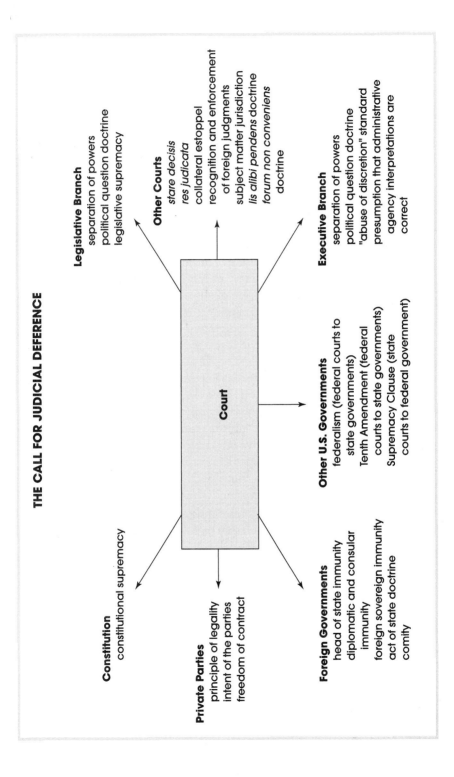

THE CALL FOR JUDICIAL DEFERENCE

Constitution
constitutional supremacy

Private Parties
principle of legality
intent of the parties
freedom of contract

Foreign Governments
head of state immunity
diplomatic and consular
immunity
foreign sovereign immunity
act of state doctrine
comity

Court

Other U.S. Governments
federalism (federal courts to
state governments)
Tenth Amendment (federal
courts to state governments)
Supremacy Clause (state
courts to federal government)

Legislative Branch
separation of powers
political question doctrine
legislative supremacy

Other Courts
stare decisis
res judicata
collateral estoppel
recognition and enforcement
of foreign judgments
subject matter jurisdiction
lis alibi pendens doctrine
forum non conveniens
doctrine

Executive Branch
separation of powers
political question doctrine
"abuse of discretion" standard
presumption that administrative
agency interpretations are
correct

sufficient ties to the court's territory (personal jurisdiction requirements), because the types of issues raised or the citizenship of the parties mandate that the case be heard elsewhere (subject matter jurisdiction requirements), because the case is in fact being heard somewhere else (the *lis alibi pendens* doctrine), or because there is a more convenient forum (*forum non conveniens* doctrine, along with rules regarding transfers and consolidations). When judges do hear a case, they are urged to defer to the work of other courts, not only by way of the doctrine of *stare decisis,* but also on the grounds of *res judicata,* collateral estoppel, and rules regarding the recognition and enforcement of foreign judgments. The work of other jurisdictions in similar cases is expected to receive thoughtful consideration.

Finally, judges are constantly being asked to defer to the will of private parties: to carry out the wishes of donors, willmakers, and creators of trusts, even in the face of technical failures of formalities, the deaths of executors and trustees, and other changes of circumstances; to enforce contracts, even in the face of uneven bargaining power of the parties; to permit private persons to engage in hazardous activity, conceding only that the persons so engaged be liable for any injuries they cause; indeed, to permit any activity, from corporate mergers to noisy parties, so long as no statute or rule clearly prohibits it.

In most cases, of course, there will be someone on the other side calling for intervention and judicial action. But there is a great deal of argument arrayed on the side of deference: the principle of legality; a tradition of liberalism that seeks constantly to expand the boundaries of acceptable behavior; and a set of constitutional freedoms — of religion, association, and speech — that (in addition to their technical legal content) reflect a spirit of tolerance. All of this presses on judges, urging them to bend to the will of others, to refrain from interfering without the most substantial reasons for doing so.

Everett's Case

In representing Everett, the principle of deference could arise in many contexts. If, for example, the legislative history of the criminal assault statute supports our position on Everett's innocence, and the judge clearly wishes it were otherwise, we would emphasize the importance of deferring to the will of the legislature. In a contract action, the tire company might try to defend Everett's firing by calling on the judge to give the company the benefit of the doubt, to defer to the company, regarding a decision so central to its operations as who works there.

The Sanctity of Rules

Rules — from constitutions, statutes, administrative regulations, and court decisions — are central to the legal enterprise. Law work is rule work: finding them, interpreting them, fighting them, and applying them. There are many other things to be done, but rule work is an essential and distinctive part of the lawyer's and judge's trade. This activity is supported and justified by the communally held belief, the axiomatic principle, that legal work is properly understood as planning and decisionmaking in accordance with rules. This axiom and its corollaries produce the frame around which the entire structure of American law is built. They define the character of the system and fix the terms of debate within it. It is thus no surprise that any threat to this system, any threat to the sanctity of rules, generates big argument on its behalf.

The rule-based concept of legal systems has an ancient pedigree that predates writing. The oldest surviving written codes, like the Babylonian Code of Hammurabi, circa 1800 B.C., clearly record preexisting rules and examples of their application. The law of Moses, Greek law, and Roman law all bear witness to this rule-based concept of law, reminding us again and again of its tenacity and appeal to the Western mind. Our current American system can be distinguished by its bookish emphasis and complexity, but the underlying conception, the essential vision is the same. On the other hand, this vision is several generations behind the times. Beginning around the middle of the nineteenth century and continuing to the present day, the notion of legal work as the application of rules has come under repeated attack: rules are not what we think they are; rule-following is conceptually incoherent; rules do not decide cases; the application of rules to facts is a mask for raw application of power; and so on. The general jurisprudential lesson of the last 150 years seems to be: decisionmaking according to rule is a joke. The only remaining questions are: Exactly what kind of a joke is it? and Should we laugh or cry?

To ignore this ferment would be a mistake, even if we find it improbable that millions of people for thousands of years have been doing something quite different from what they thought they were doing. But improbable doesn't mean impossible. For thousands of years we were quite certain that our flat earth lay at the center of the universe. Attacks on the orthodox, rule-based conception of law might be right. Even if they are, however, we need not pack up our offices and chambers and go home. There are intellectually sound reasons to stay put.

The critical attacks of the past 150 years are *meta*-critiques, that is, critiques from outside the system, looking at legal process as an entomologist might study a colony of ants. But what the entomologist discovers is not necessarily relevant to the ants. What jurisprudential thinkers discover is not necessarily relevant to lawyers and judges. Statements made *about* a system are logically different from statements *in* a system, and one cannot simply assume that true statements in one realm have direct implications in the other. While working within a system, it is intellectually honest to ignore external critiques, at least until it is demonstrated that the external critiques have a particular relevance to internal practice. One can believe, for example, that the law masks relations of power, between the oppressor and oppressed, and still file a brief on Thursday with citations to the federal tax code. *Inside* the legal system, it is important to help clients and decide cases, neither of which is aided, in any obvious way, by the insight that the law strengthens the oppressor. Maybe it does, but so what? Meta-critique *can* generate practical advice (for example, in efforts at legal reform), but its ability to do so must be demonstrated and not presumed.

Let us therefore take things as we find them, without further inquiry into philosophical merit: lawyers and judges take rules seriously. That being the case, we are always sensitive to the argument that for rules to have meaning they must have "bite." That is, they have to be applied even in the cases where their application results in decisions we might find unpalatable. If they are not so applied, then they are not rules at all, but only guidelines or presumptions, easily overcome at the first sign of trouble. We exult in having created a government "of laws not of men," but a government of guidelines is different and far more dangerous. Guidelines and presumptions do not form a bulwark against a powerful government nor do they provide predictable outcomes upon which our citizens can rely. One can't have one's rules and ignore them, too.

Such an argument generates predictable opposition. Rules, the opponent might say, are not important for their own sake. Justice is the end; the laws only the means. We must always be on guard against a mechanical jurisprudence that takes no account of the purposes the law serves. When a rule fails in its purpose, we must not hesitate to act — to limit a doctrine, to apply an exception, to create an exception if none can be found, to apply a broader principle that trumps a harsh rule, to overturn a line of cases. No matter how carefully we craft our statutes and common-law rules, they will pull in cases to which they should not apply. We cannot ignore the limits of generalization, our stark inability to treat the boundless possibilities of human behavior in general terms.

Some variation of this "big" argument appears in almost all legal debate: one side for hard rules, the other for soft. The spirit of the times suggests that the second view is substantially more attractive, and yet it does not always succeed. Judges sometimes apply hard rules, reaching decisions that they say they would rather not have reached. With surprising frequency, judges free convicted felons because earlier searches of their homes or offices were illegal; uphold penalties on taxpayers even though they were only five minutes late to the tax office; strike down wills (though no one contests their authenticity or the capacity of their testators), because there was only one witness instead of two; refuse to enjoin the march of neo-Nazis, because they filled out all the proper forms; and so on.

This behavior is driven by the belief that the too-easy escape from rules, even in just one case, does *systematic* harm to legal process. Thus, we do an occasional hurtful thing to preserve a system we believe worth saving. It is a difficult and highly dramatic position to take. On such grounds did Socrates famously drink hemlock, carrying out his own death sentence in obeisance to court judgment. One of the most eloquent defenses of the position appears in Robert Bolt's play *A Man for All Seasons*. In that play, Bolt recounts the story of Sir Thomas More, Lord Chancellor of England, in his resistance to King Henry VIII's demands that More assent to the King's (then illegal) divorce from Anne Boleyn, a resistance that ultimately cost More his head. At one point in the play, Bolt imagines the following quarrel between Sir Thomas More and his son-in-law Roper:

> *Roper:* So now you'd give the Devil benefit of law!
> *More:* Yes. What would you do? Cut a great road through the law to get after the Devil?
> *Roper:* I'd cut down every law in England to do that!
> *More:* Oh? And when the last law was down, and the Devil turned round on you — where would you hide, Roper, the laws all being flat? This country's planted thick with laws from coast to coast — man's laws, not God's — and if you cut them down . . . d'you really think you could stand upright in the winds that would blow then? Yes, I'd give the Devil benefit of law, for my own safety's sake.[5]

Serious doubts, of course, can be raised about whether rules need to be given a hard edge in order to preserve the legal system. Even so, judges are frequently drawn to the hard-edged view. By their positions, training, and temperament, they are drawn to a style of judging that promises the preservation of the legal system, constitutional integrity, social advantage, and a virtuous recognition of one's own limits. As a consequence, debates about hard and soft rules are more equally balanced — and hard rules applied more frequently — than one might expect.

---

[5]Robert Bolt, *A Man for All Seasons* 66 (First Vintage International ed. 1990) (1960).

Everett's Case

If Everett's actions constituted a battery under current case law, we might argue that the judge should create a new exception to the old rules, which take account, for example, of cases where the defendant was taunted ahead of time by the plaintiff or where the plaintiff evidenced no physical manifestation of injury. The co-worker's attorneys would emphasize the importance of keeping the law as it is (and has been for many years), arguing that the addition of new exceptions would destabilize this area of law.

Tradition and Change

We close this chapter, and this book, with the biggest argument of all. The law always comes to us from the past — statutes enacted, regulations promulgated, cases decided — and its application always lies in the present. The tension is obvious and well known. We constantly worry about whether the answers of the past, despite our institutional respect for them, are the proper answers for today. In almost every legal dispute, there is someone calling for change — that a statute be applied more broadly or narrowly than before, that an exception be created, that a doctrine be modified or eliminated entirely — simply because times have changed. And there is almost always someone to oppose the change, emphasizing the need for predictability in the law, reliance by the citizenry, and administrative efficiency.

Because we presumptively handle things today as we handled them yesterday, legal analysis is by nature conservative. This conservatism is neither politically charged nor optional. It has no particular political content: conservatism in anarchic, socialist, and capitalistic states promotes anarchy, socialism, and capitalism, respectively. Nor is this conservatism a matter of choice. If one starts with the law, one unavoidably starts with the past, with its structures, content, and terms of debate. Deciding when to break with the past, when to stop conserving and begin building, has no easy answer. We can never be sure we are right. We can only do our best, as lawyers and judges, arguing and deciding with all the honesty, intelligence, and even bravery we can muster.

IN SUMMARY

- The *answers* to legal questions, like the questions themselves, fall into predictable patterns.

- Legal arguments are judged *primarily* on the bases of:
  - truth
  - precision
  - coherence; and
  - logic

- A *second* kind of argument, also common, calls upon major themes and principles of American law:
  - morality
  - public policy
  - deference to others
  - the sanctity of rules

- Most *moral arguments* in legal writing focus on the simple virtues of honesty, fair dealing, and promise-keeping, and often have a cursory, rudimentary character.

- Arguments about *public policy*, though malleable and often abused, can sometimes reflect real choices the law has made.

- Judges are called upon with surprising frequency (and success) to *defer* to others: other branches (legislative and executive), other courts, other governments, and the parties themselves.

- A very common legal argument centers around the *sanctity of rules*, with competing claims that:
  - a rule must be strictly applied (to preserve that rule and rules generally); and
  - an exception should be made (to preserve justice in this particular case)

- Law is always in tension, balancing *tradition* against the need for *change*.

Glossary

Absolute liability Liability to which there is no defense or the defenses have been severely limited; once such liability is found, a remedy is appropriate. *Cf.* Strict liability.

Administrative law The law governing how the executive branch of government creates and applies regulations, as well as how the executive branch enforces congressional or state legislation.

Agency The theory by which one person can represent another.

Alternative dispute resolution A generic term covering all methods of resolving legal disputes other than through formal court action, such as mediation and arbitration.

Appellate courts Courts that do not make original determinations of liability and remedy, but instead review such determinations for errors important enough to reverse the decision.

Arbitration A form of dispute resolution in which a neutral individual or panel of individuals is chosen by disputing parties to judge their claims; if the parties have chosen binding rather than nonbinding arbitration, the final award of the arbitrator(s) can be enforced in court.

Black letter law A concise summary of common-law rules, the precise language of which is not binding on any court, but is often used as the starting place for legal analysis.

Burden of proof The obligation to establish the truth of a fact, the correctness of a legal interpretation, or more broadly, every element of one's claim before a court.

Canons of construction Rules and presumptions used in interpreting the language used in contracts, statutes, and constitutions.

Comity The principle under which courts and governments sometimes defer to the rules and decisions of other courts and governments, even when they are not legally required to do so.

Common law The law that develops through court decisions, in cases where the court is not applying constitutional provisions or legislative enactments.

Conciliation A form of dispute resolution in which the parties choose a

...tral individual or panel of individuals to help them reach agreement and settlement; often used synonymously with mediation, but when distinguished from that process, conciliation suggests a more active role for the conciliator, pressing the parties to resolve their dispute rather than simply acting as intermediary.

Conflicts of law The branch of law governing the decision of which law to apply, in cases where the laws from more than one jurisdiction, state, or nation could be applied to a dispute.

Contract Along with status, one of the two great methods by which persons gain legal rights and obligations. In contract, such rights and obligations are created by voluntary agreement of two or more parties; the term can also refer more specifically to the document in which such an agreement is contained.

Custom A very old source of law, growing out of the expectation that long-standing patterns of behavior will continue to be honored; historically important in almost every society and in international law today, but seldom used in contemporary, domestic matters.

Damages The judicial remedy for the violation of an obligation or right consisting of a money payment to the aggrieved party. *Cf.* Injunction.

Declaratory relief A judicial decision that a person has or has not violated a particular right or obligation, without imposing any remedy; similarly, a judicial decision on the status of persons or property, again without any element of remedy.

Due process The regular procedures followed by executive and judicial bodies in the normal course of their work, departures from which can invalidate the actions taken by those bodies; the phrase is also understood to comprise notions of basic fairness and justice, which can be violated by executive or judicial bodies even if all the proper procedures are followed.

Equal dignity rule Important in private lawmaking, the principle that a legal obligation or right can be modified or terminated only by following the same steps or requirements needed for its creation in the first place.

Estate All the property of a person who cannot, or is not permitted to, take care of it personally, as in estates of decedents, mental incompetents, and bankrupts; usually considered a distinct legal entity and therefore needing a representative to speak for it.

Estoppel A preclusion; a doctrine pursuant to which a person can be precluded from denying a state of affairs or bringing a claim or defense, often because of ethically questionable action or inaction on the estopped person's part. *Cf.* Waiver.

Hypotheticals A favorite in law school classrooms; imagined situations that are usually similar to, but not quite the same as, the situations students have read about ahead of time in judicial cases.

Injunction A judicial remedy that requires a party to the lawsuit to act or refrain from acting in a particular way. *Cf.* Damages.

International law A body of law separate from any single nation's laws, which governs the relations between nations and, to some degree, between nations and individuals.

Jurisdiction to adjudicate A government's authority to make individual determinations of liability or to make individual determinations about the legal status of persons or property.

Jurisdiction to enforce A government's authority to force compliance with its law and regulations.

Jurisdiction to prescribe A government's authority to prohibit or otherwise attach legal consequences to the behavior of persons.

Juristic persons Legal entities such as countries and corporations that are subject to legal regulation. *Cf.* Natural persons.

Legislative history The record of reports, comments of legislators, and other documents pertaining to the passage of a particular law; used to gain insight into what the legislature intended the resulting statute to mean or to accomplish.

Liability What a person incurs for violating a right or obligation. *Cf.* Remedy.

Litigation The process of resolving disputes through formal court action, in international, foreign, or domestic forums.

Mediation A form of dispute resolution in which the parties choose a person or persons to act as intermediary, helping the parties to reach agreement on an acceptable resolution; in contrast to arbitration and arbitrators, mediators do not themselves decide on the proper resolution, but spur the parties on to that result.

Natural persons Human beings; the term is used in contrast with juristic persons, also subjects of the law, who have no physical body.

Natural law Law derived from the very nature of human beings, either discovered by reason or revealed by God; historically important source of legal obligation and right infrequently used in contemporary legal analysis.

Obligation   The general term to describe any legal requirement that a person do or refrain from doing a particular thing; depending on the context, obligations could also be called duties, disabilities, requirements, or liabilities.

Office practice   Another name for transactional work; the work of lawyers outside of the courtroom, as they help to plan and execute the personal or business objectives of their clients.

Plain meaning rule   The rule of interpreting legal documents that gives primacy to the meaning that ordinary persons, in the normal course of life, would give to the language at issue.

Positivism   The idea or argument that law cannot be created except by the affirmative act of an authoritative ruler or governmental body; in contrast to natural law and custom as sources of law.

Principle of legality   A presumption of legality; the principle that all actions are permissible unless prohibited.

Private law   The law governing relationships between private persons, such as contracts and torts, where governments are involved only as umpires rather than as one of the parties governed. *Cf.* Public law.

Private lawmaking   The creation of legal rights and obligations by private persons, as by entering into a contract or creating a trust.

Public law   The law governing relationships between governments, and between governments and private persons, such as international law, constitutional law, criminal law, and taxation. *Cf.* Private law.

Public lawmaking   The creation of legal rights and obligations by governments, such as through congressional statutes, state legislation, and city ordinances.

Public policy   The moral, social, or political values that underlie law generally or a particular area of law; the ends sought to be achieved or the purposes sought to be accomplished by a particular area of law or in a particular statute or rule.

Remedy   The law's response to a finding of liability, usually aimed at making the aggrieved person whole, either by compensating him or her for the losses suffered or by attempting to return the situation to the *status quo ante.*

Rights   The general term to describe the legal permission to do or refrain from doing a particular thing; depending on the context, rights could also be called claims, privileges, licenses, powers, immunities, or liberties.

Separation of powers The division of governmental powers among the three branches of government, the legislature, the judiciary, and the executive; the actions of one branch can be questioned on the ground that it has thereby usurped the powers of another branch.

Specific performance The judicially imposed remedy for the violation of an obligation or right by which one of the parties is required to act as originally required, such as to sell a painting or repair an automobile.

Stare decisis The principle under which courts are bound by past decisions of other courts, particularly higher courts in the same jurisdiction.

Status A legal category or classification such as "citizen" or "spouse"; along with contract, one of the two great methods by which persons gain legal rights and obligations. In the status mechanism, rights and obligations are attached to a particular status; persons can move into and out of this status.

Status quo ante The situation before; usually the situation before someone violated a right or obligation, and to which a court might try to return the parties.

Statute of frauds A law, found in some form in every state, that makes certain common transactions unenforceable unless supported by a signed written document.

Statute of limitations A law, found in some form in every state, that prohibits aggrieved persons from bringing a lawsuit if they wait too long after their grievance arose, no matter what the merits of their complaint.

Strict liability Liability without fault; liability that arises out of one's involvement in a transaction or series of actions resulting in injury to others, without having breached a duty or rule; defenses to liability, like self-defense, are still available. *Cf.* Absolute liability.

Subjects of the law Those persons and entities that are regulated by the law.

Substantial compliance The principle or doctrine that actions not completely satisfying a particular set of requirements will be deemed to satisfy those requirements anyway.

Term of art A word or phrase which, from its use among those knowledgeable in a particular field, has taken on a specialized meaning that could not have been anticipated by nonexperts.

Tort A civil, noncriminal, wrong; a wrong committed by one person against another and that, unlike a criminal offense, is not deemed a wrong against the state.

Tortfeasor One who commits a tort.

Transactional work   Another name for office practice, the work of lawyers outside of the courtroom, as they help to plan and execute the personal or business objectives of their clients.

Trust   A special form of property ownership in which one person, the trustee, is the legal owner of the property, but is bound to use it for the benefit of another, the beneficiary; once formed, the trust is usually treated as a separate legal entity.

Ultra vires   A description of actions that are taken without or beyond the authority of the actor; often used in the context of corporations or agents who are accused of exceeding their legal power.

Vicarious liability   The process of holding one person liable for the actions of another, commonly found in the employment context, where employers are often held to account for the actions of their employees.

Void   Of no force or effect, a nullity; in describing a transaction, one treated as if it never occurred.

Voidable   Currently valid, but subject to invalidation; in describing a transaction, one that currently enjoys full force and effect, but is subject to someone's power to declare it void. If voided, the transaction will be treated as if it were void from the very beginning.

Waiver   A voluntary relinquishment of a known legal right; waived rights cannot be violated or enforced. *Cf.* Estoppel.

Suggested Readings

I. LEGAL SKILLS

James A. Gardner, *Legal Argument: The Structure and Language of Effective Advocacy* (Michie, 1993).

Edward H. Levi, *An Introduction to Legal Reasoning* (University of Chicago Press, 1962).

Karl N. Llewellyn, *The Bramble Bush: On Our Law and Its Study* (Oceana, 1991).

II. FOUNDATIONS OF LAW

John Chipman Gray, *The Nature and Sources of the Law,* 2nd ed. (Peter Smith, 1972).

H.L.A. Hart, *The Concept of Law,* 2nd ed. (Clarendon Press, 1997).

John Stuart Mill, *On Liberty and Other Essays* (Oxford University Press, 1998).

Leo Strauss, *Natural Right and History,* reissue ed. (University of Chicago Press, 1999).

Ernest J. Weinrib, *The Idea of Private Law* (Harvard University Press, 1995).

III. LEGISLATIVE AND JUDICIAL PROCESS

Benjamin N. Cardozo, *The Nature of the Judicial Process* (Yale University Press, 1960).

Jerome Frank, *Courts on Trial: Myth and Reality in American Justice* (Princeton University Press, 1973).

Charles W. Johnson, *How Our Laws Are Made* (H.Rep. Doc. 106-197, Jan. 31, 2000).

IV. HISTORY OF LAW

Lawrence M. Friedman, *A History of American Law,* 2nd ed. (Simon & Schuster, 1986).

Grant Gilmore, *The Ages of American Law* (Yale University Press, 1979).
T.F.T. Plucknett, *A Concise History of the Common Law*, 5th ed. (Lawbook Exchange, 2001).

V. FICTION

Harper Lee, *To Kill a Mockingbird*, reissue ed. (Warner Books, 1988).
Jerome Lawrence and Robert E. Lee, *Inherit the Wind*, reissue ed. (Bantam Books, 1982).

Index